Narrative in the Icelandic Family Saga

Narrative in the Icelandic Family Saga

Meanings of Time in Old Norse Literature

Heather O'Donoghue

BLOOMSBURY ACADEMIC
LONDON • NEW YORK • OXFORD • NEW DELHI • SYDNEY

BLOOMSBURY ACADEMIC
Bloomsbury Publishing Plc
50 Bedford Square, London, WC1B 3DP, UK
1385 Broadway, New York, NY 10018, USA
29 Earlsfort Terrace, Dublin 2, Ireland

BLOOMSBURY, BLOOMSBURY ACADEMIC and the Diana logo are trademarks of Bloomsbury Publishing Plc

First published in Great Britain 2021
This paperback edition published in 2022

Copyright © Heather O'Donoghue, 2021

Heather O'Donoghue has asserted her right under the Copyright, Designs and Patents Act, 1988, to be identified as Author of this work.

For legal purposes the Acknowledgements on p. viii constitute an extension of this copyright page.

Cover Design: Ben Anslow
Cover image: Kvöldvaka in Icelandic Farm House, H. Aug. G. Schiøtt (1823–1895)
(© National Museum of Iceland)

All rights reserved. No part of this publication may be reproduced or transmitted in any form or by any means, electronic or mechanical, including photocopying, recording, or any information storage or retrieval system, without prior permission in writing from the publishers.

Bloomsbury Publishing Plc does not have any control over, or responsibility for, any third-party websites referred to or in this book. All internet addresses given in this book were correct at the time of going to press. The author and publisher regret any inconvenience caused if addresses have changed or sites have ceased to exist, but can accept no responsibility for any such changes.

Every effort has been made to trace copyright holders and to obtain their permissions for the use of copyright material. The publisher apologizes for any errors or omissions and would be grateful if notified of any corrections that should be incorporated in future reprints or editions of this book.

A catalogue record for this book is available from the British Library.

Library of Congress Cataloging-in-Publication Data
Names: O'Donoghue, Heather, author.
Title: Narrative in the Icelandic family saga : meanings of time in Old Norse literature / Heather O'Donoghue.
Description: London ; New York : Bloomsbury Academic, 2021. | Includes bibliographical references and index. | Summary: "Representative of a unique literary genre and composed in the 13th or 14th centuries, the Icelandic Sagas rank among some of the world's greatest literature. Here, Heather O'Donoghue examines the singular textual voice of the Sagas while also exploring their important underlying ideas about the passage time. Bringing fresh and lively insights to the foundation texts of Old Norse and medieval Icelandic heritage, this book is an essential discussion the luminous oral tradition of a migratory people and an iconic canon of Western culture"– Provided by publisher. Identifiers: LCCN 2020039279 (print) | LCCN 2020039280 (ebook) | ISBN 9781788312875 (hardback) | ISBN 9781350211636 (paperback) | ISBN 9781786726254 (epub) | ISBN 9781786736314 (ebook)
Subjects: LCSH: Time in literature. | Sagas–History and critcism. | Old Norse literature–History and criticism. | Narration (Rhetoric)–History–To 1500.
Classification: LCC PT7193.T56 O36 2021 (print) | LCC PT7193.T56 (ebook) | DDC 839/.63–dc23
LC record available at https://lccn.loc.gov/2020039279
LC ebook record available at https://lccn.loc.gov/2020039280

ISBN:	HB:	978-1-7883-1287-5
	PB:	978-1-3502-1163-6
	ePDF:	978-1-7867-3631-4
	eBook:	978-1-7867-2625-4

Typeset by Integra Software Services Pvt. Ltd.

To find out more about our authors and books visit www.bloomsbury.com and sign up for our newsletters.

For my students, past and present

Contents

Acknowledgements	viii
Introduction	1
1 The representation of external time	11
2 The management of narrative time: Duration	47
3 The management of narrative time: Order	75
4 The voice of the silent narrator	113
5 Withheld knowledge	153
Conclusion	183
Notes	187
Further reading	214
Index	216

Acknowledgements

I am grateful to everyone who has helped me, directly or indirectly, with this book: family, friends and colleagues (especially Carolyne Larrington and Siân Grønlie, who have provided unstinting practical help and unfailing moral support in the often difficult circumstances of present-day academia), students, and my husband, Bernard. I owe particular thanks to Matthew Roby, who, with his technical expertise, wide knowledge of Old Norse literature and apparently limitless patience, has guided this book from messy script to print. Any remaining messiness is down to me.

Introduction

Icelandic family sagas – the *Íslendingasögur* – are a unique literary genre. Written in Iceland, for the most part in the thirteenth and fourteenth centuries, they are lengthy prose narratives – sometimes interspersed with carefully positioned stanzas of poetry – which tell of people and events in Iceland in the period between its settlement in 870 CE and its Christianization, following conversion in the year 1000 CE. Although there is very little in the way of historical or archaeological record with which to compare these sagas, the indications are that at least some of the people and events within them have a basis in historical actuality, while others, and probably most of the dialogue, are invented. Certainly, the society depicted in the family sagas – their setting – is a plausible recreation of a possible reality. This is largely due to the subject matter of family sagas. Their focus is squarely on human society. Indeed, even when they portray supernatural or otherwise unrealistic phenomena, these tend to be limited to entities of human size and shape – such as witches or ghosts – rather than the dragons or giants common to other saga genres. Family sagas are very unlike myths or fairy tales. Instead of invention and fantasy, we are presented with a real-feeling world of deceptively familiar human characters in everyday and domestic – though often very dramatic – circumstances. And in part, this impression of actuality arises from the confident and comprehensive but above all remarkably consistent portrait of early medieval Icelandic society, as if saga authors were working with an authentic and detailed picture of their ancestral society accurately transmitted via oral tradition.

So far, the characteristic literary mode of the family saga might appear very little different from that of the post-medieval historical novel. And indeed family sagas – as extended, secular, naturalistic prose narratives – have sometimes been compared with nineteenth-century European novels. But what sets apart – definitively – saga and novel is the distinctive narrative mode of the family saga, and this distinctiveness lies in its authors' apparent avoidance of almost all of those literary techniques which Wayne C. Booth termed 'the rhetoric of fiction'. Booth identifies these rhetorical tropes as characteristic of fictional works, especially novels, but it is important to be clear that their use by authors is not confined to or definitively diagnostic of invented, that is, fictional, subject matter. By the same token, the absence of such tropes does not mean that the subject matter of a work is necessarily *not* invented, however one might define the distinction between history and fiction. The issue is one of narrative style, or mode. So it's not just the appearance or possibility of historicity of person and event which defines the family saga, but rather, in the absence of rhetorical tropes characteristic of fictional narrative, a striking historicity – or better, non-fictionality – of narrative mode. Whether or not the events actually happened, or characters actually existed, they are represented as if they did, or at least might have. So whether family sagas may be regarded – or may have been regarded – as history or fiction, and indeed what the distinction between the two may be – or may have been – is not at issue in this book, although it is of course an important question in other contexts and has rightly preoccupied many scholars. Following the French literary theorist and philosopher Paul Ricœur in *Temps et Récit* (translated into English as *Time and Narrative*), I see narrativity itself as a bridge between, or interleaving of, history and fiction.

There are two techniques which are central to the rhetoric Booth associates with fictional narratives. One is the establishment of a controlling narrative voice guiding the audience's responses, describing in detail characters' inner lives and perhaps even intervening in the narrative with comments based on privileged knowledge of what is happening. The other is the creation of what the Russian formalists termed *sjuzhet* – the order in which events are narrated, or perhaps more simply plot – as distinct from *fabula* – the order in which these events, whether fictional or actual, would have taken place if they had happened in a real world, or a simulacrum of one. We might imagine that absence of these two narrative devices would leave us with a narrative akin to historical reportage, in which events are distantly and objectively narrated with no sense of a narrator manipulating for dramatic or emotional effect the order in which they happened, or engaging our sympathy or judgement by giving us privileged access to the minds and hearts of the characters, or intervening in the narrative. But family sagas are very much not detached or minimal narratives. They are rich and detailed, full of psychological subtleties and the vivid dynamics of social and family life; they score very highly on readability and audience engagement.

I shall be looking at ways in which saga authors, even though employing a self-effacing narrative voice, nevertheless maintain the urgency and complexity

– essentially, the readability – of an emotionally engaging fictional narrative. But further, I will move beyond the superficial impression of this self-effacing and detached narrator to bring to light how saga authors devise ways of allowing their narrators to offer insight into the inner lives of their characters and judgement on events or characters, and to handle the narrative line so as to modulate the chronological even-handedness of historical narrative or chronicle. To demonstrate this, I will use the tools of modern narratological theory, especially that of Gérard Genette. And as we shall see, the distinctive role and stance of the narrator are a crucial factor in our experience of how the authors of family saga narratives create and represent time – the primary subject of this book. In this, I will rely on the work of Paul Ricœur, and especially *Time and Narrative*.

I want to pause for a moment to clarify my use of the terms 'saga author' and 'saga narrator'. By narrator – or more impersonally, narrative voice – I mean what Paul Ricœur sees as an abstract unity of consciousness which we as audience apprehend as allowing us to experience the narrative. It's the voice we imagine and construct from the words of the narrative, and which listeners may hear directly in an oral recitation. In family sagas, as I have outlined, we rarely hear the voice of individuated narrators speaking directly to us, intruding in the story as they may do in other literary genres, especially novels, to offer comments or judgements, implicitly or explicitly, or to ask leading or rhetorical questions of the reader, either as fictional constructs in themselves or as *personae* adopted by an author. In fact, the saga story may sometimes seem to have a prior and independent existence of its own, the narrative voice apparently simply passing it on without intervention or involvement. The role of a creative author is squeezed out, and the universal anonymity of family saga authors reinforces this impression of absence. Thus, in family sagas, the conventional narratological distinction between author and narrator is not often a useful one. Nevertheless, I shall use *narrator* or *narrative voice* when my emphasis is on how the story is being told, and *saga author* when I am trying to highlight more distantly compositional issues – although of course the distinctions here are far from absolute. I shall work throughout with the assumption of the individual authorship of family sagas, whilst recognizing that we may in fact be dealing with a series of prior authors, perhaps oral as well as literary, and that the written version of the text which has come down to us may have been built on or changed by a succession of authors, redactors or copiers. Multiple authors would then be jointly responsible for the effect of a given example, but this does not affect my analysis, which is concerned with narrative effects, evident in the texts we have, rather than with who originally or finally produced them.

I hope, therefore, following on from my previous work on the poetics of saga prosimetrum, to take the first steps towards describing what could be built into a comprehensive poetics of family saga prose in an attempt to capture those distinctive literary strategies which their invisible authors adopt and advance with such consistency, energy and poise: in short, to begin to redefine the literary rhetoric of family saga narrative. I have limited the analysis in this book to just six family sagas: *Njáls saga, Laxdœla saga, Grettis saga, Eyrbyggja saga, Hrafnkels saga* and *Gísla saga*. My selection of texts was based on three criteria: these sagas (with the possible exception of *Grettis* saga, which has been regarded as something of an outlier) are generally accepted as representative of the family saga genre; being so celebrated, they are relatively well known and easily accessible; and finally – a somewhat self-indulgent reason – they are sagas I greatly admire and love to work with.

Throughout, my starting point is that in constructing a narrative saga authors are both representing and creating a block of time. As we shall see, the status of the narrator and the stance of the narrative voice determine how we as readers or listeners experience this block of time.

I begin, like so many others who have written on the representation and creation of time in narrative, with Augustine's celebrated articulation of the paradox of time – that logically, it defies definition, because its three elements have no existence in real life as we experience it: the past no longer exists, the present has no duration and the future does not yet exist. Augustine's response to this aporia was a concept he calls the *distentio anima* (the time of the soul), with the three elements refigured as memory, attention and expectation. Lived time is 'all in the mind' (in a sense this anticipates phenomenology, as expounded by such philosophers as Husserl and Heidegger). We can contrast this with Aristotle's concept of time: 'the time of the world' – time as external to human consciousness, measurable by cosmology, that is, the movement of heavenly bodies. Following the work of Paul Ricœur, I will look at Icelandic family saga narratives as examples of what Ricœur calls a 'third time' – that is, the time produced by narrative itself.

A narrative text can give us a specimen of time, and we can apprehend what we cannot experience in real life. This allows us a perspective on time which Boethius called *totum simul* (everything at once) – the divine perspective on human time. In the form of narrative, the slice of time is similarly simply *there*. Readers can even see it – physically and materially – as a whole, and are outside it. Even if the text is not realized physically, once the process of composition or recitation is underway the author or narrator will almost certainly be able to envisage it and, having heard it, listeners can envisage it in its entirety too. Within the confines of a narrative, past, present and future will all three be equally available at one time, in one text. Augustine imagined human time as being bounded by eternity, God's timelessness; the narrative text similarly is set in and distinct from a timeless eternity outside it which is paradoxically our real world.

But this is not our experience of actually reading or listening to a narrative, in which there is a present 'moment of attention', as Augustine terms it, and also a passed past and an unreached (even if predetermined, and unalterably laid out) future. We are experiencing as we read or listen a sort of recreation of Augustine's human, impossible-to-define time – it's rather like following the ever-moving dot on a karaoke screen. Nevertheless, even as we read or listen, we know that the text also exists outside of and distinct from our own time, and has its own integrity as a block of time. Moreover, if we know the story, we are aware of what is going to happen in its future, which is not like living our life in real human time. All this means that at the same time as viewing a text from the *totum simul* perspective, we also live through its narrative time. Ricœur calls this duality the 'double temporality' of narrative. I intend to analyse the representation and the creation of time in family saga narrative in terms of this double temporality.

When representing external, chronological time, saga authors, positioned above and beyond the narrative, implicitly assume the all-knowing *totum simul* perspective. This perspective is also implied when authors depart from the natural, or chronological, order of events, and transform a notional *fabula* into an actual narrative *sjuzhet*. But for first-time readers or listeners who are experiencing an ongoing saga narrative as if living through real time, the characteristically self-effacing saga narrator is largely absent and does not always actively betray this all-knowing position. This leaves readers and listeners to make what sense they can of what is happening – much as we do when we live in real human time ourselves, knowing little of others' motives and inner lives, and in ignorance of many salient facts and circumstances. In fact, as I shall ultimately show, saga authors may go a step further and conspicuously withhold information, so that we experience even more vividly the uncertainty of living through real time.

My first chapter will consider the representation of external time in saga narrative. Family sagas typically present to their audience 'the time of the world'. This is characteristic of historical narrative, though not limited to it, and gives family sagas their distinctively historical feel. It is often said that it is the actuality of the physical setting which gives the family sagas their air of historicity; I shall argue that equally significant is the patent actuality of their chronology. Most obvious is the overall time frame – the *söguöld* (saga age, the period in which the family sagas are set) – which is tied to major historical events (settlement, conversion, the reigns of Norwegian rulers), and events in the narrative are in turn tied to them. This stretch of time is also often ultimately tied to the present time of the narrator, who is outside the narrative, and thus, by implication, the reader or listener. It is in no sense an imaginary time, not like the distant and dream-like imagined past of the heroic or mythological poems of the Old Norse *Poetic Edda*, nor like the heroic past of other saga genres such as the *fornaldarsögur* ('sagas of olden times') – what Bakhtin called the 'walled off' past of epic – and it is recounted in largely chronological order.

No less prominent is the emphasis in family saga narratives on the realistic passage of external time within the *söguöld*: day versus night; the interplay of winter and summer; and the slow succession of calendrical cycles, both Christian and pre-Christian: Yule, Easter and so on. Furthermore, individual family sagas shape the main body of their narratives within distinctive limits of time and place. For example, the passage of time in *Laxdæla saga* is generational, the *longue durée* of a community, a set of families in a district. In *Grettis saga*, the primary span is the life of Grettir, and the cycles of measured time reflect his own circling of the island of Iceland. In all this, the narrative voice seems to be recounting – from a perspective analogous to Boethius's *totum simul* position – a completed, 'passed' past, and is necessarily heterodiegetic, that is, outside the world of the narrative, not part of it. However, narrators very rarely explicitly betray this all-knowing, quasi-divine standpoint, although, as I shall show, their position above and beyond the narrative world is often evident.

But against the backdrop of externally measured time, all authors can play a number of what Gérard Genette called 'games with time', and so my next two chapters will explore the management of narrative time in family sagas. As outlined by Genette, the chief games involve concepts of duration and order. *Duration* is very familiar and relatively simple – it's the disproportion (usually) between the time events would take in a real world, and the time the narrator takes to narrate them. Take, for example, the brief statement: 'several years passed'. This is perfectly familiar in all manner of narratives, including saga narrative. The opposite disproportion is much less common in saga narrative, because it involves giving narrative space (and therefore time) to such things as description, authorial comment and interiority, which do not advance the course of events, at least not in conventional ways. And as we shall see, there is not much of this in saga narrative. However, family saga narratives are rich in dialogue, and dialogue offers an example of isochrony: the times of action and report are roughly equal.

Order explores the difference between the sequence in which events would have taken place in a real world, and the order in which the narrative presents them to us – often figured as the fundamental distinction between *fabula* and *sjuzhet*. In family sagas, there is very little narratorial anachrony – that is, no flashbacks and/or flashforwards. But there is a wide range of intimations of the future in family sagas, such as the prophetic dreams of Guðrún in *Laxdœla saga*, in which the dreaming and the re-telling and interpretation of the dreams happen in chronological time, although their narrated content functions as a sort of coded flashforward. The key issue here is that the evocation of future events by characters in the saga – prophecies, predictions, promises, curses and so on – is not narratorial but is part of the diegesis; that is, it takes place within the storyworld because it is attributed to a character or characters in the narrative. In much the same way, references to the past are very often framed as recollection by saga characters. Whether they allude to the past or the future, all these references take place in the present time of the narrative.

In these three chapters, then, I shall explore the distinctive rhythms and patterns of external time, and the games played with time, in my selection of family sagas. In these chapters, as in the ones which follow, I shall be engaged in an oddly contradictory process: I begin by defining and analysing the characteristic narrative strategies of family sagas such as the apparently absent or at least self-effacing narrator, and the chronological ordering of the narrative, but then selecting for special emphasis and analysis the departures from this norm.

In the next two chapters, however, I want to shift the focus from the presentation of the narrative as a continuous and external whole, from the perspective of a narrator situated outside it, to the construction of the audience's experience of moving through a narrative, an experience which corresponds to Augustine's 'moment of attention' in our experience of real human time. I turn again to Ricœur, this time to his theory of 'imperfect knowledge' – the state in which the first-time reader moves through the narrative (as if riding the karaoke dot) along with some or all of the characters, in uncertainty about or actual ignorance of what is to come, and in partial knowledge of what has occurred. The reader or listener who already knows the story is in a complicatedly equivocal position, as I shall discuss. I shall argue further that there are two distinct kinds of imperfect knowledge, both conditioned by the representation or creation of time, and both manipulated by the narrator, and that both are separate from the imperfect knowledge which arises simply from not knowing what will have happened by the very end of the saga. In the first, the narrator avoids commenting on the narrative, or guiding the audience's responses to it. In the second, the narrator conspicuously fails to impart certain kinds of information about characters and/or events. These two kinds of imperfect knowledge form the basis of Chapters 4 and 5.

In Chapter 4, I will consider the voice of the silent narrator. The unheard, implicit or self-effacing narrator is paradoxically a crucial and very powerful element in saga narrative; indeed, this effacement lies at the root of the distinctive narrative mode of the family sagas. We can distinguish a number of linked features. Saga narrative is apparently objective, lacking what Mieke Bal calls 'colouring', that is, the use of emotive adverbs which indicate the narrator's ethical standpoint. Interiority – narratorial omniscience with regard to a character's feelings or motives – is typically avoided. There is almost always zero or external focalization, that is, events are not very often presented from the point of view of one or more of the characters, which would, in itself, be a version of interiority. Finally, an individualized or characterized narrative voice is largely absent. The narrative voice seems to have no designs on us, to preach no moral message, or to advance no over-arching theme, but simply to record what happened.

These sorts of narratorial absence produce a narrative which seems to move through time without the explicit manipulation or intervention of an author or narrator. The story seems to tell itself, and on occasion it is explicitly accorded autonomy and even a sort of agency with formulae such as 'as the story says'. These formulae – along with information about past times and places, and sudden allusions forward to the narrator's present day – clearly locate the situation of the narrative voice outside the temporal range of the story itself, and further, the narrator seems to avoid taking responsibility for the subject matter being related. But without the mediation or guidance of a narrator, readers and listeners move through the time of a saga narrative in a state of unusually imperfect knowledge, with an uncertain understanding of how to regard or respond to characters and events. I shall argue further that ambiguity is a carefully crafted effect in saga narrative, and not merely the result of an absence of explicit narratorial comment, although it is perhaps exacerbated for a post-medieval audience by our own ignorance of the social norms of the narrative or its setting. Naturally, there will be differences between the reception of saga narrative by a post-medieval audience and an original audience, and these differences may be considerable. But mostly, we can do no more than speculate about them. Wherever it seems possible that we might be able to gauge the distinctive response of a medieval Icelandic audience, perhaps because of social or historical determinants, I will note the possibility. Otherwise I shall use the term 'audience' – or even, anachronistically, the first person pronoun 'we' – with reference to a supposed common response to events, characters and narrative strategies. In fact, this common response will prove to be a key element in my application of Ricœur's theories of time and narrative. And as we shall see, a more significant distinction for my purposes is the distinction between a first-time audience and those who know the story in advance.

Imperfect knowledge occasioned by a self-effacing narrator is not concerned with the facts of what happened but with our response to, or reception of, what happened. However, in Chapter 5, I shall explore the ways in which the saga author, from the *totum simul* perspective, actively withholds full knowledge of what happened from the reader or listener. The saga author already knows what happened but not only the audience but also the characters in the narrative do not. I am particularly interested in a fascinating technique which also reveals the conscious artistry behind the apparent absence of a narrator: the disingenuous deployment of conspicuous silences, in which the narrative voice tells us that a conversation, for example, took place, but that no one beyond the secret speakers knew what was said. As I shall show, sometimes what has happened is disclosed sooner or later in the narrative. Sometimes we never find out. I conclude that delaying the release of or conspicuously withholding information signals the essence of what we recognize as plot.

The celebrated narrativity of family sagas is partly produced by the pull (or push) of causality, which gives the sequence of events its clear irreversibility and thus onward velocity through time, and partly through the necessary engagement of the reader or listener, who feels required to fill in what is missing: to interpret, assess and understand the import of events in the absence of narrative voice providing this information or commentary, or to fill out what the text does not say. I am well aware that this latter action is anathema to literary purists, but I shall argue that saga narratives not merely invite but require it.

In conclusion, I shall return to Ricœur's double temporality: readers or listeners can see a narrative, either physically (in the form of a book or text) or conceptually, as a mental construct, as a block of time, and this affords them a *totum simul* perspective, especially if the story is well-known to them. But they can also experience the passage of this third time along with the characters and may either be actually in a state of imperfect knowledge along with the characters, or, in a willing suspension of advance knowledge, share in that experience. All this constitutes Ricœur's 'third time', which is the temporality created by narrative itself. In sagas, the third time of narrative provides a collective experience – it's always available and is by definition a shared resource – and ideally it causes what Ricœur calls 'an alteration of consciousness' – a gradual or sudden insight into what the world looks like to others, a 'thought experiment' to quote Ricœur again. This is the fundamental resource of narrative, and only narrative can furnish us with it. It's not only being informed about the past, or being presented with a vision of an alternative world, but also being privileged to imagine, or relive, the experience as others might have experienced it. In this sense, it is the individual reader or listener who draws on and benefits from engagement with the saga narrative. But as Ricœur explains, '[both] individual and community are constituted in their identity by taking up narratives that become for them their actual history'. So it is that the narrative itself – and with it, the history in which it is situated – is transformed and accorded its full potential by and through an audience's collective reception of it.

1

The representation of external time

The *Íslendingasögur*, or family sagas, are set primarily in Iceland, in the so-called *söguöld* (saga age), that is, roughly the period from the settlement of Iceland in 870 CE to the beginnings of its Christianization in the decades following the conversion in the year 1000 CE. This location in space and time is universally regarded as the defining feature of their genre. They probably reached their final form – that is, the form in which they have come down to us – in the thirteenth and fourteenth centuries, although some of their narrative elements may very well have originated in an earlier, oral period, perhaps even close in time to events narrated in the sagas. The *Íslendingasögur* are thus not merely narrated in the conventional preterite tense of storytellers but are actually *about* the past, and this past is both in a continuum with the present time of the narrator and original audience, and conterminous with their own actual geographical location, Iceland.

Partly as a result of the largely accurate topographical detail in the sagas, and partly because in many places the topography of Iceland has changed relatively little since the Middle Ages, the settings of these medieval narratives are readily accessible to a modern audience. The attention paid to accurate topographical detail is one of the features of saga narrative which bolsters the impression it gives of historicity, or authenticity, and this inclined early saga scholars to regard the *Íslendingasögur* as historical documents. I shall argue in what follows that attention to actual historical chronologies, and to realistic temporal detail – from the passing of individual seconds to the broader sweeps of Icelandic and Norwegian history, or the naturalistic interplay of night and day, or summer and winter, and the impact their different conditions necessarily have on the lives of saga characters – contributes no less to the apparent historicity of the narrative. However at the same time, I hope to show that the representation of external, or objective, time in saga narrative is no mere inflexible scaffolding for the events of the saga but is exploited for literary ends, to promote the themes and issues which occupy each individual saga.

I shall consider in the course of this chapter the distinctive contributions of the genealogies so characteristic of the *Íslendingasögur*, and how through them the time span of the main action of certain sagas reaches both further back and further forwards in time. I shall explore how the saga author ties the events of individual sagas to established dates in Icelandic and Norwegian history. I shall look at the use of familiar naturalistic alternations in time, such as day and night or winter and summer, and also at annual calendrical markers – Christmas or Easter – and the use of Christian time labels as opposed to secular ones. I shall look too at the careful timings associated with the legal system. I shall discuss the intersection of the passage of time with geographical distance in some saga narratives, and conclude with a summary of how the distinctive concerns of individual sagas are both reflected in and augmented by their authors' representation of external time.

It is worth making clear at the outset that I shall not be concerned with the accuracy or otherwise of a saga author's chronology as set against actual historical dates, or against the timings attested in law codes. I am not even especially concerned with how far any saga's internal chronology is either consistent in itself, or consistently aligned with other saga narratives. My aim is simply to demonstrate how fundamental the explicit representation of the passage of external time is to saga narrative. More than half a century ago now, M. C. van den Toorn published an article on time and grammatical tense in the sagas which incidentally anticipated much of what has been so far written on time and saga narrative. He was emphatic about the fundamental importance of specific references to time in family sagas, asserting that 'die Verfasser nicht ohne Zeitangaben erzählten, ja, höchstwahrscheinlich nicht erzählen konnten ohne zu berichten, ob ein bestimmtes Gespräch an einem Morgen oder an einem Abend stattgefunden habe, ein Umzug im Herbst oder im Frühjahr vorgenommen wurde, eine Reise drei oder vier Jahre nach einer vorigen Reise angetreten wurde' (authors did not narrate without time references, indeed were most probably incapable of narrating without reporting that a certain conversation took place in the morning or the evening, that a move happened in autumn or spring, that a journey was undertaken three or four years after a previous one).[1] The detailed representation of the passage of external time is fundamental to family saga narrative.

Genealogies

As every reader or listener soon discovers, the *Íslendingasögur* are full of genealogical material. Much of it is 'front-loaded', that is, whole sagas, or distinct sections of whole sagas, open with an account of the forebears of what are usually the characters in the main body of the story. This technique has not always been regarded positively: Vésteinn Ólason, for example, speaks of family sagas as 'notorious for the[ir] abundance of genealogical information'.[2] Kathryn Hume, in her article about beginnings and endings in the *Íslendingasögur*, summarizes some of the most negative reactions to the amount of genealogical detail: that authors reveal their 'weakness' for genealogy, as Stefan Einarsson put it; that they 'apparently give information for information's sake', according to Theodore M. Anderson; or that, in W. P. Ker's damning and sweeping conclusion, genealogies are 'felt as a hindrance ... by all readers of the Sagas; as a preliminary obstacle to clear comprehension'.[3]

Genealogies are not in themselves a narrative form but still very clearly indicate the passage of time, an irreversible and inevitable succession of generations which is nevertheless presented in reverse order, that is, running from the forward-moving present backwards through time. The primary effect of an opening genealogy is definitively to situate the narrative which follows in the framework of actual time, the narrative emerging, as it were, from a connected list of names which was very likely to be familiar to a contemporary audience.[4] Hume marks off the genealogical material from what typically follows in the saga as a 'pre-beginning', and also discusses, as I shall in due course, the material constituting what she terms 'post-ending'.[5] Thus, the genealogies which open saga narratives stretch the time span of the saga back to earliest times, sometimes even beyond the time of the first settlers and deep into the era of their Norwegian forebears. The closing genealogical information – what Hume calls the 'post-ending' – is usually shorter, but still stretches the saga's time span forwards, sometimes far enough forward in time to reach the present time of the narrator and the saga's first audience. Both kinds of material anchor the main body of the narrative in a framework of known time. The narrative seems to constitute a distention of part of the history of Icelanders between two usually unequal genealogical summaries, like a hammock slung asymmetrically between two trees, suspended from narrow ropes.

Vésteinn Ólason concludes his discussion of saga genealogy as follows: 'Undoubtedly the most important function of the [introductory genealogical material] is to establish the impression that a reader or listener will be engaging with a truthful narrative.'[6] It seems therefore counter-intuitive to claim that the genealogies do not in fact merely function as an objective temporal scaffolding for the saga narrative, but rather make a purposeful contribution to its themes and concerns. However, opinion has more recently turned to a more favourable

– though perhaps still somewhat grudging – assessment of the contribution of genealogies. Hume herself noted that even if (or perhaps *because*) genealogical material is not integral to whatever one distinguishes as the body of the narrative – Hume defines this as 'contributing to the conflict story' – it must 'apparently [be] considered necessary to saga aesthetic'.[7] In line with W. P. Ker's focus on the experience of a reader, Vésteinn Ólason states that the genealogies are essential for those who want to 'immerse themselves fully in the saga world', and Hume concludes that sagas themselves 'satisfied psychological cravings extrinsic to aesthetic appreciation of a well-shaped plot' and that the opening and closing material contributes to that satisfaction.[8] Vésteinn goes on to argue that the genealogies can 'help to explain the origin of confederacies and alliances' – evidently what Hume had in mind as 'the conflict story' – and that from the point of view of a contemporary Icelandic audience, genealogies very often 'reveal ancestral excellence'. Finally, he quotes Einar Ólafur Sveinsson's slightly double-edged appraisal that genealogies 'endow the saga with an air of pomp and ceremony'.[9]

These affirmative judgements still assume – even if implicitly – the essential historicity of the genealogical material. Given that the twelfth-century Icelandic *Fyrsta málfræðiritgerðin* (*First Grammatical Treatise*) claims that genealogies were currently being read and written in Iceland, it seems likely that there were some secure written as well as oral genealogies available to saga authors – and probably, the population more widely.[10] No one has seriously questioned the essential authenticity of the genealogies in the sagas, and Gísli Sigurðsson rightly insists that it is 'highly improbable' that the genealogies are wholly invented.[11] But Margaret Clunies Ross adds 'carry[ing] a number of [a] saga's key themes' to the genealogies' primary function of stretching the narrative backwards and forwards in time, although she does not go into detail.[12] However, in a very detailed comparison of the genealogies in several sagas, Gísli makes a strong claim for artistic rather than factual priority: 'The differences in information offered by the various sources on families and genealogies are generally motivated by purposes specific to each occasion, with modifications and selection dictated by the needs of the narrative rather than any aim to provide a strictly historical record of the actual family connections among Icelanders in the 10th century.'[13] In what follows I shall examine some saga genealogies which in my view strongly support, and even extend, Gísli's claim.

The very nature of a genealogy – the basic structure of a family tree – means that with every generation back, there is an increasing degree of selectivity open to the saga author. One can, for example, make a decision to follow the paternal or the maternal line in each generation. Moreover, the inclusion of names at the margins of the chosen central genealogical thread – an otherwise unrecorded spouse, say, or an extra sibling, or the addition of a significant nickname – offers ample room for introducing figures who may underline or reflect the themes of the saga as a whole. It is very striking how far some family saga genealogies do appear to have been tailored to match what is narrated in the body of the saga.

Laxdæla saga, for example, opens with a genealogy of two characters whose stories figure prominently in the first part of the saga: the half-brothers Hrútr Herjólfsson and Höskuldr Dala-Kollsson. As in a number of family saga genealogies, the family is traced back to the celebrated settler Ketill flatnefr (flat-nose). Ketill is himself described as the son of a prominent Norwegian, the *hersir* (leader) Björn buna (stream), and Ketill's wife Yngvildr is also said to have come from a distinguished Norwegian family.[14] A similar genealogy is also found in *Njáls saga*, in which Hrútr and Höskuldr again feature prominently, but there is no mention there of Ketill's highborn wife or her family.[15] Five children of Ketill and Yngvildr are named in *Laxdæla saga*. One daughter married the settler Helgi inn magri (the lean), who is featured in a number of saga genealogies, but in *Laxdæla saga* his mother is also cited: she is named as Rafarta, the daughter of the Irish King Cearbhall.[16] It has been suggested that Helgi's nickname is Irish[17]; one of Ketill's sons, also Helgi, certainly had an Irish nickname: he is Helgi bjólan (probably from the Irish word *beóllan*, diminutive of the Irish word for 'mouth'). One of Ketill's daughters is the celebrated matriarch Unnr in djúpuðga (the deep-minded) – she is said to have been married to Óláfr inn hvíti (the white) who as Amhlaibh conung features in Irish annals as a prominent ruler in Ireland, though he is not mentioned in Unnr's genealogy in *Eyrbyggja saga*. Finally, Unnr's sister Jórunn is nicknamed 'manvitsbrekka' (wisdom-slope).[18]

Domination by Irish elements on the one hand, and impressive women on the other, matches perfectly the main themes of *Laxdæla saga* itself, with its celebrated heroine Guðrún Ósvífrsdóttir, and her lover Kjartan, whose grandmother was an Irish princess bought as a slave by his grandfather Höskuldr. However, the Irish princess Melkorka, Kjartan's grandmother, is not presented, even by implication, as a descendant of the Irish figures named in the genealogy, and Guðrún is only very distantly related to her powerful predecessor Unnr. In other words, the genealogy is primarily connected *thematically*, rather than by descent, to what follows in the main body of the saga.

In fact, the opening genealogy is not completely separated from the main body of the saga, as what Hume calls a 'pre-beginning'. Instead, the saga author soon begins to expand his list of names, moving into narrative mode with a detailed and lively re-enactment of Ketill's decision to emigrate to Scotland, where he is feted as a famous Norwegian aristocrat, and an account of the death of his grandson Þorsteinn, who had become king of half of Scotland before being betrayed and murdered in Caithness. The narrative then moves on to tell of Unnr who, having married two granddaughters into renowned Orcadian and Faroese dynasties, finally settles in Iceland.

In Iceland, this celebrated matriarch – an impressive woman even by the standards of saga heroines – organizes a lavish wedding feast for her great-grandson Óláfr feilan (whose nickname derives from the Irish for 'wolf'). In spite of her advanced years, she impresses all the guests with her upright and dignified bearing, but retires early to bed and is found dead – though still sitting up – the next morning.[19] She is thus the first of the powerful women for which the saga is famous. However, as we have seen, Unnr's power is expressed not only – however impressively – in her personal, domestic sphere, but also in the extraordinary management of her family dynasty. One of the enduring themes of *Laxdœla saga* is the increasing wealth and ambition of the Laxárdalr families down through the generations – sometimes, to an overweening degree. This theme meets the Irish element in the storyline when Höskuldr Dala-Kollsson buys the slave Melkorka, who turns out to be an Irish princess. The scene in which he negotiates the purchase can be read as revealing rash bravado on Höskuldr's part: it seems that his primary aim is to catch out the trader by asking to buy something which the trader does not have to sell – a slave woman – in order to show off to his companions.[20] Höskuldr and Melkorka's son Óláfr is nicknamed 'pái' (the peacock). When he travels to Ireland he is accepted as an heir to an Irish throne by his maternal grandfather King Myrkjartan.[21] But he returns to settle in Iceland and becomes the owner of a magnificent farm, Hjarðarholt, stocked with such a vast number of livestock that when they are driven from their old farm to Hjarðarholt, the narrator tells us – possibly hyperbolically – that the first animals to leave reached the new farm as the last were leaving the old one several kilometres away.[22] And towards the very end of the saga, the two strands of descent come together when Guðrún marries her fourth husband, Þorkell Eyjólfsson – he is the great-great-great grandson of Unnr.[23] Like many of his predecessors in the saga, he travels abroad to buy goods – in this case, timber from the king of Norway, as Óláfr pái did years earlier. But Þorkell shows himself to be too ambitious: he annoys the king by measuring the dimensions of a great church the king himself has had built, so that the church he, Þorkell, means to build back in Iceland will be no smaller.[24] The king accuses Þorkell of arrogance in vying with him. Before he left for Norway, Þorkell had related to his wife Guðrún a strange dream he'd had: that his beard was so enormous that it stretched over the whole of Breiðafjörðr, the largest fjord in the west of Iceland, where Unnr in djúpuðga originally settled. Þorkell characteristically supposes that the dream means that his influence and power will extend over this vast area. But the following year he is drowned in the same fjord – though not before he has made a farcical attempt to buy up the great estate of Hjarðarholt from Óláfr's son. We can see all of these long-running themes adumbrated in the opening genealogy of *Laxdœla saga*, and as I have shown, this cannot simply be ascribed to inherited traits. The genealogy must have been carefully tailored by the saga author.

The genealogy which opens *Eyrbyggja saga* traces the same ancestry for its principal characters – who are, however, not quite the same set of characters we meet in *Laxdœla saga*. Down through the generations, descendants multiply exponentially: one couple may have two children who each have two children and so on, and the increase may often be much faster than this steady rate, even allowing for unmarried and/or childless individuals. This means that very large sections of the population may trace their ancestry back to the same distant ancestors and explains why a large cast of characters in one saga may be shown to descend from the same original settlers as another almost wholly different descent group in another. But the same happens in reverse: every individual has an array of ancestors which increases exponentially back *up* through the generations. Choosing which line to follow in each generation – whether moving backwards or forwards through time – will make a significant difference to the genealogy outlined in a saga, and offers more scope for a genealogy to foreshadow the themes and events of the narrative which follows it.

Both *Laxdœla saga* and *Eyrbyggja saga* begin by tracing the genealogy of their principal characters back to Helgi inn magri and Ketill flatnefr. But even what is roughly the same genealogy can be slanted in different ways to resonate with the larger concerns of the main body of the narrative. In *Laxdœla saga*, Ketill's decision to leave Norway and the tyranny of King Haraldr, who was fighting to unite Norway under his sole rule, is attributed to the king's attack on his power and status. We are told that because Ketill was so well-born and so celebrated himself, he was welcomed in Scotland by the rulers of that country.[25] In *Eyrbyggja saga*, however, the conflict with Haraldr is concerned much more with being driven out of ancestral estates. Ketill travels not to mainland Scotland but to the Hebrides, as commanded to by the king, and in his absence Haraldr seizes his family land. When Ketill's son Björn attempts to reclaim it, he too is driven out of Norway, and he eventually settles in Iceland.[26] This is a narrative of dispossession and resettlement, rather than a story of aristocratic independence.

In *Laxdœla saga*, Ketill mocks Björn's decision to go to in Iceland and is openly disparaging about Iceland as a place to settle, dismissing it as a mere *veiðistöð* (fishing place).[27] Ketill sneers at fishing, and we should remember the story of his descendant Óláfr pái with his prestigious herd of livestock and enormous farm. And when Óláfr organizes a wedding feast there for his daughter, as part of the entertainment, he employs a skaldic poet to sing his praises – and the praises of the magnificent hall – just as the great Norwegian kings and earls had done. The Laxárdalr people like to see themselves as the equals of wealthy landowning Norwegian aristocrats. By contrast, the overall theme of *Eyrbyggja saga* is the settlement and development of a community, of how the initial rivalries and conflicts – often culminating in collective violence – are at length resolved, and how the community comes together to deal as a united front against an aggressor from outside.

To return to Ketill and his son Björn, it is with Björn's flight from Norway that the narrative of *Eyrbyggja saga* begins to follow a different genealogical line, for Björn is helped by a chieftain called Þórólfr, who also flees to Iceland and settles there. Björn's flight is not only dated to the reign of the Norwegian King Haraldr but also described as happening ten years after the first settler, Ingólfr Arnason, came to Iceland – thus reinforcing the settlement themes of the saga.[28] And finally, in view of Ketill's scorn for Iceland as merely a place to fish from, it is intriguing that Þórólfr's son Þorsteinn, although presumably named after his maternal grandfather Þorsteinn inn rauði (the red) who became joint ruler of Scotland, is nicknamed *þorskabítr* (cod-muncher).[29] In fact, the genealogical link between Þórólfr's family – which includes this fish eater – and Ketill's dynasty is a rather fragile one: we are told that Þórólfr married a woman called Unnr who is said to have been Þorsteinn inn rauði's daughter, although the great Icelandic historian Ari Þorgilsson, from whom much genealogical lore is derived, does not name her as one of Þorsteinn's children, as the narrator points out.[30] This weak link in the genealogical chain is the only connection between one of the major families in the saga – the descendants of Þórólfr – and Ketill flatnefr.

Their rivals are the family known as the Kjalleklingar, named after Kjallakr, who is the son of Björn inn austrœni (the easterner), Ketill's son, Unnr in djúpúðga's brother and thus the cousin of Þorsteinn inn rauði. The genealogies given in *Eyrbyggja saga* demonstrate the key factor underlying the conflict between these two settler families: they are fierce opponents, and yet connected – if rather distantly – by their descent from the original family who left Norway three or four generations earlier. Here, then, we can see that the opening genealogies both help us to negotiate the origins and development of feuding amongst the settlers, and also pick up on the themes of the saga as a whole – in the case of *Eyrbyggja saga*, the dynamics of settlement itself.

In spite of their usual English name, not all family sagas focus on large families of settlers and their descendants. I want now to consider another themed genealogy, this time one which opens a saga named for its protagonist: *Grettis saga*. Grettir himself is a violent, anti-social hero who is outlawed to Norway, and, on his return, survives for decades as an outlaw in Iceland itself – according to the saga, both the longest-surviving outlaw in Iceland, and also the cleverest and the strongest. As such, he is set apart from society and from his own family, and associates with those on the very fringes of human society, befriending trolls, fighting berserks and confronting aggressive revenants. It will perhaps be no surprise, then, that, as we shall see, the genealogy with which the saga opens reflects his singularity: both his isolation and his pre-eminence.

The saga begins with Önundr, Grettir's great-grandfather. His descent is not explicitly linked with that of Unnr and Ketill, although there is a distant family relationship here. However, two paternal antecedents are named: his father, Ófeigr burlufót (clubfoot) and his grandfather Ívarr, nicknamed 'beytill' (horse-prick). These two men are very far from being the representatives of aristocratic Norwegian families, with their unflattering nicknames (Ívarr's may be a foreshadowing of Grettir's sexual appetites, or even an ironic foreshadowing of the claim made later in the saga that Grettir has a surprisingly small penis), which are recounted in the saga, and possibly an echo of Grettir's own name, which can mean either 'face-puller' or 'serpent/penis'). However, Önundr's sister has unexpectedly distinguished descendants, for her daughter was the grandmother of Óláfr inn helgi – King Óláfr the saint, perhaps the most eminent Norwegian of all.[31] Further out on the other side of the family, following the distant and distinctly separate link with Unnr, it is even possible to trace Grettir's descent to the notorious legendary Viking Ragnarr loðbrók (hairy breeches). Grettir is associated with extraordinary individuals.

An even more striking impression given by the genealogy is of a mass of colourful figures with outlandish nicknames. For example, a little further on from the opening genealogy of Grettir's great-grandfather Önundr, we are offered family histories of the rebels who join with him in attempting to oppose King Haraldr. They include Ófeigr Grettir Einarsson, whose father is Ölvir barnakarl (child-man). One of Ölvir's granddaughters is married to a man called Þorbjörn laxakarl (salmon-man) and a couple of generations on, we hear of Ketill inn einhendi (the one-handed) and Ásmundr skegglauss (beardless).[32] This genealogical lore is not invented by the saga author – much of it comes from *Landnámabók,* the Book of Settlements, with its vast quantities of apparently factual information about the early settlers in Iceland.[33] But it is of a piece with the use of nicknames rather than patronymics in narrative passages: the chief opponents to Haraldr's rule are Kjötvi inn auðgi (the rich) and Þórir haklangr (long chin). Like Geirmundr heljarskinn (Hel-skin), who drops out of the rebellion, they are familiar figures in Old Norse historical traditions.[34] The opening chapters of *Grettis saga* are similarly full of intriguing nicknames and absent patronymics. Önundr himself takes on two Vikings named simply as Vígbjóðr and Vestmarr, from the Hebrides, and we are introduced to Öndóttr kráka (crow), Auðunn jarl geit (nanny-goat earl) and Eiríkr ölfúss (ale-eager).[35] The overall impression is of a wealth of barely historical but intriguing popular stories just beneath the surface of the narrative. This preponderance of animal nicknames prefigures Grettir's own marginal status as an outlaw from human society, and there is clear theming of the nicknames in the genealogical material itself: Önundr's father, as we have seen, is nicknamed 'clubfoot', and Önundr, when he loses a leg in a sea-battle, is nicknamed 'tréfótr' (wooden leg).[36] Grettir's unparalleled outlawry is brought to an end when he is unable to defend himself successfully because he is weakened by an infection in a leg injured when he was chopping a piece of driftwood cursed by a witch. What the narrative recounts of Önundr – not only the loss of his limb, but also his propensity to express his emotions in verse – clearly prefigures his great-grandson Grettir. Furthermore, his acknowledged exceptionality – the saga author notes that 'hann hefir frœknastr verit ok fimastr einfœttr maðr á Íslandi' (he has been the most courageous and nimble one-legged man [who ever lived] in Iceland) – also anticipates the saga author's summing up of Grettir's own career.[37] Even the mention of one-handed Ketill in the genealogy foreshadows the events surrounding Grettir's death, when his enemies have to cut off his hand to release his sword.[38]

Grettis saga exists, like its hero, on the margins – it contains within it a number of episodes more characteristic of the Icelandic *fornaldarsögur* than of the sober naturalism of many family sagas. The opening genealogy, together with the very first narrative chapters, is peopled with Vikings and berserks, awash with evocative nicknames and notably lacking in the kind of historical sobriety which we might expect. So yet again, we can see that what might have constituted an objectively historical framework to the main action seems in addition to reflect the major issues – and, indeed, the whole premise – of the saga.

Together with introductory narratives about the antecedents of a saga's main characters – Unnr in djúpúðga, say, or Önundr tréfótr – who prefigure the careers and concerns of the central characters in their sagas, genealogical material slanted in the ways I have described contributes to a highly allusive and tightly themed story. But there are much more radical twists on the standard opening genealogies. Most notoriously, *Njáls saga* does not begin with a genealogy at all but plunges without any preamble into the present time of the beginning of the main story: 'Mörðr hét maðr ... ' (There was a man called Mörðr ...).[39] Although Mörðr's father is named, the saga author almost at once turns to his daughter, Unnr, another of the major players in the first half of the saga. This is an extraordinarily bold move. The story moves on to Höskuldr Dala-Kollsson, whom we will remember from *Laxdæla saga*, and thence to the familiar genealogy reaching back to Unnr in djúpúðga and Ketill flatnefr. Why then does the saga author begin with Mörðr and his daughter Unnr? Could it be because the saga has broken away from a postcolonial mindset, which insists on anchoring the settlement of Iceland to Norway as a first move? Or even, as Theodore M. Andersson has suggested, because *Njáls saga* is a text which reveals – however obliquely – a collapse of confidence in the golden age of the first settlers, such that its author no longer feels the need to begin the narrative there but insists on bringing to the fore Icelandic events after that settlement?[40] One final possibility is that genealogical material, as I have noted, is often 'front-loaded', that is, a great mass of characters are introduced together at the beginning of the narrative, though they may not have a part to play in the action until further on. This produces the implicit impression that these characters somehow actually exist – that is, that they are in place in a past actuality (or simulacrum of one) independent of the course of the narrative, and are not simply brought into being when the narrator needs them for the ensuing action. It is with Unnr that the sexual, or marital, themes of the saga begin; introducing her and her father at the very outset of the saga privileges a fundamentally fictional strategy: the establishment of an overriding theme to the narrative.[41]

Events outside Iceland

Another striking departure from the customary settlement genealogy is the opening of *Hrafnkels saga*. The author begins with a genealogy, but it is not a genealogy of Hrafnkell's antecedents, of whom we know practically nothing, but of King Haraldr himself, spliced in between a statement of the date of

Hrafnkell's father's emigration to Iceland – 'Þat var á dögum Haralds konungs ins hárfagra ... ' (It was during the reign of King Haraldr finehair ...) – and the emigration itself – 'at sá maðr kom skipi sínu til Íslands ... er Hallfreðr hét' (that a man called Hallfreðr came with his ship to Iceland).[42] Here, the saga author reaps all the rewards of genealogical information as earlier scholars saw them: a sense of occasion, historical authority and fixing the narrative in external time. But at the same time, the saga author introduces his story of a settler in Iceland who does not arrive with the cultural baggage of a distinguished Norwegian family, who precociously makes his own way in the new country, and who comes to care little for the old rules or inherited pieties.

Hrafnkels saga is unusual in that this opening reference to the rule of King Haraldr is the only one in the saga linked to a dateable historical event outside Iceland. As we shall see, family sagas typically play out against the background of actual history, most often Norwegian, in the form of references to whoever was ruling Norway at the time. But Hrafnkell himself has cut his ties with Norway; thus, even external historical time references are tailored – like the genealogical material – to the themes of individual sagas.

When Icelanders in the *Íslendingasögur* travel to mainland Scandinavia – especially Norway – they are invariably presented as being received, usually with honour, by the current ruler there. This automatically provides a historically verifiable backbone to the saga even if it was not necessarily the saga author's primary purpose. The bold opening of *Njáls saga*, lacking the customary genealogy, and with no reference to the tyranny of King Haraldr as a motivating factor for the settlement of Iceland, has been interpreted as signalling a move away from the traditional postcolonial tie with Norway. But even here, whenever a character goes abroad, we are kept up to date with Norwegian rulers. When, for instance, Gunnarr goes to Norway with his brother Kolskeggr, we are told that Hákon jarl Sigurðsson has succeeded Haraldr gráfeldr (grey cloak), thus dating the journey to sometime after 965 CE.[43] It is perhaps significant that Gunnarr chooses at first to go raiding rather than become one of Hákon's retainers. But when he travels on to Denmark, he is warmly received by King Haraldr Gormsson, nicknamed 'blátönn' (bluetooth), and eventually goes back to Norway to be lauded by Hákon jarl.[44] After Gunnarr's death, his brother Kolskeggr travels to Denmark and enters the service of King Sveinn tjúguskegg (forkbeard), and later still in the saga, his kinsman Þráinn Sigfússon also travels to Norway, and as Gunnarr's kinsman is well received by Hákon in Norway.[45]

This pattern is repeated in many family sagas. In *Eyrbyggja saga*, for example, Vermundr and his brother-in-law Þórarinn are said to be received in Norway by Hákon jarl, which serves to date their journey by his rule from 965–95 CE.[46] But as we might expect, the trope is particularly prominent in *Laxdœla saga*, in which Icelandic families habitually measure themselves against Norwegian royalty. Höskuldr Dala-Kollsson is said to have been a retainer of King Hákon Aðalsteinsfóstri, and some manuscripts add that he spent alternate winters with the king in Norway and at home in Iceland.[47] His half-brother Hrútr, who has not yet settled in Iceland, is a retainer of Haraldr gráfeldr, the grandson of Haraldr inn hárfagri (the fine haired), and son of the notorious Eiríkr blóðøx (blood-axe).[48] But throughout the saga, successive generations of Icelanders perpetuate these links with Norway in rather different ways. Óláfr pái is warmly welcomed by Hákon jarl, but when his son Kjartan travels to Norway, Hákon has been succeeded by King Óláfr Tryggvason, with whom Kjartan – the proudly independent Icelander – at first clashes.[49] And as we have already seen, towards the end of the saga, Guðrún's husband Þorkell travels to Norway to buy timber and angers King Óláfr with his ambition to build a huge church back in Iceland to rival Óláfr's great minster in Trondheim.[50]

A sentence of outlawry may also cause a saga character to travel abroad, though a warm welcome from the current ruler is less likely. Grettir travels to Norway when he is first outlawed. Amongst his adventures there is an encounter with a group of berserks who have themselves been outlawed by Earl Eiríkr, the son of Hákon jarl. Grettir is staying in Norway with one of the earl's allies, who is thus the target of the berserks' aggression. Although Grettir is not himself received by the earl, in explaining his part in the campaign against the berserks the saga author effectively ties his outlawry to Norwegian dates.[51] Flosi in *Njáls saga* is outlawed as the leader of those who burned Njáll and his sons inside their house, and though he means to go to Norway, he is blown off course, and to his discomfiture finds himself in Orkney, which is now under the rule of Earl Sigurðr Hlöðvísson (991–1014 CE), one of whose followers was Helgi Njálsson, who was killed in the burning. Although initially furious when Flosi identifies himself, the earl and the burner are in due course reconciled.[52]

Sigurðr Hlöðvisson of Orkney is one of the major players in the Battle of Clontarf, in 1014, an account of which constitutes a major part of *Njáls saga*.[53] These connections tie Icelanders, especially Flosi's company of burners, and events in Iceland to a very widely known and dated historical event. While, as we have seen, Grettir himself is connected to real historical time in Norway, the epilogue to the saga – in which, in a romance-derived episode, Grettir is avenged in Byzantium – is carefully dated to the reign of the Emperor of Byzantium Michael Katalak, who ruled from 1034 to 1041 CE. And although no precise date is adduced, in *Eyrbyggja saga* we are told that Björn Breiðvíkingakappi, outlawed after a controversial love-affair which ended in Björn killing the woman's husband's supporters, travels via Denmark to Jómsborg, a celebrated Viking stronghold on the Baltic coast. The leader of the Vikings there is named as Pálna-Tóki, which similarly places Björn's journey to Jómsborg within a known historical period.[54]

As with the link between the settlement of Iceland and the reign of King Haraldr of Norway,[55] the other great Icelandic event which is linked to the regnal dates of a Norwegian ruler is the evangelization and conversion of Iceland to Christianity, initiated by King Óláfr Tryggvason (995–1000 CE). The author of *Njáls saga* prefaces his account of Iceland's conversion to Christianity with an unambiguous historical reference: 'Höfingjaskipti varð í Nóregi. Hákon jarl var liðin undir lok, en kominn í staðinn Óláfr Tryggvason' (There was a change of ruler in Norway. Hákon jarl had died, and Óláfr Tryggvason had succeeded).[56] This introduces news of the conversion of Norway and prepares the way for Iceland's own conversion in the year 1000 CE.[57]

All of these historical references to the rulers of Norway set the family sagas against a well-known backdrop of actual history. It seems likely that the regnal dates of Norwegian rulers were common knowledge amongst educated people in Iceland. Ari Þorgilsson in his *Íslendingabók* claims that this work is an abridgement of a longer work of his own (no longer in existence) which included the regnal dates of Norwegian kings. He also makes reference to the Icelandic historian Sæmundr (1056–1133), whose work, though now lost, was a history of the Norwegian kings which greatly impressed later historians such as Snorri Sturluson, and was the basis of the twelfth-century genealogical poem *Noregskonungstal* (List of Norwegian Kings).[58] Saga authors saw their narratives unfolding in tandem with actual history.

Events in Iceland

I want now to turn to the internal chronologies of saga narratives, to show that in spite of some glitches, saga authors had a strong sense of the steady, naturalistic passing of past time, and a strong desire to reflect this in their narratives. What happens in sagas is linked not only to Norwegian dates, but also to major internal Icelandic events. Thus, for example, the death of Snorri goði (the chieftain), who features in *Laxdæla saga* and *Eyrbyggja saga*, is linked in both to the death of St. Óláfr. The dating is part of a final rounding off, or summing up, of events: the sentiment is that with the death of two great men – one in Iceland and the other in Norway – the *söguöld* (saga age) has come to an end. *Eyrbyggja saga* states that Snorri died in Sælingsdalstunga (in Iceland) one year after the death of St Óláfr, and that he was buried in the church which he himself had had built.[59] In *Laxdæla saga*, the saga author recounts different details: the circumstances of Snorri's last illness, noting that he was at that time sixty-seven years old, and that this was one year after the death of St Óláfr, adding that Ari is the source for this information.[60]

The internal chronology of *Laxdæla saga* is much more detailed than that of many other family sagas: ages, in years, and relative datings, and intervals of time, are often specified. In fact, this internal chronology is not wholly consistent, and the saga author's desire to include so much chronological detail may well have created the problem. What interests me is not the author's success or otherwise in presenting a consistent chronology, but the evident ambition to show how a series of internal time scales fit together and run parallel to external events. Events are dated relative to two main events, one internal – Iceland's conversion to Christianity – and the other external – the death of St Óláfr. But as Einar Ól. Sveinsson points out in the introduction to his edition of the saga, the two chronologies do not match up.[61] Furthermore, the saga's internal chronology is contradictory.

Given the saga author's practice of relative dating, it isn't easy to give individual, isolated examples of inconsistency; whole networks of events are interconnected, and the knock-on effects are extended. But one particularly straightforward instance involves the dating of Bolli Bollason's vengeance against his father's killer, Helgi Harðbeinsson. When Bolli senior was killed, we are told of a dramatic, even histrionic, gesture on the part of Helgi, who wipes the blood off the weapon he has used to kill Bolli on his widow Guðrún's shawl. Helgi prophetically remarks that his own nemesis is lying under the shawl, and indeed, Guðrún is pregnant with Bolli Bollason.[62] Twelve years later, the prophecy is fulfilled when the boy kills Helgi. But this stretch of twelve years is very difficult to fit into the saga's narrative chronology. To disguise the gap, after Helgi's prediction the saga turns to the man who is to become Guðrún's fourth husband, Þorkell Eyjólfsson. Þorkell goes to Norway for a year, but when the narrative returns to Guðrún, in Iceland, twelve years seem to have passed by, for we are told that the boy Bolli is now twelve years old.[63] This fold, or pleat, in the narrative chronology has a number of disruptive effects, most obviously concerning the age of Guðrún and Þorkell's first child Gellir, whose birth, according to other relative datings in the saga – and some of them external ones – must have been much earlier than twelve years after Bolli's death. But if Guðrún and Þorkell did indeed have a child shortly after Bolli's death, this would make a nonsense of Helgi's dramatic gesture, and young Bolli's precocious role as his father's avenger, for Guðrún has made it quite clear that she will not marry again until her late husband Bolli has been avenged, and she has been waiting for her sons to grow up. In short, as Magnus Magnusson and Hermann Pálsson suggest, the whole vengeance episode 'seems to have been invented for the purpose of enhancing Bolli Bollason's prestige'.[64] Moreover, as they point out, 'the whole of the marvellously detailed account of the vengeance wreaked on Helgi Hardbeinsson for the death of Bolli Þorleiksson seems to have no historical basis at all'.[65]

We are left with a contradiction: the very chronological markers which ostensibly serve to situate the saga narrative in real time are inconsistent and possibly even sometimes subservient to the probably fictional drama of the narrative. There are a number of similar inconsistencies in *Laxdæla saga*, and indeed in many other sagas. Perhaps it's inevitable that with such complex and multi-stranded narratives as full-length family sagas, chronological inconsistencies will arise, and we do not need to attribute every case to a saga author deliberately sacrificing chronology to fictional effects. Nevertheless, it is clear from at least this one example in *Laxdæla saga* that the author's primary purpose was not to document a historically viable chronology, but rather to set a fictional narrative within a context of apparent chronological actuality.

As we have seen, the settlement of Iceland and its association with the tyranny of Haraldr inn hárfagri provides a clear historical situation, as well as a date, for the beginnings of many family sagas. The conversion of Iceland to Christianity may also occur as an event in saga narrative itself, but may on occasion be used simply as an external dating point. In *Grettis saga*, we are told that Grettir's father came to Iceland to settle in the Vatnsdalr district. The leading settler there is Þorkell krafla (scrabbler), who features prominently in *Vatnsdæla saga*, and this connection links the two sagas. Þorkell, we are told, was given provisional baptism (he was 'prime-signed'), and the saga author links the settlement of Grettir's family in Iceland with events leading up to the conversion – specifically, the missionary work of Þorvaldr Koðránsson and Bishop Friðrekr. The saga author adds that although there are many stories associated with their mission, this saga is not the place to tell them – the saga author is not bringing in the events preceding the conversion on their own account, but simply as a date marker.[66] Similarly, incidentally, in *Eyrbyggja saga*, we are told that Snorri goði lived at Helgafell for eight years after Christianity was made law in Iceland. After this, he apparently exchanged farms with Guðrún.⁶⁷ This ties the chronology of *Eyrbyggja saga* to the already shaky framework of *Laxdœla saga*, and there are a several such explicit links between the two sagas. But there is also a sense that the ancient link between Helgafell, the sacred mountain of the original pagan settlers of Þórsnes, and the descendants of that side of the family has, following the conversion, faded and been dismantled; we are told in *Laxdœla saga* that Guðrún later builds a Christian church there.⁶⁸

There are a number of other instances of dating saga events to historical dates in the history of Iceland, and many of them are similarly resonant with the themes of the saga in question. In *Grettis saga*, for instance, we hear early on about a violent conflict over a beached whale in a time of famine. Rights to the whale are disputed – the issue rests on the land rights granted by the original settler in the area to Grettir's then newly arrived great-grandfather Önundr. But fighting breaks out and men are killed and severely wounded on both sides. When, eventually, a truce is called, the current lawspeaker Þorkell máni (moon) is called in to make a ruling.⁶⁹ From the work of the historian Ari, we can date Þorkell's term of office – and thus, the episode more generally – to 970–84 CE.⁷⁰ In *Grettis saga*, Þorkell's ruling over who has rights to the beached whale is reached by reference to a similar case involving Þorkell's grandfather Ingólfr – the first settler in Iceland. Þorkell establishes an important legal point even though the fight over the whale may have seemed an undignified brawl. Ironically, it has been calculated that the famine alluded to at the beginning of the episode more likely dated to the first half of the tenth century – well before Þorkell became lawspeaker.⁷¹ So again the impulse to provide explicit dating for events in the saga narrative has overridden – whether by accident or design – historical accuracy.

In *Njáls saga*, we see an even more striking example. Njáll has fostered Höskuldr Þráinsson, as part of an ambitious, but ultimately doomed, peace settlement; Höskuldr's father had been killed by Njáll's son Skarpheðinn. Höskuldr is presented as a paragon of virtue and accomplishment, and Njáll becomes extremely fond of him. In an attempt to arrange a prestigious marriage for him, Njáll approaches Flosi – who is later to lead the men who burn Njáll and his family to death in their farmhouse – about his impressive niece Hildigunnr. Hildigunnr, however, refuses a match with a man who does not have a formal chieftainship. According to the saga, Njáll, famed for his legal acumen, hatches a plan: that summer, he deliberately causes the lawsuits he is involved in to come to an impasse, and then argues the case for an extra court – the so-called Fifth Court – to deal with such lawsuits such as this one, which cannot be resolved in the normal way. The lawspeaker, Skapti Þóroddsson, is persuaded; new chieftainships are set up to service it; Njáll's foster-son Höskuldr is – of course – appointed to one of them; and he is duly married to Hildigunnr.[72] However, according to all other sources, the Fifth Court was actually set up some years later – *c*. 1005 CE – and Skafti himself, who was lawspeaker from 1004 to 30, instituted it, not Njáll.[73] Perhaps the author of *Njáls saga* was either working from alternative sources, or muddled in his chronology. But this story of Njáll's procurement of a chieftainship for his own foster-son, by what is evidently legal chicanery, adds very greatly to the irony, fatalism and moral ambiguity of the saga as a whole.

One final example of dating by domestic history involves – perhaps unexpectedly – the settlement of Greenland. In *Eyrbyggja saga*, a case of unlawful wounding is heard at the local Þórsnes assembly. This case is a small part of the widespread feuding in the district, involving as it does the powerful chieftain Snorri goði. But we are then told that at the same assembly, a case was heard against Eiríkr inn rauði (the red). This case is intertwined with local alliances, but the saga author goes on to explain that Eiríkr leaves the assembly and journeys to Greenland; that he stayed there for three years; and that after returning to Iceland for one year, he returned to Greenland to settle there. The saga says that this was fourteen years before the conversion.[74] It all fits with what we know from elsewhere of Eiríkr's discovery and settlement of Greenland, and the dating roughly matches what Ari sets out in his *Íslendingabók*.[75] In one respect, then, the author of *Eyrbyggja saga* has simply attached an event in his narrative to a secure and probably well-known historical date. But the references to Greenland promote the saga's thematic focus on settlement. The settlement of Greenland is carefully recorded in Ari's *Íslendingabók*, and as Siân Grønlie points out, Greenland would have held a prominent place in Icelanders' sense of a national identity as emigrants themselves becoming emigrants and settlers in their turn, since its settlement 'establishes Iceland as no longer a periphery of Norway ... but a centre for migration elsewhere'.[76]

I want to turn now to the way saga authors represent and exploit not merely the passage of historical time, but the passage of what might be called 'natural', or 'environmental time' in daily life – the passing of seasons, and of days and nights. Following this, I will explore the representation of what might be called 'cultural' time – segments of time which are used to determine social dates in daily life such as the dates of assemblies, the sentences of outlawry or the major Christian festivals.

Natural time: The seasons

Throughout the family sagas, there is a strong sense of the movements of seasons, the alternation of summer and winter and the weather conditions which go with them. I have never noticed a discrepancy between the weather conditions depicted or implied and the time of year required by the course of the narrative. This in itself lends sagas a convincing air of actuality and plausibility. Saga authors are also attentive to the time taken to cover distances. Most obviously, this relates to travelling times: the time taken to sail from Norway to Iceland, or vice versa, or the time taken to travel to the Alþing. The necessity of acknowledging in the narrative the time the journey would take is very seldom overlooked, and realistic estimates are almost always provided. Again, *Hrafnkels saga*, which takes movement across Iceland as one of its major themes, provides a number of examples. We are told, for example, that Hrafnkell's coastal route from the remote eastern fjords to the annual Alþing is a seventeen-day journey on horseback, while Sámr's perilous shortcut between inland glaciers enables him to arrive at the assembly before Hrafnkell gets there, even though he sets off after him.[77] Most dramatically, when Hrafnkell pursues Sámr's brother Eyvindr across moorland and bog, and Sámr pursues him in turn, not only is the route meticulously detailed, but so too is the effect on the speed of all three parties of the terrain, whether mud, a downhill slope or a treacherous rocky surface; the mesmerizing tension of the pursuit depends for its effect on the saga author's confident mastery of the interrelationship of time, speed and terrain.[78]

Realistic intervals of time for news to spread, either from one part of Iceland to another, or from abroad, are also characteristic of saga narrative. In *Njáls saga*, for instance, the news of Gunnarr's death reaches Norway from Iceland only after a reasonable interval (and significantly, only when travel between the two countries becomes feasible in the spring).[79] And at the very end of the saga, Hrafn inn rauði (the red) brings news of the Battle of Clontarf to Flosi in Orkney a week after the battle.[80]

Given the adverse weather conditions in winter in Iceland and Norway, travelling, especially by sea, almost always takes place in the summer. This is easy enough for the saga author to accommodate in the narrative: we frequently hear of Icelanders who begin preparations for a journey to Norway in late spring or early summer, or wait out a winter in Norway before setting sail back to Iceland. Conformity to this seasonal imperative is taken so much for granted that it barely needs a mention in some instances. In *Grettis saga*, for example,

Sveinn jarl Hákonarson is persuaded to banish Grettir from Norway after a series of killings, rather than actually killing him, but in spite of his anger, he tells those who have pleaded for Grettir's life that he will be free to go 'þegar skip ganga' (as soon as ships are sailing).[81] In *Laxdæla saga* Óláfr pái decides to travel to Norway one spring and is invited to spend the winter with a retainer of Hákon jarl. The following spring, Óláfr travels to meet Hákon, to carry out the purpose of his journey: to request timber to take back to Iceland. He sails back to Iceland in the summer and builds a great hall at Hjarðarholt. Hákon's retainer with whom he had spent the winter travels back to Iceland with him that summer and marries Óláfr's daughter in late winter.[82] The seasonal rhythms are almost intuitively observed. And failure to abide by them generally ends badly. It is just before Easter that Þorkell Eyjólfsson, Guðrún's fourth husband, disregards advice not to sail in bad weather, and he and all his men are drowned when his boat is overturned in Breiðafjörðr.[83]

Emigration to Iceland and subsequent settlement invariably follow the same seasonal rhythms. In *Hrafnkels saga*, Hrafnkell's father first sets up a farm called Arnþrúðarstaðir and spends the winter there – so we assume he sailed out the previous summer – but when he moves again, he waits until spring.[84] This pattern is repeated in any number of family sagas. Once in Iceland, saga characters are shown managing their lives against this slow, unchanging annual pattern: travelling to legal assemblies in the spring, making journeys abroad in the summer, and waiting out a long winter punctuated by feasts and festivities. Inevitably, events in Iceland are determined and advanced by these temporal markers: agreements and disagreements, betrothals and violence, happen at assemblies and gatherings; characters leave and return to Iceland in summer, when the weather is fit for travelling. But within this ineluctable seasonal round, which lends a solidly plausible foundation to family saga narratives and involves the whole Icelandic community, saga authors often reveal an acute attentiveness to more minor and even individual entailments of seasonal change. Sometimes, these allusions to season or weather seem merely incidental, maintaining the characteristic naturalism of saga narrative. Sometimes, however, the saga author exploits to dramatic – and yet still plausibly naturalistic – effect the influence of seasonal conditions on his characters and events.

As we have seen, in *Laxdæla saga* Guðrún takes over Snorri goði's farm at Helgafell. When her father Ósvífr falls ill and dies, he is buried in the church which Guðrún has had built at Helgafell. His friend Gestr falls ill the same year, and tells his son that he too wants to be buried at Helgafell. Gestr has been living in the west, at Barðaströnd, and when he dies during the winter – winter is always a bad time for old people – moving the body to Helgafell is problematic, because the weather has been particularly harsh. The fjord is iced over, and ships cannot set sail to cross it. Manuscripts differ in their account of the number of days Gestr's body remained unburied but agree that a fierce wind suddenly blew up, cleared away the ice and just as suddenly dropped, producing a perfect day for travel across the fjord. Gestr's son sets sail, with the body on board, and – with that close attention to realistic time we have been observing throughout – arrives at Helgafell in the evening. The following morning, Gestr is duly buried, in the same grave as his old friend Ósvífr. A day later, the storm returns; the ice is blown back to the shore and Breiðafjörðr is rendered impassable once more, remaining so for the rest of the winter. As the narrator pointedly remarks, 'þóttu at þessu mikil merki, at svá gaf til at fara með lík Gests, at hvárki var fœrt áðr né síðan' (People thought it very remarkable that transporting Gestr's body had proved possible when it could not have been moved either before or after).[85] This unlikely co-operation of the weather falls somewhere between an uncanny occurrence and the sort of weird natural coincidence which might just have actually happened and, if it did, would certainly have lodged itself in popular memory. In fact, the story might even have acquired its quasi-supernatural quality as it was orally retold, with the period of good weather being shortened to create a more striking episode. And we must pay attention to Gestr's reputation for prophecy. It is Gestr who is shown earlier in the saga as interpreting Guðrún's dreams as a prefiguration of her four marriages, as I shall discuss in Chapter 3. Her father Ósvífr is not present at their meeting, but Guðrún presses Gestr to stay with them that evening. However, Gestr – on his way to the Alþing, with an arduous and time-constrained itinerary – politely refuses, prophesying that he and Ósvífr will end up as much closer neighbours, with all the time in the world to talk together. This is the context of the strange behaviour of the winter weather, and just to make sure, the saga author reminds us of Gestr's prophecy as he concludes his account.[86]

Winter conditions play a similarly crucial role in *Gísla saga*. As an outlaw, Gísli is of course particularly subject to the passing of the seasons, hiding out in the countryside during the spring and summer, and being sheltered by supporters in the winter. Gísli's brother-in-law – his wife's brother – and closest friend Vésteinn has been murdered, and Gísli claims to know who the culprit is.[87] Gísli's brother Þorkell, and his and Gísli's brother-in-law Þorgrímr – Gísli's sister's husband – are holding a feast with sacrifices to the god Freyr in their farmstead adjoining Gísli's at the traditional time of the 'Winter Nights' (around the middle of October). Travelling is initially possible, at least for neighbours in the district, but late in the evening of their arrival, we are told that it begins to snow, with the careful detail that it laid on the ground. Gísli leaves his house in the middle of the night and wades along the bed of stream which runs between the two holdings. He makes his way into Þorgrímr's farmhouse, Sæbol, and in a very celebrated scene, stabs him in bed, where he is lying next to his wife, Gísli's sister Þordís. Þordís wakes, thinking that her husband has touched her, and remarks that his hand is cold – as, indeed, Gísli's hand would be on that snowy night. Gísli does not make the same mistake twice and warms his hand while he waits for the couple to fall asleep, before making a second attempt. After the killing, Gísli makes his way back to his own house, and only now does the narrator point out that by wading through the stream he will have left no tracks in the newly fallen snow. With the saga's usual attention to diurnal rhythms, Gísli is said to go back to bed, while over at Sæbol people rush to light lamps and try to apprehend the killer. But it is too late, and it is not until the next morning that Gísli's brother Þorkell and his guest Eyjólfr make their way to Gísli's house, ostensibly to break the news of the murder. Gísli pretends to know nothing about what has happened, but his brother Þorkell spots that the snowy weather might yet give Gísli away, for his shoes are covered in snow and ice. Þorkell, impossibly caught between loyalties, secretly pushes the telltale shoes under Gísli's bed.[88]

Here, weather and time of day entirely naturalistically serve the sequence of events. In the winter following the autumn of the killing, the narrator notes, frost and snow never settle on Þorgrímr's burial mound (unlike the snow on the ground between the two farms on the night of the murder). The narrator tells us that some people say this is because the god Freyr was so gratified by Þorgrímr's sacrifices that 'hann myndi eigi vilja, at frøri á milli þeira' (he didn't want frozen earth to come between them).[89] The narrative exploits to the full the entailments of the season in which it is set, and the time of day at which the events take place.

Wintry conditions naturally produce a dramatic backdrop to events. Perhaps the most memorable is Skarpheðinn Njálsson's winter killing of Þráinn Sigfússon. The Markarfljót river is described in detail: partly iced over, but still flowing, and bridged at intervals by arches of ice. Skarpheðinn sees Þráinn and his men on the other side of the water. He leaps across the river, skims at speed – 'svá hart sem fogl flygi' (as fast as a bird in flight) – over the smooth slab of ice on the other side, and catches Þráinn such a fierce blow that his head is split open and his teeth scatter across the ice.[90]

Summer does not usually produce such dramatic effects, but its own particular conditions are often exploited in saga narrative. For example, in a farming community, midsummer haymaking is the busiest time of year, and this often has significant implications in sagas. In *Laxdœla saga*, for example, Bersi Véleifsson, bedridden through an illness, is left at home minding a baby in a cradle when the rest of the household are out saving the hay. When the cradle upsets, and the baby rolls out, Bersi speaks a little verse lamenting his inability to help the baby which cannot help itself, and noting wryly that at least the baby will improve.[91] This verse is also quoted in *Kormáks saga* but is less well contextualized there.[92] Here in *Laxdœla saga* the realistic detail of the busy midsummer household working outside, leaving indoors only the very old and the very young, provides the perfect naturalistic context, whether that represents some actual context for the verse, or is due to the art of the saga author.

Haymaking also has the effect of leaving farmsteads undefended. One of the two great climaxes in *Njáls saga*, the killing of Gunnarr, takes place when his household are away from the farmstead, finishing off the haymaking.[93] And when, in *Hrafnkels saga*, an old woman rushes into the farmstead to alert Hrafnkell to the approach of Eyvindr Bjarnarson and urge her master to take immediate vengeance on him, Hrafnkell himself, like Gunnarr, is asleep at home with his closest retainers while the rest of the household are busy in the fields.[94] In *Gísla saga*, there is a dramatic twist to this trope. Gísli's brother-in-law Vésteinn is on his way to the feast held to celebrate the Winter Nights – the celebration which eventually leads to Gísli's murder of Þorgrímr, discussed above. Vésteinn has been abroad, in England; he has returned to Iceland and is making his way to the feast at Gísli's, although Gísli, fearing that his life is in danger, tries hard to prevent him. A few nights after his arrival, a sudden squall in the middle of the night blows part of the thatch off the farmhouse, and it begins to rain very heavily.[95] Gísli's first thought is to save his stock of winter hay – vital fodder to keep his livestock fed over the coming winter. He and all the farmhands rush out to cover the hay, leaving Vésteinn (whose offer of help is politely refused by his host Gísli), his sister, Gísli's wife, and a cowardly slave alone in the farmhouse. It is now that someone creeps into house and murders Vésteinn.[96]

In this episode, we can appreciate the perfect harmony of narrative event and natural time. The feast is held at the traditional time of year, around the middle of October. Vésteinn must have returned to Iceland from a period abroad in the summer, when the conditions for an ocean journey would have been optimal. But winter is on its way, and the weather turns suddenly bad. After the summer's haymaking, any competent farmer's barn would be packed with hay in the hope of being able to feed the livestock over a long harsh winter. October would be a disastrous time to suffer the loss of it. The events of the narrative do not merely take place against the backdrop of a seasonal pattern but are inextricably intertwined with its conditions. This tight interweaving can be interpreted in two ways. The narrative is so solidly plausible that it may reflect actuality: that Vésteinn was actually murdered in the circumstances and at the time of year the narrative depicts. The alternative is to credit the saga author – or the creator of some tradition preceding the narrative as we have it – with a very remarkable ability to produce a seamless simulacrum of actuality.

In the medieval period, Iceland was essentially a subsistence economy, and shortages of produce – especially given Iceland's isolation during the winter months – are shown in the sagas to lead to tensions, violence and sometimes fatality. But again, the saga author is revealed to be constantly alert to the issue and often explores it in conjunction with the underlying themes of particular sagas. In *Njáls saga* and in *Hrafnkels saga*, we see two very striking instances of the crucial role of food supplies in Icelandic society – and thus in saga narrative. In the former, we are told that there was a serious famine, and that supplies ran very short throughout the whole country. Gunnarr shares what he has with his neighbours, but when these supplies run out, he turns to a neighbour, Otkell, and asks if he can buy hay and food. Otkell, egged on by a malicious friend, refuses to let Gunnarr have any supplies. Njáll condemns this selfish and anti-social behaviour, and makes Gunnarr a hugely generous gift from his own store: he has fifteen horses loaded with hay, and another five with food supplies. All this takes place in the spring, at a time when winter supplies might indeed be nearly exhausted, but before even early harvests could replenish them. In this context, the saga narrative sets up a pointed contrast between Otkell's meanness and Njáll's admirable generosity.[97]

In the summer, Gunnarr rides to the local assembly and, while he is away, his wife Hallgerðr sends a slave to steal butter and cheese from Otkell's farmstead; Otkell, like Gunnarr, is at the assembly. Her attempts to cover up the theft with arson are initially successful, but Gunnarr realizes that she must have stolen the food. Clearly Hallgerðr was not short of provisions because when challenged by her husband, she brings out an alternative meal. A couple of weeks afterwards, she is caught out in the theft when she tries to get rid of the stolen property by giving the cheese to some travelling women sent to her as a trap. The cheese, in a stunningly realistic detail, is even shown to fit the mould usually used by Otkell's wife.[98] In this second episode, the theft of foodstuffs is not linked to seasonal considerations; food is by now not in short supply. Instead, the theft seems to be simply an act of vengeance – there is no suggestion that Hallgerðr is in desperate need of the foodstuffs, even though she has previously been described in the saga as 'fengsǫm' (prodigal with provisions).[99] What we see here is a telling distinction: Hallgerðr is not responding to the exigencies of daily life in a subsistence farming economy, but to the superseding imperative of vengeance, linked to but separate from an episode which arose naturally from the necessities of the agricultural year.

In *Hrafnkels saga*, the old man Þorbjörn is made a startlingly generous offer of informal, out-of-court compensation for the killing of his son by the powerful chieftain Hrafnkell. The basis of the offer is the lifetime provision of milk in the summer and meat in the autumn, for his whole household.[100] If we see this offer against the episodes from *Njáls saga* recounted above, we can understand how, if Þorbjörn accepts the offer, he will be freed for the rest of his life from the tyranny of struggling to survive each agricultural year, and the relative comfort of his whole family, for whom he is responsible, would be assured. In fact, this dramatic annexation of his function as head of the household may be the very reason why Þorbjörn refuses the offer, which otherwise remains one of the many unanswered questions in the saga, and propels the narrative along its oddly morally ambivalent path.[101] In both *Njáls saga* and *Hrafnkels saga*, we can see that stepping outside the requirements of the steady seasonal round, however gruelling that round might be, could prove a catalyst for disruption and, ultimately, tragedy.

By contrast, in *Laxdœla saga*, we see families at the height of their power and success working with the constraints of the environment to stage display. When the great matriarch Unnr is arranging a magnificent wedding feast for her son Óláfr, she takes care to fix a date towards the end of the summer, 'því at þá er auðveldast at afla allra tilfanga' (because that's when [it will be] easiest to get all the provisions).[102] The same timing is also clearly a consideration for Óláfr pái's wedding feast, which similarly takes place at the end of summer, and with appropriate munificence.[103] But equally and oppositely, when Óláfr pái's father Höskuldr dies, his sons plan a grand feast in his memory but decide to put off holding it until the following summer, because they want the feast to be as magnificent as possible, and – in words which closely echo Unnr's – 'er nú mjök á liðit í haustit, en ekki auðvelt at afla fanga til' (it is now well into autumn, and it's not easy to get the provisions).[104] These examples may very well reflect or even record how medieval Icelanders actually responded to seasonal constraints. But in the same saga, an event is related which may have much more literary origins. When Unnr first arrives in Iceland, she visits her brother Helgi bjólan, expecting to be invited to spend the winter with him, in accordance with the usual pattern of taking land and establishing settlement the spring after arrival in Iceland. In an intriguingly close echo of the story of King Lear – which itself seems to have origins in Geoffrey of Monmouth's twelfth-century *Historia Britonum* – Helgi is only willing to offer hospitality to half of her retinue, and Unnr angrily turns to another brother, Björn, who welcomes her with all her followers and provides them with hospitality for the whole winter.[105] An original Icelandic audience would surely be fully alert to the extent of Björn's generosity, and perhaps inclined to be forgiving towards Helgi's reluctance. It's tempting to speculate that the saga author came across the story and realized that it might play very differently in the context of an Icelandic subsistence economy.

The most striking collocation of natural season and narrative event involves supernatural episodes: specifically, hauntings that take place in winter. I want now to examine three examples of midwinter hauntings. There is an obvious congruity between the activities of supernatural creatures such as ghosts or trolls, and the darkness dominating the winter months. But there are other factors at work. It may be the case that the increased supernatural activity depicted around what has been transformed in the course of some sagas from a pagan midwinter festival to the Christian celebration of Christmas is designed to show the denizens of pre-Christian Iceland flexing their power in response to the new Christian festival. Even further, one might see ghosts and revenants as symbolic of the fear and hostile conditions characteristic of winter itself.

Gísli Súrsson, having been an outlaw for a considerable time, is spending his last summer with his wife Auðr, in an underground hiding place, as has previously been his custom. Towards the end of the summer, he has a series of bad dreams which he understands as presaging his approaching death. These dreams increase in frequency as the summer wears on, and we are told that, like Grettir, 'hann gerir svá myrkhræddan, at hann þorir hvergi einn saman at vera' (he becomes so afraid of the dark that he dare not by any means be on his own).[106] This is indeed a perilous condition for an outlaw in winter. As autumn comes near, Gisli's dreams become even more frequent and, on 'sumarnótt síðasta' (the last night of summer), he cannot sleep at all, and decides to move on to another refuge.[107] We are given an evocative description of the autumnal weather conditions: 'Veðri var þann veg farit, at var á logn mikit; hélufall var ok mikit' (The weather had turned out like this: it was very still, and there was a heavy frost).[108] As Gísli, together with his wife Auðr and his foster-daughter Guðríðr, makes his way across the hillside, the women's clothes leave a trail in the frost, an ironic recall of the care Gísli once took not to leave his own tracks in the snow when he set off to kill Þorgrímr. He seems to be fatalistically failing to take the precautions about which he was once so careful. Moreover, he carves runes on a stick as he walks, so that the wood shavings add to the already evident tracks.

Gísli's enemies have no trouble following the track; indeed, the narrator adds, it was as if 'vísat væri til' (the way were being pointed out).[109] Gísli is cornered and is killed. The fatal ambush even has a carefully time-defined aftermath: six attackers are killed at the scene, one dies later the same night, and another dies of his injuries a year later.[110]

The author of *Eyrbyggja saga* also recounts an extended episode of winter hauntings and, in keeping with the saga's overall themes of settlement and agriculture, emphasizes the effect of the supernatural activity on the local farming community. Þórólfr bægifótr (twisted foot), a difficult and sinister character, has died, and his neighbours feel at first an unspecific unease: 'þótti mǫrgum mǫnnum verra úti, þegar er sólina lægði' (it seemed to many people to be better not to be outside when the sun had gone down).[111] However, it becomes clear as autumn approaches that his ghost is haunting the district, and that indeed 'máttu menn þá aldri í friði úti vera' (people were not safe to go outside).[112] In the autumn, the shepherd fails to return home one evening and is found dead near to where Þórólfr is buried; attentive as always to the time of day, the narrator notes that no search is made for him until the next morning.[113] The naturalistic threat of darkness is neatly conveyed in the detail that rumbling noises are often heard in the area, but no explanation is given of what exactly might be causing them. In the winter, Þórólfr himself appears, frightens his former wife to death and causes the whole household to leave the farm. He terrorizes the district more widely to such an extent that, for the whole winter, 'engir menn þorðu at fara ferða sinna, þó at ørendi ætti' (nobody dared to make any journeys, even if they had business to do).[114] Once winter passes, and spring arrives, the ground becomes soft enough for Þórólfr's son to be able to exhume his corpse and bury him away from the district, on a headland facing out to sea. Here we see hauntings correlated to seasonal changes: the darkness of winter brings on Þórólfr's depredations, while their termination is dependent on the softer ground of spring.

The winter hauntings in *Grettis saga* gather together all these elements. In the summer – the standard time for ocean-going travel – a mysterious Swede called Glámr arrives in Iceland. A farmer called Þorhallr has had trouble with hauntings and, the next summer, he asks advice at the Alþing about how to deal with his supernatural presence, since it is making it difficult for him to hire farmhands. The lawspeaker, Skapti Þóroddson, arranges to send him the Swedish stranger. Þorhallr hires him to mind the sheep, warning him that the farm is haunted. Glámr is scornful of ghosts, and he starts work in mid-autumn – 'at vetrnóttum' (at winter-nights).[115] Glámr refuses to celebrate Christmas as a Christian festival, dismissing it as 'hindrvitni' (new-fangled superstition).[116] When he – like the shepherd in *Eyrbyggja saga* – fails to return home, no one makes a search for him until daylight comes the next day; we are told that a combination of the darkness and a violent snowstorm prevents an immediate search.[117] The explicitly anti-Christian Glámr, having been killed, now himself becomes a ghost who haunts the area in winter.

Natural time: Night and day

The same balance of naturalistic detail on the one hand, and exploitation of it for literary effect on the other, is evident in the treatment of diurnal rhythms in family sagas. In just the same way as the passing of the seasons can provide a robustly naturalistic temporal backdrop to events in the saga narrative, so too the alternation of night and day is both naturalistically observed and exploited in all family sagas. Since experience of the alternation of night and day, darkness and light, is common to all human societies – with one startling exception, which I will discuss in due course – the strict observance of this alternation in saga narrative makes saga society seem comfortingly familiar in its attitude to daily times. To return to Unnr, for example, we learn that towards the very end of her life, she stays in bed until midday, retiring early in the evening and maintaining absolute privacy unless she is up and dressed.[118] This strikingly realistic detail of geriatric behaviour lends naturalism to the saga's portrait of Unnr's old age, and narrative tension is subtly increased as we are told that on the day of her grandson's wedding, she stays in bed even later than usual. Although she is up to greet the guests, she goes to bed before everyone else, and is found the next morning – for it has already been made clear that she is never to be disturbed between retiring and rising – dead in bed, sitting up like a warrior in his burial mound.[119] Here, what seems at first to be no more than a touchingly recognizable detail of an elderly routine is developed into an unforgettable portrait of female dignity and stoicism. And we should not forget that one of the dominant themes of the whole of *Laxdæla saga* is the representation of powerful women.

The narrative climax of *Njáls saga*, the burning of Njáll and his family at Bergþórshváll, is similarly attentive to naturalistic diurnal detail. Flosi and his group of burners gather within reach of Njáll's farmstead by mid-afternoon, and wait there until early evening.[120] Two of Njáll's sons are away from home, visiting their children who were being fostered nearby. They get news of the burners gathering and, though they had intended to stay away overnight, set off home to Bergþórshváll. There, Njáll's wife is preparing what she foresees as being the household's last meal together; she offers each of them a choice of food.[121] As we have seen, saga authors are constantly alert to the scarcity of provisions; Bergþóra's indulgence in the matter of individual food provision is completely out of character and goes against the norms of saga society, although of course Bergþóra's unspoken grim presentiments mean that there will be no need to husband their food supplies any longer. The narrative is clearly preparing us for the extraordinary event which is to follow. There is in addition a curiously anachronistic echo of the trope of the condemned person's last meal, and a less anachronistic biblical echo of a Last Supper. Njáll's sons return home just as the evening meal has finished, and Njáll tells his household not to go to bed. Meanwhile – in a relatively rare but perfectly engineered example of managing parallel narratives in a saga – we are told that Flosi and his supporters are setting off for Bergþórshváll, planning to arrive before dark. After a preliminary skirmish, Flosi takes the momentous decision to set fire to the farmhouse and burn to death everyone in it. In one of the most celebrated scenes in all saga literature, Njáll, Bergþóra and their young grandson, as if going to bed, lie down under an oxhide and commit themselves to God's mercy.[122]

Here we can see the precise harmony of a naturalistic representation of time and the symbolic resonances associated with those times. One final detail of timing concludes the account of the burning of Njáll: the fire burns all through the night, and Flosi and his men stay there until the fire dies down, which is not until well into the following morning. With the coming of the day, the extent of the destruction and loss of life is clear; Flosi and his men ride away, and the narrative turns to the aftermath of this momentous episode.[123]

The alternation of day and night can also be used in saga narrative for comic effect. An example of this is the story of Gísli's attempts to thwart the efforts of two men hired by his enemies to discover his hiding place, Njósnar-Helgi (spy-Helgi) and a man called Hávarðr, newly arrived in Iceland. Hávarðr is said to have arrived in Iceland that same summer, so we can assume that events are taking place in autumn.[124] One evening, they spot a fire in the distance, but 'þat var um dagsetrsskeið ok niðmyrkr sem mest' (it was nightfall and as pitch dark as it could be).[125] Helgi's cunning plan is to mark their spot by building a cairn so that the next day, 'er ljós dagr er' (when it's daylight) they can reposition themselves and calculate the location of the fire. But Helgi's companion Hávarðr is related to Gestr Oddleifsson, whose mother Þorgerðr sheltered Gísli earlier in the saga in her farmhouse with a secret underground passage; Hávarðr is working against Helgi. They take turns to keep watch during the night, and when it's Helgi's turn to sleep, under cover of the darkness Hávarðr dismantles the cairn. He then throws a heavy stone to land near the sleeping Helgi's head, pretending that they have come under attack from Gísli himself. They beat a hasty retreat, but the next morning, when it is light, they return with Gísli's enemies to look for the cairn, which has of course disappeared. Hávarðr's explanation is that Gísli must have been watching them watching him, and when day broke, and the two of them left, must have dismantled the cairn himself.[126] This is a simple enough piece of trickery and tomfoolery, but it depends for its narrative success on a confident and secure handling of day and night, light and darkness.

In *Eyrbyggja saga*, we have another example of would-be assassin trying to take advantage of dusk for an attack, but the strategy is more sophisticated and is planned not by its perpetrator, a slave called Egill, but by the redoubtable Snorri goði – or at least, as the saga author cagily suggests, 'Þat er sumra manna sǫgn' (that's what some people say).[127] It is autumn again, and men are gathered for the ball games traditionally held at this time of year. The slave Egill is to hide in one of the temporary huts erected to house those coming to the ball games from some distance away. He can approach the huts by coming down a mountain pass, but must wait until the conditions are just right for him not to be seen or identified. In the evening, when fires are lit for the supper, the wind comes in from the sea, and the smoke will be channelled up the mountain pass, and conceal his movements.[128] This is an elaboration one step further from the mere use of the cover of darkness: evening implies not simply darkness, but cooking, and cooking implies smoke.

Family saga narratives are of course full of simple, one-off instances of people operating secretly under cover of darkness. For example, Njáll advises his friend Gunnarr about summonsing Hrútr Herjólfsson for the recovery of Unnr's dowry: he hatches an elaborate plan which involves Gunnarr and his men riding only at night, so that his enemies cannot follow where he has gone, although in fact the deception seems oddly unnecessary to the eventual outcome.[129] By contrast, early morning is often shown as a good time to mount a surprise attack: in *Hrafnkels saga*, for instance, Hrafnkell's adversary Sámr leads supporters to Hrafnkell's farm in Aðalból at break of day, catching Hrafnkell himself and all his household in bed.[130] When Hrafnkell turns the tables on Sámr, the element of surprise is similarly based on time of day: Sámr has retired for the night, but Hrafnkell eats his evening meal and then sets off to catch out Sámr at his farm.[131]

Natural times of winter and summer, of day and night, need no mechanical or formal means of measurement: their conditions – climatic, or darkness versus light – are more than sufficient as markers of difference and succession. But we also find smaller segments of days defined by either the movement of the sun, or by the routines of daily life. In *Hrafnkels saga*, with its much shorter overall time span limited to the life of Hrafnkell himself, there are a number of examples. Einarr the shepherd rides the sacred horse Freyfaxi 'allt frá eldingu ok til miðs aptans' (right from dawn to mid-evening) and, by the time Freyfaxi gallops back down to Hrafnkell in Aðalból, Hrafnkell is sitting down to his evening meal.[132] When Sámr's brother Eyvindr makes his way from his ship to Sámr's new residence in Aðalból, he is spotted riding past Hrafnkell's new farm at Hrafnkelsstaðir, and we are told that 'þá var jafnnær rísmálum ok dagmálum' (it was halfway between rising time and mid-morning).[133] In the same saga, it is said that the court of confiscation has to be held when the sun is due south – that is, at midday.[134] Perhaps most significant of all, the mound which Hrafnkell respectfully raises over the body of Einarr, whom he has murdered, can be used by other shepherds to mark mid-afternoon – presumably, as the setting sun catches its outline on the hillside when they are standing outside their shieling, much as prehistoric standing stones can be shown to mark solstices and equinoxes.[135] Einarr's burial mound, in conjunction with the movement of the sun in summer, plays the role of a sort of primitive clock.[136] Periods of time roughly equivalent to seconds can be dramatically measured out by human means: in *Laxdœla saga* Þorgils Hǫlluson is murdered just as he is counting out pieces of silver. As he gets to ten, his murderer cuts off his head with an axe, and onlookers claim to hear the head call out eleven. The narrator does not comment on the trustworthiness of this claim.[137]

With reference to the alignment of daily routine and cosmological time – that is, day and night, and the seasons, measured by the movements of the sun – I need to raise one puzzling aspect of the naturalistic representation of the 'natural' alternation of day and night in saga narrative. One of the most remarkable features of the Icelandic calendar is that around midsummer there are almost twenty-four hours of daylight, while in winter, conversely, there is a very short period of proper brightness. There are remarkably few episodes in family saga narratives which acknowledge – let alone exploit – this asymmetry. Indeed, some sagas seem incongruously to ignore it. Dawn breaks in summer as in winter; and evening heralds nightfall. In *Eyrbyggja saga*, Arnkell is described as working his slaves hard because he makes them work continuously 'alla daga milli sólsetra' (all day from sunrise to sunset), but since the context of this remark in the saga is winter, the time between sunrise and sunset would not actually have been very long.[138] Interestingly, in a statement made in reference to that same winter, Arnkell is also said to make it his practice to move hay from one farm to another 'un nætr, er nýlýsi váru' (at night, by the light of a new moon) and is described as getting out of bed and waking his slaves to do this, so it seems that the middle of the night in the conventional sense, and not just some part of the long winter hours of darkness, is intended here.[139] Elsewhere in saga literature, we are told in *Egils saga* that Haraldr and his men row night and day, and that they are able to do this because 'nótt var þá farljós' (the night was light enough for travelling), a notion that is repeated in *Fóstbrœðra saga*: 'Þá var svá misserum komit, at nótt var farljós' (it had come to the time of year when it was light enough to travel at night).[140] And as we have seen in *Gísla saga*, Gísli's dreams return in autumn: 'kemr nú á þref um draumana, þegar er lengir nóttina' (the dreaming comes again when the night lengthens).[141] However, in general, the saga narrative does not make special allowance for the remarkable difference in day length in Iceland between summer and winter. As with the notoriously scant references to volcanic activity, it seems that saga authors avoided drawing attention to these distinctive features of Icelandic life.[142]

As Ari makes clear in *Íslendingabók* in his discussion of how the settlers worked out a way of making lunar weeks and months accord with the solar year, units of seven-day weeks and approximately thirty-day months were perfectly familiar to early medieval Icelanders. This too was connected to the natural changes in the seasons: as Siân Grønlie explains, 'the need for a reliable calendar probably arose in conjunction with the establishment of regular meetings at the Alþing as well as being important for agricultural activities'.[143]

I will now turn to the representation of what I will term 'cultural time' – units or segments of measured time over and above the seasonal or diurnal rhythms of the natural world, the necessary markers of cultural or societal functions.

Cultural times

The legal proceedings which form the central core of so many family saga narratives inevitably involve various kinds of timings. Most obviously, as Grønlie has made clear, calendar times needed to be established for both local assemblies and the all-Iceland assembly, the Alþing. Unsurprisingly, the dates set for these assemblies were in spring and summertime, for ease of travelling, and the length of the meeting was also specified. Many of these timings are spelled out in the Icelandic law codes, which are then reflected in saga narrative. In *Hrafnkels saga*, for example, which, as we have already seen, is particularly attentive to timings, we are told that before Sámr's case against Hrafnkell comes to the Alþing in the summer, he must meet the deadline for serving the summons on him – the *stefnudagar* (summonsing days), which were fixed at a specified period four weeks before the Alþing itself.[144] When the court finds against Hrafnkell, Sámr is legally allowed (or obliged) to hold a court of confiscation to ratify Hrafnkell's sentence of outlawry, and this must take place within fourteen days of the end of the assembly.[145] As we have seen, the precise time of day when the court is to be held is also specified: when the sun is due south. This piece of information is presented extra-diagetically – that is, the narrator informs the audience of the stipulation directly, rather than showing the saga's characters acknowledging it, as if actual law codes were being referenced. Most crucially, we have already been told that Hrafnkell's route to the Alþing from the Eastern Fjords takes seventeen days, but that Sámr takes a short cut so that he arrives shortly before him.[146] Thus, Sámr and his supporters have just enough time to get back east and set up the court of confiscation on Hrafnkell. The saga author has timed the narrative to perfection.

Sentences of outlawry in saga narrative also involve the measurement of time, most commonly, the necessary three-year exile from Iceland known as *fjörbaugsgarður* (lesser outlawry).[147] Again, saga authors invariably take into account the tally of absent years when constructing the narrative. Interestingly, a familiar trope in the so-called poets' sagas, which we also see in *Laxdœla saga*, which shares some of their fundamental storylines, is that before travelling to Norway, the hero is betrothed to a woman in Iceland and undertakes to return in the space of three years. Kjartan fails to return to Guðrún within the stipulated period, fails to make any excuse for the delay, and tragedy ensues. The three-year period seems to be used as a token measure of a major absence – in much the same way as a three-day period often crops up as a measure of promptness: in *Gísla saga*, for example, we are told that in Norway, at a time before the settlement of Iceland, a duel should take place three days after the challenge has been issued.[148] In *Eyrbyggja saga*, a farmhand lies on his deathbed for three nights.[149] There are any number of similar and various examples. The significance of these fixed intervals for our purposes is not to what extent they correspond with any actuality, or any textual source such as the law codes, but how saga authors make realistic and often very precise allowance for them in their narratives.

In *Grettis saga*, the length of Grettir's survival as an outlaw is also a matter of record. Just before his final sanctuary on Drangey, we are told that he had by this time survived as an outlaw for fifteen or sixteen years – and this tally is referred to the extra-diegetical authority of Sturla Þorðarson, the celebrated thirteenth-century Icelandic historian and author of *Íslendinga saga*.[150] The saga concludes with a summary of Grettir's pre-eminence, claiming that he survived longer than any other outlaw in Iceland.[151] In chapter 77, we are told that it was agreed no one should be made to serve more than twenty years as an outlaw in Iceland, and that Grettir's term had reached that. However, Grettir's enemies argue that he has only served nineteen years, since the year between his lesser and full outlawry should not be counted.[152] Remarkably, the chronology of the saga supports these calculations with total precision. Legal processes demand a similar precision, as when, much earlier in the saga, the lawspeaker Skapti Þóroddson rules that Grettir cannot be involved in a manslaughter case because he had been an outlaw for one week before the killing took place.[153] It seems more than likely that such precise timings would have been crucial in early medieval Iceland, and saga authors attend to them too.

Family sagas also make reference to what might be termed 'semi-legal' dates: *fardagar* (moving days), for example, the days in May – a good time, of course – when it is legal to move house.[154] In *Gísla saga*, when the moving days come round, Gísli and his brother Þorkell get together to discuss momentous business: dividing up their joint property, and Þorkell moving to share a farm with his brother-in-law Þorgrímr, thus formalizing the split between the two brothers which lies at the heart of the saga.[155] Again, the issue is not how well or otherwise the timings tally with the legal sources, but only with how the timings – whatever they are – are handled by the saga author. In this instance, the narrator is careful to allow for the passing of summer following the moving days, and to pick up the narrative with the *vetrnætr* – the so-called Winter Nights, the traditional time for many festivities in saga Iceland. The author of *Gísla saga* helpfully explains the origin of the feasting: 'Þat var þá margra manna siðr at fagna vetri í þann tíma ok hafa þá veizlur ok vetrnáttablót' (it was a popular custom at that time for people to celebrate the coming of winter and hold feasts, and Winter Night sacrifices).[156] The Winter Nights festivities might have already lost their pagan significance; indeed, we are told that, although Gísli himself had given up the element of sacrifice, he still gave the feasts, and just as lavishly as before.[157] But their place in the agricultural year – when it was prudent to slaughter livestock in preparation for the coming winter – ensured their continued place in the social calendar. One might speculate similarly that the pagan midwinter festival of *Jól* (Yule) could smoothly mutate into the Christian festival of Christmas. In Grettir's Christianized Iceland, for instance, the festival is still called *Jól*, although the observances as described in the saga are manifestly Christian ones.[158]

The coming of Christianity to Iceland is represented as a major event in the narrative of several family sagas, and the family sagas, whatever their origins, are overwhelmingly the work of Christian writers depicting a period of radical transition from a pre-Christian to a Christian society. Of course, in actuality there could have been no short sharp move from one to the other, but rather a relatively extended period of transition and accommodation. Furthermore, we do not know how reliable the presentation of the pre-Christian features of Iceland's past by saga authors might have been. For instance, Gabriel Turville-Petre noted that the description of the pagan temple at the beginning of *Eyrbyggja saga* probably owes more to the saga author's experience of Christian church architecture than to his knowledge of pagan temples.[159] However, saga authors do not customarily present all their material stubbornly refracted through a lens of Christian terminology and morality. I would like to conclude this section, though, with a striking counter-example: an analysis of the use of terms from the Christian liturgical calendar in the account of what is undoubtedly presented as a quasi-martyrdom – the death of Kjartan in *Laxdœla saga*.

Following her extended humiliation after Kjartan's failure to return from Norway to marry her, Guðrún, in the paradigm of her heroic eddic predecessor Brynhildr, incites her husband Bolli to kill Kjartan. The underlying story pattern is manifestly that of the murder of the hero Sigurðr in the poems of the *Poetic Edda* and the saga deriving from them, *Völsunga saga*.[160] In *Laxdœla saga*, this archetypal dynamic is doubly transformed: firstly, from its context in the heroic past to the quasi-historical past of the family sagas, and secondly, from its pre-Christian heroic ethos to be represented as culminating in a Christian martyrdom.[161] In a long chapter at the heart of the saga, we are told of Kjartan's exploits in Norway and his encounters with the militantly Christian King Óláfr Tryggvason. Kjartan's conversion to Christianity begins slowly. His first winter in Norway is a harsh one, and the saga author tells us that 'heiðnir men' (heathen men) – presumably including the Icelanders – attribute the bad weather to the anger of the gods in the face of King Óláfr's attempted Christianization of the country.[162] Kjartan is at first in fact strongly opposed to the new faith, but eventually concedes that his faith in Þórr, once he returns to Iceland, will be diminished.[163] He continues to watch Christian ceremonies, and we are shown his response from his own perspective: he and his men argue about the king's preaching at the time 'er kristnir menn kalla næst inni mestu hátíð' (which Christians call their second most important festival) – that is, Christmas, or Jól, the most important being Easter.[164] Christian terminology is not yet being used in the narrative, and Christ is referred to as a 'höfðingi' (chieftain).[165] But Kjartan is eventually baptized and, subsequently, Iceland is itself converted to Christianity. From this point, the narrative invariably and insistently uses Christian liturgical time references, and as the day of his killing by Bolli approaches, the time is measured in insistently Christian terms. Kjartan humiliates Bolli in a purchase of land, but we are told that nevertheless the rest of *Langafasta* (Lent) passes quietly.[166] Kjartan rides home 'inn þriðja dag páska' (on the third day of Easter) and spends the fourth day of Easter (Wednesday of Easter Week) at Hóll.[167] On the fifth day of Easter week, he leaves on his last journey. He is ambushed by Bolli and killed in what is plainly presented as a Christian martyrdom, telling Bolli 'miklu þykki mér betra at þiggja banaorð af þér, frændi, en veita þér þat' (I think it a great deal better to receive my death at your hands, than to give you yours).[168] The temporal framework of Kjartan's Christian martyrdom is expressed in ostentatiously Christian terminology.

2

The management of narrative time: Duration

In the previous chapter, we saw how events in family sagas play out against a steady and consistently realistic backdrop of external time, whether a historical framework or the familiar rhythms of daily or seasonal rounds. But the authors of family sagas do not allocate narrative space strictly proportional to the time represented – one line per day, say, or one page a year, as diarists or chroniclers might. Instead, they vary the pace of their narratives, sometimes covering a long period of time very briefly, and sometimes relating in close detail and corresponding length an episode which would have happened in a relatively brief period of time. I want to explore the relationship between these two measures of time: the time taken for events to happen and the time taken to narrate what happened. Gérard Genette has defined the two as *story* – the signified or narrative content – and *narrative* – the discourse itself, the narrative text or signifier.[1] Paul Ricœur, whose work on time and narrative owes a good deal to Genette, also stresses the importance of this relationship. He cites the earlier work of Günther Müller, who uses the terms *erzählte Zeit* – the time the episodes or events would have taken if they had taken place in a real world, or a simulacrum of one – and *Erzählzeit* – the time or space taken up by the narrative text when an episode or event is being narrated.[2] Jonathan Culler uses the terms *story* and *discourse* to make the same distinction.[3]

This relationship between story and narrative, a relationship which is most often a disproportionate one, is one of the most familiar features of narrative. Perhaps the commonest kind of disproportion is the virtual ellipsis – 'X years passed' – in which narrative time (or space) is minimal, but the story time is not only much longer but also has the potential to be infinitely longer. Genette, under the heading of 'Duration', distinguishes four basic possible relationships between story and narrative: *ellipsis, summary, scene* and *pause*.[4]

With *ellipsis*, in which the narrator simply passes over some period of time in the narrative, little or no narrative time is taken up, while in the story, what might have happened during the ellipsis may have taken any amount of time, long or short.⁵ Genette adds that what he calls an 'explicit ellipsis' – in which, as in the above example, the narrator draws attention to the action of passing over a period of time and specifies how much has been passed over – is actually an extreme form of the next category, *summary*.⁶ *Summary* is the very familiar practice of using a relatively short amount of narrative time/space to narrate a longer segment of story time, which has the effect of seeming to 'speed up' the narrative. Genette uses the term *scene* to denote a detailed narrative which comes close to taking the same amount of time to relate – that is, to actually or mentally enunciate – as the events themselves might have taken to unfold. This equality of time, or isochrony, as Genette terms it, can only ever be approximate, but by and large the reading or reciting of dialogue, one of the usual features of *scene*, produces something close to isochrony.⁷ The careful alternation of these three temporal relationships is especially fundamental to the creation of longer narratives, and family saga narratives are no exception. Given the conventional extended time span of the family saga – from the settlement of Iceland (sometimes including a Norwegian prelude) to the generation following the conversion to Christianity – there is plenty of scope for the interplay of ellipsis, summary and scene.

Genette's fourth relationship – *pause* – has a trickier application to saga narrative. Genette understands *pause* as essentially descriptive: story time pauses while the narrative continues with a description – perhaps of a person, or a setting – which takes up little or no story time, that is, it does not move the narrative forwards through time. Pauses may also be the result of interventions from the narrator, who may voice an opinion, ask a rhetorical question of the implied audience or offer some background information. However, following Genette, I will concentrate in what follows on the descriptive pause.

Genette is not primarily concerned with the voice in which the description is articulated – that is, whether it seems to be produced directly by the narrative voice, or is spoken by a character in the story. Strictly speaking, descriptions voiced by characters in the diegesis are in and of themselves narrative events, that is, speech acts, even though the time characters take to articulate them does create a pause in the onward sequence of the narrative events. Extended descriptions of any kind are also relatively rare, and I shall show that when they do occur, sometimes the narrative voice carries the description, but at other times the descriptive passage is displaced on to one or more of the characters in the saga. This is for me a crucial distinction. In the present chapter, I shall be most concerned with the descriptive pause *per se* and its effect on the rhythm and pace of saga narrative. But in distinguishing the descriptive pause in the narrative voice from descriptions displaced on to characters, I will be forced on occasion to anticipate my analysis of narratorial voice in Chapter 4.

Genette based his analysis of narrative duration very largely on Proust's *Á la Recherche du Temps Perdu* and observed that the variation of ellipsis, summary and scene is not random throughout Proust's long novel. Rather, the interplay between the three gradually develops a distinct rhythm which Genette described as one of 'increasing discontinuity … built of enormous scenes separated by immense gaps … thus [tending] to deviate more and more from the hypothetical "norm" of narrative isochrony'.[8] Noting – crucially – that Proust did not write his narrative in the order in which it appears in its final form, Genette argues that Proust must have planned this 'ever more abrupt rhythm' from the outset, and was aiming for a contrast in temporal texture between the early part of the novel – and thus the narrator's more distant past, recounted as summary – and later, more detailed and at the same time more widely spaced, memories.[9]

Scholars of Old Icelandic sagas have not often analysed narrative temporality.[10] However, over the course of whole family sagas, one can discern a very basic underlying durational pattern. The brevity of genealogical information, in contrast to the time span of the generations it signifies, gets many family sagas off to a brisk start, but then the narrative settles into a slower pace, with scenes linked by summary. The narrator then often concludes the saga with a brief summing up of what happened to the descendants of the major players in the body of the narrative. In his article 'Passing Time and the Past in *Grettis Saga Ásmundarsonar*', Jamie Cochrane specifically considers what he calls the 'pace or rhythm' of this saga in particular – essentially, the effect which Genette analyses as the relationship between story and discourse. Cochrane's detailed analysis bears out the general impression made by typical saga narratives: 'In the early chapters, time passes relatively quickly with only a few events narrated in detail … As one approaches the climactic portions more of the events are narrated in detail, with greater use of direct speech … [and], as one approaches the end of the saga, the style once again becomes synoptic and years pass more quickly.'[11] Cochrane also makes the important point that events are mostly related in chronological order in saga narratives, an observation I will discuss in the next chapter.

Ellipsis

I begin my analysis based on Genette's four categories of relationship between story time and discourse time with ellipsis – when the discourse time is minimal, while the story time may vary from relatively short to infinitely long. Genette makes some further distinctions within this category: he notes that ellipses can be either definite or indefinite – that is, the narrator can specify or not the duration of the ellipsis; and explicit or implicit – that is, the narrator can acknowledge or not that some story time has passed without narration. Furthermore, Genette distinguishes what he calls the 'characterizing ellipsis', in which the story time which passes un-narrated is nevertheless briefly characterized. This is very familiar from family saga narrative, as when the narrator tells us that a certain winter passed 'quietly', or 'without incident'.[12] This would, I think, be a definite, explicit and characterizing ellipsis according to Genette's classification, but other kinds of simple ellipsis are just as familiar from saga narrative.

As I noted earlier, all narratives are in practice elliptical to some degree, since it simply isn't possible to relate every detail of every moment in story time. Family sagas typically cover in their narration a period of several centuries – from the settlement of Iceland, and sometimes the settlers' prehistory in Norway, to the decades following the establishment of Christianity at the beginning of the eleventh century – so saga writers have ample scope to alternate between ellipsis, scene and summary, their narratives moving from one key scene to another, filling in the intervening times with summaries of varying degrees of length and detail. The naturalistic representation of external time, as discussed in the previous chapter, necessitates the use of ellipsis: most events cannot follow on from each other without a break, since they are dependent on legal timings, weather conditions, the building of alliances and much else.

Definite ellipses specify how much time has been skipped. For example, from the earliest chapters of *Njáls saga*: 'tveim nóttum síðar' (two days later); '[l]itlu síðar' (shortly afterwards); 'en er váraði' (when spring arrived); or, based on the legal calendar, '[n]ú líða stundir, þar til er stefnudagar kómu inir síðustu til alþingis' (now time passes until the last days for summonsing to the Alþing arrived).[13] Such ellipses contribute very considerably to the impression that saga narrative is a record of events which actually happened, in real time, and that the narrator is carefully accounting for the passing of time even if it was uneventful. These ellipses are usually relatively short; the authors of family sagas do not routinely skip long stretches of time, in order to bring the past and present of the narrative into contrastive or comparative collision, as some novelists do, but rather prefer the contingent causality of successive events.

There are very particular kinds of uneventful periods in saga narrative, because, as we have seen, certain events take place in annual or bi-annual cycles: assemblies, Yule feasts, haymaking and so on. During the winters, when there is little travelling, the outdoor encounters which might lead to or facilitate violence and other noteworthy interactions are less likely to occur. By contrast, during the long summer evenings, the threat of hauntings and troll visitations is likely to wane, only to build up again in the autumn. We hear in *Grettis saga* about a series of hauntings at Sandhaugar, in the north of Iceland. One Christmas, the farmer there disappears in mysterious circumstances. Nothing happens until the following winter: 'Liðu svá in næstu misseri' (Things went on as before for the whole year).[14] The following winter, a farmhand disappears. Grettir arrives just before Christmas and lies in wait for the troll woman who has been haunting the farm and killing its menfolk. We would not of course expect to hear about events at Sandhaugar between the episodes of haunting – the storyline is focused on Grettir. But since the hauntings only happen in winter, we see the narrator use a definite explicit ellipsis to take the story from one haunting to the next.

Longer (and more frequent) ellipses, as Cochrane noted in reference to *Grettis saga*, tend to occur near the beginnings of family saga narratives, for instance when the long lead up to and process of settlement is very briefly narrated. In *Eyrbyggja saga*, for instance, we are told that Björn inn austrœni, son of the settler Ketill flatnefr, 'var tvá vetr in Suðreyjum' (spent two years in the Hebrides) before he went to Iceland, but the saga author is not concerned with what might have happened when Björn was there, since his subject is the settlement of Iceland, and this remains a simple temporal ellipsis.[15] Björn's sister, Unnr in djúpúðga, joins him in Iceland, and this ellipsis seems longer: 'Nǫkkurum vetrum síðar' (A few years later).[16] The exact length of time is not important. In *Laxdœla saga*, as we saw in the previous chapter, the saga author seems especially anxious to correlate and organize the saga's chronology, and several times the narrative moves forwards in time elliptically to follow the careers of the main characters. Thus, for example, we are told that Óláfr pái is fostered at the age of seven, after which the narrative jumps forwards to his first appearance at the Alþing, '[þ]á er hann var tólf vetra gamall' (when he was twelve years old); his precocious pre-eminence at the assembly is the next notable event in his life.[17] Similarly, having set up the close relationship between the foster-brothers Kjartan Óláfsson and Bolli Þorleiksson, the narrator elides their shared childhood and notes simply that Kjartan's father Óláfr remains on his farm 'svá at vetrum skipti eigi allfám' (such that for [some] years, not much changed). The narrative picks up again with events 'eitt vár' (one spring ...).[18]

Towards the end of *Eyrbyggja saga*, we hear the story of the malevolent and mysterious bull Glæsir, who grows so precociously quickly (but not wholly improbably so) that when he was two years old, he is as big as a five-year-old animal.[19] The narrative then jumps two years, to the point when the bull is fully mature. At this point, the narrative slows dramatically to recount the ominous prophecies of the old woman who had advised the farmer to kill the bull when it was a calf. Then, in a very detailed (and therefore scenic) passage, the deadly confrontation between the farmer and the bull is related.[20] Our focus has been on the precipitous growth of bull, and of course there is no reason whatever to detail (whether inventing or recounting) random events during that period. Ellipsis is an almost automatic technique when one story strand – in this case, that of the malevolent bull – is being pursued: the bull was born, grew preternaturally rapidly, and large, and turned on the farmer four years later. Ellipsis may also be especially evident when the saga is following the story of a single character – such as Grettir – or a very closely defined group, as in *Hrafnkels saga*. But in the case of most family sagas, there are many more than one story strands in play. The astonishing skill of the saga author is to keep all of the strands in synchronization.[21]

One technique for achieving a synchronized chronology is explicitly to return the narrative to the point at which the ellipsis in one strand began – what we might call the 'meanwhile' strategy.[22] Another way of achieving the synchronization of story strands is to use indefinite ellipses in other narrative strands. Again, we can produce an illustrative list from *Njáls saga*: 'Þat var einn dag' (It happened one day); 'Þat var eitthvert haust' (It happened a certain autumn); or simply, 'Þat var einu hverju sinni' (It happened on one occasion).[23] In such cases – and there are very many in family saga narratives – the saga author alerts us to the fact that some time has been elided but leaves open, or indefinite, just how much. This allows a degree of flexibility so that the progress of other narrative strands can be progressed or held back to keep pace.

What Genette termed 'characterizing' ellipses can be used to significant effect in saga narrative. For example, in *Laxdœla saga* after the death of Bolli Þorleiksson, his widow Guðrún mourns his death but is widely believed to be capable of planning and inciting revenge, and indeed she refuses to accept compensation for his death. She discusses with Snorri goði the possibility of exchanging farms with him, so that she doesn't have to live in the vicinity of Bolli's killers, but Snorri tells her that this will have to wait until the following spring. A narrative ellipsis – the uneventful passing of the rest of the year – is significantly characterized: it 'var kyrrt at kalla' (was quiet in name only), ensuring that the tension inherent in the narrative is not lost in the gap.[24] The saga author uses exactly the same technique earlier in the saga, when the audience's awareness of bad feeling between Hrútr and his nephew Óláfr pái is not allowed to fade even though there is no physical altercation.[25]

In *Eyrbyggja saga*, the narrative is characterized by a series of violent confrontations, an interrelated set of feuds within the community, which are temporarily halted, but which then flare up again, like a fire which smoulders and then sparks into life. Breaks in the feuding – represented as temporal ellipses in the narrative – sometimes occur after episodes of violence until the right time comes for a legal challenge. Thus, for instance, when Arnkell, Snorri goði's rival, kills Snorri's follower Haukr, we are told 'Spurðusk nú þessi tíðendi; stóð allt kyrrt þessi misseri' (These events were much talked about; [but] everything remained quiet that year).[26] Time is skipped to the following spring, when both parties bring a case to the spring assembly. Sometimes the ellipses simply represent the tantalizing stop-start nature of the feuding. Arnkell wins the case (the dead man is judged to have struck the first blow) and things go quiet again, although 'váru þá dylgjur miklar með mǫnnum um sumarit' (there were ill feelings amongst people throughout the summer).[27] In the autumn, an outlaw begs to be taken in for the oncoming winter, petitioning first Snorri, who sends him away, and then Arnkell, who is also reluctant to have him. The man attacks Arnkell, and it is rumoured in the district that Snorri was behind the attack. Nevertheless, time is said to pass uneventfully – another temporal ellipsis – until the following autumn, the season for feasting. Snorri and his supporters meet and determine to kill Arnkell; the killing is duly carried out that winter.[28]

While some ellipses help to manage the complex and often multi-stranded narratives typical of family sagas, others may also increase narrative tension and further contribute to the sense that events are being played out against a backdrop of actual, or real time, whose passage must be carefully accounted for even during quiet periods: nights, winters, uneventful years or standard childhoods (whether bulls' or boys'). Furthermore, the impression that events actually happened is created or reinforced by a narrator's explicit observations, found in many family saga narratives, that there is nothing worth relating from some specified period of time. Here we need to pause to consider the commonest element in such narratorial observations: the word 'tíðendi' and its derivatives, which are cognate with the archaic English word 'tidings'. In the sagas, such 'news' is invariably disseminated by oral report – that is, in itself in the form of a narrative. As used by saga authors, furthermore, it carries the extended meaning of 'newsworthy event' – a happening itself worth reporting, not merely the report of such a happening.

In *Grettis saga*, which, as a late saga narrative, is notably self-conscious and self-reflexive about its own narrative processes and conventions, the saga author repeatedly uses variations on the concept of 'tíðendi' in narrative ellipses, creating an impression of some prior discourse, perhaps an oral tradition, which is being re-presented and incorporated into the saga narrative we are receiving. So, for instance, when Grettir is made an outlaw in his absence from Iceland – significantly enough, when news of his misadventures in Norway arrives as an oral report from Norway just before the Alþing – the saga author announces an ellipsis with the observation that 'Varð nú tíðendalaust fram yfir miðsumar' (There were now no *tidings* right up to midsummer).[29] One might understand this to mean that, within the storyworld, nothing happened – nothing worth recounting, anyway. But there is also the sense that there is no existing report of anything having happened, no fragment of story which the saga author might incorporate. Some formulations in the saga suggest event rather than report: 'bar þá ekki til tíðenda um vetrinn' (nothing happened during the winter).[30] Others stress rather the report: 'Eigi er sagt, at þeir fyndisk Kormákr síðan, svá at þess sé getit' (It is not stated that [Grettir] and Kormákr had any further encounters, [at least] as far as is reported).[31] On occasion, both possibilities are invoked: 'var hann spakr um vetrinn, svá at ekki bar til frásagnir' (he was well-behaved during the winter, such that nothing happened that could be related).[32]

In family saga narrative, then, ellipsis – a familiar feature of all kinds of narrative, historical as well as fictional – serves numerous functions. It can help synchronize complex interwoven story threads, as well as imply meaningful juxtaposition between periods of relative and/or ostensible calm and others of greater moment. But in designating periods of time in which nothing happened, it also contributes to that powerful impression of historicity, or actuality, which characterizes family saga narrative; the passage of time is not determined by the content of the narrative, as in fiction, but has the appearance of an external reality.

Summary and scene

Summary in saga narrative entails the dispassionate relation of events stripped of rhetorical devices associated with fiction and is consonant with the narrative style and tempo of historical record, in which the representation of the interiority and dialogue of the participants are also likely to be limited.[33] In addition, summary, with its relative paucity of detail (relative, that is, to the amount of detail in scenic narrative), has the effect of distancing the narration, and thus, the narrator, from events; to borrow a time-honoured distinction, the narrative voice will shade towards 'telling' rather 'showing'.[34] This too tends to figure the narrator more as a historian than as a storyteller, conveying information through narrative rather than using the rhetoric of fiction imaginatively to recreate how the past happened. However, as Genette has explained, there is no clear dividing line in terms of duration between virtual ellipsis, summary and scene: they are all on a spectrum of the possible disproportions between story time and discourse time. Summary is fuller than even characterizing ellipses, and scene is fuller than summary. Carol Clover, in her seminal article 'Scene in Saga Composition', definitively distinguishes a compositional unit in saga narratives, which she describes as a scene: 'a kind of miniature, visual drama'.[35] But as the title of her article makes clear, Clover is primarily interested in the scene as a structural or compositional unit. While she analyses very persuasively what she views as its distinctive narrative structure, she does not specifically discuss its temporal aspect, though she rightly notes the significant part played in scenes by direct or indirect discourse, a key aspect of slowing the narrative down to near isochrony. I will single out some examples of scene in saga narrative on grounds of an evident shift in the tempo of the narrative, a marked shift from simple, brief summary towards the isochronous end of the spectrum. But as we shall see, it is scenes which allow the literary art of the saga author – that is, the utilization of much more of what Booth terms the rhetoric of fiction, and especially dialogue – to come to the fore, and it is also in scenes that the voice of the narrator becomes more evident to an audience.

Family sagas are full of celebrated and memorable scenes which stand out prominently against summary narrative. I will examine four such scenes in this chapter, but first, I want to look at two departures from the characteristic norms of saga narratives, according to which scenes are created only once the narrative is well underway. In these two cases, the opening of a saga moves suddenly from genealogical information to scenic mode rather than simply specifying or summarizing the outlines of the settlement of Iceland.

Laxdœla saga begins conventionally enough with the familiar genealogy of the settlers descended from Ketill flatnefr. But the narrative unexpectedly loops back to Ketill himself and summarizes the historical background to the earliest emigration from Norway: the ambition of King Haraldr inn hárfagri to be sole ruler over the whole of Norway, effectively dispossessing and subjugating the Norwegian aristocracy. We are then told that Ketill calls a meeting of his kinsmen and makes a speech outlining their options, explaining that although he would like to stay in Norway, he understands that this is a risky course of action and doesn't want to endanger his closest allies by committing them to it. His son Björn speaks next; he is determined by contrast to leave Norway, and he and his brother Helgi decide to relocate to Iceland. As we have seen, Ketill dismisses Iceland as a mere 'veiðistöð' (fishing ground) and chooses to go to Scotland.[36]

Ketill's first speech is represented directly, and at some length. Björn's is shorter, but still narrated as direct speech, as is Ketill's scornful judgement on Iceland. Such a cluster of direct speeches is unusual so early in a saga narrative and effectively dramatizes the motives behind the original settlers' decisions, as well as illustrating the dilemmas they must have faced. From the near ellipsis of genealogy and the speedy narrative of early saga summary, this sudden deceleration to the near isochrony of direct speech is very marked. Beyond simply creating a novel effect from the use of scenic time so early in a saga narrative, the saga author is successfully foregrounding from the outset the saga's enduring theme of the power and autonomy of ambitious individual leaders, and showing how the distinguished settlers in the north west of Iceland did not simply flee the tyranny of King Haraldr but made reasoned choices and had impressive options; Ketill for instance was warmly welcomed in Scotland and his son became ruler over half of it by conquest. Since sustained stretches of direct speech, by their very nature, are not likely to represent what was actually said, this is another indication that the saga author is not merely relaying information, but rather, actively shaping the way the story is being told. But as the story continues, the narrator reverts to classic historical summary style.

Better known as a radical departure from the norms of saga narrative is the opening of *Njáls saga*, which is, as I have already noted, distinctly atypical, in that it begins not with emigration from Norway, or the genealogies of settlers, but simply introduces Mörðr gígja (fiddle), the son of Sigvatr inn rauði (the red) and his daughter Unnr, who was the best match in the whole district. The narrative then turns abruptly to another part of Iceland and introduces Höskuldr Dala-Kollsson who, as we have seen, plays a prominent role in *Laxdœla saga*. Now we get the genealogy familiar from that saga, as Höskuldr's antecedents are traced back to Ketill flatnefr, as I have already discussed. Höskuldr's half-brother Hrútr is also briefly introduced. And then the narrator launches into distinctly scenic mode, and the narrative suddenly becomes much more detailed and circumstantial. Höskuldr is hosting a feast, and he and his brother Hrútr are watching his beautiful daughter Hallgerðr playing with other children. Höskuldr proudly calls her to him, and 'tók undir kverkina ok kyssti hanna' (held her chin and kissed her).[37] He asks his brother Hrútr whether he thinks Hallgerðr is beautiful, but Hrútr delivers a shocking verdict: 'Œrit fögr er mær sjá, ok munu margir þess gjalda; en hitt veit ek eigi, hvaðan þjófsaugu eru komin í ættir várar' (The girl is pretty enough, and many will pay for this, but what I don't know is, where the thief's eyes came from into our family).[38] Whether Hrútr's devastating judgement – delivered so dramatically in the heart of a peaceful family occasion – is reported in the saga as a survival of oral tradition, the memorability of which might well secure its place in history as a snatch of direct speech, or whether the saga author invented it for the purposes of his narrative, it resoundingly closes the scene. But I would draw attention to the relaxed depiction of the setting and preceding conversation: the children playing, the obedience of Hallgerðr in coming up when her father calls, Höskuldr's affection towards her and pride in his question to Hrútr (a question to which he of course expects simple assent). All this is elaboration from a saga author, a detailed imagining of the scene to provide the most dramatically incongruous setting for Hrútr's brutal prediction.

These two women, Unnr and Hallgerðr, will in due course prove to be sources of disorder and death in *Njáls saga*. In an exceedingly complex narrative, the roots of conflict in the first half of the saga can be traced back to them. Unnr marries Hrútr, thus uniting the bifurcated opening of the saga, but their marriage is spectacularly unsuccessful. Unnr's subsequent appeal to one of the saga's two male protagonists, Gunnarr Hámundarson, to reclaim her dowry from Hrútr brings him into fatal conflict with powerful forces. His own ill-advised marriage to the beautiful Hallgerðr might well be seen as the ultimate fulfilment of Hrútr's grim double prophecy, for she too entangles her husband in violent interactions with others, not least when, as mentioned above, she steals cheese from her neighbours.[39] As in *Laxdæla saga,* the precipitous move into scenic mode, and the atypical arrangement of the genealogical material, focuses attention on the origins of crucial narrative themes. Furthermore, because of the substance of the scene involving Hallgerðr, and the preceding introduction of Unnr, the saga author draws immediate and insistent attention to issues that will prove central to the concerns of the body of the narrative: marriage, sexuality and gender. As Ursula Dronke so memorably demonstrated almost forty years ago now, *Njáls saga*, far from being an unselective and wide-ranging chronicle of a period of Icelandic history, is in fact purposefully constructed to explore sexual themes – and precisely those adumbrated by these two women, Unnr and Hallgerðr.[40] The creation – or at least development – of theme in narrative is without doubt the result of literary craft, the hallmark of a purposeful author selecting, imaginatively elaborating, or inventing characters and events.[41] And finally, we see in Hrútr's prophecy a clear example of a powerful narrative cataphor – a 'textual reference pointing to subsequent information in the text'.[42] I shall discuss narrative cataphora again in Chapter 5; for the moment, we need only recognize cataphor as a literary device to excite an audience's desire to read or hear more: to create suspense. The author of *Njáls saga* begins not simply by telling us what happened, but by impelling us to find out what *will* happen, that is, by instigating suspense.[43]

The two examples discussed above stand out because it is unusual to find scenes at the very beginnings of sagas. But we can see the same degree and quality of scene-setting and emotional depth throughout the family sagas, as summary narratives either suddenly or gradually give way to intensely imagined and detailed scenes. I will describe two scenes which involve dramatic interactions between a small number of protagonists, and one in which violent actions in battle are recounted in such detail that the narrative seems almost to pause at crucial moments. Finally, I will examine one scene in which evocative descriptive detail is carefully woven into the presentation of events to almost symbolic effect.

Hrafnkels saga contains an unusually large amount of dialogue, even by the standards of family sagas, and this has long been regarded as a measure of its fictionality.[44] For this reason, it is tricky to isolate distinct scenic units, because they do not stand out so markedly against a background of intermittent summary narrative, as scenes in other family sagas do. Furthermore, the brevity of the whole saga and the relatively limited *erzählte Zeit* do not allow the same scope for larger-scale or repeated variations in duration. The narrative recounts how the shepherd Einarr, on the hunt for missing sheep, flouts the autocratic chieftain Hrafnkell's taboo on riding the stallion Freyfaxi. The horse escapes from Einarr, and gallops, exhausted and mud-spattered, to Hrafnkell's farm. After a brief exchange with one of his serving women, Hrafnkell vows vengeance.[45] This vow prepares us for the significant narrative action to come. But first of all, we are told that Hrafnkell goes to bed and sleeps well. What is remarkable here is that we might expect not a reference to Hrafnkell's sleep, but an unremarkable, uncharacterizing ellipsis at this point, such as 'the next morning ... '. But the careful reference to Hrafnkell's sound sleep contrasts with the anxious insomnia of those who try to counter his bullying tactics and underlines his decisiveness – he does not lie awake all night worrying about what to do. I would argue that a scene – as defined by a distinct change in narrative tempo – begins the next morning. There is detailed reference to Hrafnkell's preparation for a journey: he has a horse brought and saddled (notice the precision with which the narrator reminds us that he has servants to help him) and is wearing a dark coloured cloak and carrying only an axe in his hand. This last detail suggests a tidy execution; Hrafnkell does not anticipate any opposition.

The scene at the shepherd's hut is evocatively depicted in naturalistic pastoral detail. We are told that Einarr has rounded up the sheep and is lying on a wall counting them. Women are doing the milking. The first exchange is ostensibly a pleasant one: everyone there greets Hrafnkell, and he neutrally asks Einarr how things are. Einarr at once tells him about the missing sheep but hastily adds that they have now all been found. Hrafnkell reveals that he is not at all concerned about missing sheep – Einarr's anxiety to find them, occasioning the use of the sacred horse, is thus revealed as a tragic misjudgement on his part – but asks Einarr directly whether or not he has ridden Freyfaxi. Of course he and the saga audience know the answer to his question; that the saga author shows Hrafnkell asking it not only adds to the depiction of Hrafnkell as a dominant and threatening figure, but also produces a tense slowing of the time of the encounter and a consequent heightening of tension. Einarr's reply is reported as indirect speech: not a simple yes, but the oblique response that he is not able to deny the charge. Hrafnkell's next portion of direct speech puts his thoughts into words, and he asks a rhetorical question which he does not expect Einarr to answer: 'Fyrir hví reiztu þessu hrossi, er þér var bannat[?]' (Why did you ride the one horse which was forbidden to you?).[46] He continues, as if voicing his thoughts: 'Þar munda ek hafa gefit þér upp eina sök, ef ek hefða eigi svá mikit um mælt' (I'd have forgiven this one offence if I hadn't sworn such a solemn oath [to kill anyone who rode the horse]).[47] Representing voiced thought processes in this way slows the narrative to near isochrony and makes the audience party to what are ostensibly tantalizing fluctuations in Hrafnkell's intentions, even though the narrative so far has implied that his mind is made up. In fact, Hrafnkell's next shift – 'en þó hefir þú vel við gengit' (and yet you have made a good confession) – gives some hope that Hrafnkell's purpose is not fixed, and that he may be inclined to spare Einarr.[48] But his conclusion – that it's unwise to break sworn oaths – seals Einarr's fate: just as the lead-up to this encounter anticipated, Hrafnkell kills Einarr with one blow. After the killing, the narrative picks up its usual speed; Hrafnkell returns home, organizes a replacement shepherd and arranges a proper burial for Einarr.

As well as focussing attention on a crucial turning point in the narrative – for the killing of Einarr sparks the legal action against Hrafnkell which initiates the substance of the main body of this little saga – the slow narrative of the scene allows a number of literary effects which transcend the straightforward reporting of action. We are privy to psychological processes, not as thoughts, through the interiority practised by novelists, but actually voiced as direct speech. The deceptively quiet pastoral scene is beautifully set, and all of this adds up to a masterly crafting of narrative suspense.[49] The relaxed pace of the narrative is both caused by and allows the employment of these literary techniques, and the production of their effects. Cause and effect are hard to distinguish.

Grettir's fight with the violent revenant Glámr constitutes a long scene in which their physical encounter is minutely detailed. As mentioned above, Glámr is a mysterious and ungodly Swedish farmhand who is hired by a farmer called Þorhallr to protect his farm against the hauntings it has been suffering. But Glámr himself falls victim to the supernatural assailant, and after his hideous corpse is discovered – 'hann var dauðr ok blár sem hel, en digr sem naut' (he was dead, as livid as hell and as bloated as a bull) – he returns as an *aptrganga* (an after-walker – a revenant in the form of an animated corpse).[50] Grettir arrives at the farm in the role of ghostbuster.

Once the night of the fight arrives, there is no dialogue until Glámr's curse at the end of the scene: the slowing of the narrative pace is done entirely through descriptive detail. Grettir's preparations for his encounter with Glámr are meticulously recounted, involving a careful description of the structure, layout and disordered state of the main room of the farmhouse, as well as Grettir's precise placement within it, in a seat near the farmer's bed closet, covered with a shaggy cloak and with his feet braced against a wooden partition. When Glámr arrives, his approach is seen from Grettir's perspective – the narrative is focalized through Grettir, rather than events being reported objectively. Grettir hears loud noises, and 'var þá farit upp á húsin ok riðit skálanum' ([something] had climbed up on to the roof and was riding the building).[51] Whatever it is – the Old Norse is framed in grammatically subjectless clauses which completely efface every aspect of the identity of the assailant – then comes to the door of the hall, and Grettir sees a creature which 'sýndisk honum afskræmiliga mikit ok undarliga stórskorit' (seemed to him [Grettir] to be extremely hideously large and horrifyingly monstrous).[52] Having allowed the audience to hear and see things as Grettir would have – to share in his experience – the narrator turns suddenly to external focalization, describing from the outside what is happening, and Glámr is named as the visitant. This allows a longer perspective, and Glámr is described as standing up inside the hall such that his head reaches the rafters, and his arms lean on the crossbeam. Next we see the scene from Glámr's point of view: he saw 'at hrúga nökkur lá í setinu' (that some sort of heap was lying on the bench) – this is Grettir under the cloak, motionless.[53] Glámr pulls at the cloak and cannot understand why the heap does not move, even when the cloak is ripped in two; he 'undraðisk mjök' (was very amazed) as to who or what was resisting him. In this brief moment of stasis, Grettir launches his attack.[54]

Their struggle is described in detail, and mostly from Grettir's point of view. At length, they both crash out of the hall, still locked in combat. The saga author now produces a moment of narrative stasis, one of the most dramatic and memorable in all saga literature. Outside the hall, the light is meticulously described: there is bright moonlight periodically obscured by cloud cover. As Glámr topples over backwards and stares up at Grettir, the clouds part and Grettir is paralysed by the supernatural gaze of the monster. In this frozen moment, Glámr delivers, in direct speech, his celebrated curse on Grettir, condemning him to bad luck, outlawry and a crippling fear of the dark which will ultimately prove fatal. The moment he finishes his speech, Grettir recovers himself and cuts off Glámr's head. The narrative speeds back into summary mode as Grettir and the farmer burn Glámr's corpse, dispose of the ashes far from the farmstead and return home.[55]

The slowing of the narrative tempo makes time for focalization (or is caused by the exercise of it), showing how the scene and events look from the perspective of one or more of the characters, and thus allowing us to imagine their experience. And the dramatic moment when a suddenly moonlit Glámr delivers his proleptic curse on Grettir (and every element of the curse comes to pass in the saga) allows for intense focus on this brief period of time. These are literary effects characteristic of fiction: the saga author cannot know how things seemed to saga characters, and indeed there were no witnesses to any part of this encounter – we are specifically told that the farmer Þorhallr only appeared once Grettir had finished off Glámr.[56] Of course, the whole episode is necessarily a fiction, fundamentally because revenants like Glámr only exist in the imagination. We do not know when that fiction originally came into being. But the scene has been told or retold to make full use of several of fiction's rhetorical devices.

I want now to turn to another scene in *Grettis saga*, which I am taking to represent the recurrent and familiar use of scenic slowdown amounting almost to narrative pause in accounts of saga battles. *Grettis saga*, as we saw in Chapter 1, opens in conventional saga style with genealogical material, but rather than the familiar genealogies of celebrated settler families, *Grettis saga* begins with a litany of Viking raiders with colourful nicknames, chief among them being the Norwegian Viking Önundr, the son of Ófeigr burlufótr (club-foot). Önundr fights against King Haraldr at the Battle of Hafrsfjörðr (887 CE) along with Þórir haklangr (long chin). In spite of Þórir's bravery and martial prowess, he is killed in the battle, along with everyone on board his ship. At this point, the narrative slows into detail. Önundr's ship is attacked by Haraldr's men, and Önundr fights bravely. We then have the near isochrony of direct speech – one of the king's men sees Önundr and comments: 'Þessi gengr fast fram í söxin; látum hann hafa nökkurar várar minjar, at hann hafi komit í bardagann' (This one is standing fast in the prow of the ship; let's remind him that there's a battle going on!).[57] This lively taunt is in no way a realistic representation or record of a battle scene, but an example of the familiar trope of a speech ostensibly delivered in the thick of the fighting.[58] The focus is now concentrated on Önundr. He is depicted in the act of hewing at one of his assailants, and he has one leg braced against the side of the boat. Another man aims a blow at him, and he crouches down to parry it. At that very moment, one of his enemies lands a blow on his leg and cuts it off below the knee.[59] This one moment in a ramified encounter is spotlit, singled out from the other actions, and the account of it may even exceed in narrative time the actual or real time it would have taken to deliver the blow.

Once Önundr is incapacitated, the battle is said to favour the king's side, and Önundr is rescued and escapes. So it might be argued that the blow to his leg marks a turning point in the battle, and that this alone justifies the focus on it. But Önundr and his subsequent wooden leg are of more significance in the saga narrative to come than in the losing battle against King Haraldr. Grettir's own demise is the result of a fatal injury to his leg, and drawing attention to Önundr's injury foregrounds this literary theme.[60] Moreover, very many accounts of fighting in saga narratives slow the tempo to focus on individual blows.[61] One might conjecture that ensuing legal procedures, determining culpability and compensation after a domestic dispute, might well have led to either a particular interest in or the traditional survival of details about who struck whom, in what order and to what precise effect.[62]

The final scene I would like to analyse is also a very celebrated one in saga literature, from *Laxdœla saga*. Höskuldr Dala-Kollsson has bought the slave woman Melkorka and taken her back to Iceland. It seems that she cannot speak. She gives birth to Höskuldr's child, whom Höskuldr – presumably to his wife's chagrin – names Óláfr, after his late uncle. The scene opens with a conventional introduction: 'Þat var til tíðenda einn morgun' (It happened one morning … or The noteworthy happening one morning was …).[63] The naturalistic detail of the setting is perfect: Höskuldr is out and about, checking his farmland; it's early in the morning and the sun is still low. He hears voices and walks down to a little stream at the bottom of the home meadow. There, he sees Melkorka and their son, and she is chatting fluently to him. Every detail of this scene seems to carry some evocative significance: the new dawn with its rising sun heralds the discovery of Melkorka's real identity; the stream echoes the free-flowing chatter of the hitherto mute Melkorka; the situation of the mother and her child at the edge of the home meadow symbolizes their liminal position on the margins of Höskuldr's household. Höskuldr asks her name, and she tells him of her origins. Here we have an exquisite example of description, dialogue, scene-setting, suspense and symbolic detail all accommodated by and at the same time causing the apparent slowing of narrative time. And as with the other scenes discussed above, the slowing of time allows scope for the saga author to depart from bare narrative and employ the rhetoric of fiction.

Pause

I now turn to a limited series of descriptive passages in sagas which have the effect of halting the narrative.[64] Such passages are relatively rare in saga narrative, and for this very reason stand out very markedly in their narrative context. I will argue that one reason for the rarity of such passages is that descriptive passages which halt the narrative normally involve an intervention by the narrator, and saga authors employ various strategies to avoid such intervention. Sometimes, as we shall see, narrators displace description on to characters in the storyworld, and thus, into the diegesis itself.

In sagas in which the topography and geography of the setting play a necessary part in the unfolding of the saga narrative, such as in *Hrafnkels saga*, description of the landscape is rarely included for its own sake, but usually limited to what is necessary to explain the events of the story. Thus, for instance, the terrain around Fljótsdalr is often briefly described, but primarily so that the actions and movements of the saga characters can be understood and envisaged: the difficulty Hrafnkell has travelling over Fljótsdalr moor to visit his father, for instance, or swampy Oxmýr, where Eyvindr and his men become bogged down, and Hrafnkell, in pursuit, begins to catch up on them.[65] Such brief descriptions still create a fleeting pause, but their function is not merely scene-setting; they help the audience to understand what is going on, and why. However, some descriptions do shade into imaginative evocations of a scene. For instance, the location of Eyvindr's last stand, against an upland hillock which is eroded to bare soil by the wind, with turf on top of it, is carefully depicted, and every detail contributes to our understanding or envisaging of the site as an almost theatrically appropriate place for a small group of men to stand – backs to the wall, as it were – and face their attackers.[66]

Even brief passages of description may have the effect of drawing attention to the narrator's own voice. Throughout *Hrafnkels saga*, the saga author implies not only his characters' mastery – or not – of the landscape's challenges, but also his own local knowledge of the landscape. Thus, when Hrafnkell finds the going too difficult over Fljótsdalr moor, he establishes a new route, easier and drier but longer. The narrator notes that this route is called Hallfreðargata, and 'fara þeir einir, er kunnugastir eru um Fljótsdalsheiði' (only those who are most knowledgeable about Fljótsdalr moor use it).[67] This establishes not only Hrafnkell's intimate relationship with the district, but also the saga author's own local knowledge and authority. Such descriptive pauses involve information conveyed extra-diegetically – that is, from outside the storyworld – by the narrator, a technique which will be examined more closely in Chapter 4.

However, passages of description may also be displaced into the storyworld. In *Grettis saga*, for example, Grettir's relationship with the environment is a crucial aspect of his itinerant outlawry. His hideouts are carefully described, and it may be that if local tradition associated a certain site with Grettir, the saga author might draw on actual topography in the descriptions. But when Björn Hítdœlakappi agrees to shelter Grettir in his own district, it is Björn himself who describes in entirely realistic detail a hideout he has in mind: 'í því fjalli, sem fram gengr fyrir útan Hítará, mun vera vígi gott ... Er þar bora í gegnum fjallit, ok sér þat neðan af veginum, því at þjóðgatan liggr niðri undir, en sandbrekka svá brött fyrir ofan, at fáir men munu upp komask' (in the mountain which rises up on the far side of the Hít river, [there] would be a good stronghold ... There are [holes] there which bore through the mountainside, and you can see that from below, because there's a road running along the bottom, but there's a scree slope above it so steep, that few men could climb up it).[68] Caves like the one described, caused by the flow of lava, can be seen in many places in Iceland. But here, whatever the saga author's actual knowledge of the local topography, the description is absorbed into the diegesis by being put into the mouth of one of the characters, not interjected by the narrator.

A little later in the saga, Grettir hides out in a remote valley called Þórisdalr, which is again described in entirely realistic terms: it is a narrow valley, 'ok lukt at jöklum öllum megin, svá at þeir skúttu fram yfir dalinn ... hann sá þá fagrar hlíðir grasi vaxnar ok smákjörr; þar váru hverar, ok þótti honum sem jarðhítar myndi valda, er eigi lukðusk saman jöklarnir yfir dalnum' (and closed in by the glaciers on all sides, such that [the ice] overhung the sides of the valley ...

he saw there pretty hillsides grown over with grass and brushwood; there were hot springs, and he thought that the underground heat must have brought it about that the glacier did not close up over the valley).[69] This little oasis in the harsh frozen highlands of Iceland represents the topographical equivalent of a short but idyllic interlude in Grettir's outlawry. However, the description is in fact subtly focalized through Grettir himself – he finds the valley, sees what it was like and ponders how it came to be like that. In this way, the description functions as free indirect speech – Grettir's own words presented without the usual dialogue markers. Later in the saga, Grettir's final refuge, on Drangey in Skagafjörðr, is also carefully described, again with the apparent aim of emphasizing its suitability as a fastness, with its sheer cliffs which can only be accessed by ladders, which could be drawn up if necessary. Its almost arcadian qualities are clear: provisions will not be hard to come by, because there are many nesting seabirds, and sheep grazing its grassy top.[70] This description is both evocative and realistic, and it is also necessary to the narrative, explaining how Grettir and his brother Illugi were able to survive there as long as they did. But again, there is an element of focalization: we are told that Grettir 'þótti þat gott' (was pleased with it).[71]

Descriptions such as these are woven into the narrative and do not abruptly halt it as a mechanism for inducing suspense or drama, although they may still create fleeting pauses. However, some descriptions of individuals do interrupt the narrative, not only by virtue of their length, but also by being pointedly positioned in advance of a key moment in that individual's story. Thus, for example, when Óláfr pái travels to Ireland in search of his maternal relatives, the Irish inhabitants attack their ship as it nears the shore. Óláfr is ready to fight them, but there is a stand off because the water is too deep for the Irish to approach. Óláfr steps forward to the prow of the ship, and in this moment of tense stasis, his appearance is vividly described: 'hann var í brynju ok hafði hjálm á höfði gullroðinn; hann ver gyrðr sverði, ok váru gullrekin hjöltin; hann hafði krókaspjót í hendi höggtekit ok allgóð mál í; rauðan skjöld hafði hann fyrir sér, ok var dregit á léo með gulli' (he had a mailcoat on, and a gilded helmet on his head; he had hanging from his waist a sword with a gold-inlaid pommel and guard; he had a barbed spear in his hand, decorated and finely engraved; he carried a red shield in front of him, and on it was a golden lion).[72] This formidably impressive figure understandably cows the advancing Irish, and they retreat, so that the description is, strictly speaking, necessary to the narrative. Nevertheless, the air of theatricality about the description betrays the saga author's careful deployment of it in the midst of the otherwise ongoing narrative.

The description of Óláfr standing at the prow of his ship in all his finery focuses attention on a crucial moment and compels the reader or listener to envisage the scene. But in addition, we see an image of Óláfr in character – Óláfr pái, the peacock, for whom outward show is a key attribute. Back in Iceland, Óláfr cuts an impressive figure at the Alþing. However, Þorgerðr, the daughter of the prestigious Viking poet Egill Skalla-Grímsson, is not persuaded that, as the son of a slave woman, he is a good enough match for her. Óláfr falls back on his finery. Wearing the brightly coloured clothes King Haraldr of Norway had presented him with, his gilded helmet and a gold-inlaid sword his grandfather King Myrkjartan of Ireland had given to him, he walks boldly up to Þorgerðr and their betrothal is assured.[73] Again, the elaborate description of Óláfr is occasioned by narrative events – Óláfr's ploy to win over Þorgerðr – but at the same time the attention of the reader or listener is captured and focused on one static image. In both cases, the descriptive passage pauses the onward flow of the narrative.

The author of *Laxdœla saga* uses a similar technique to focus attention on the outstanding individual in the saga's next generation: Kjartan Óláfsson. This time, the description is of Kjartan's fundamental physical attributes and consequently does not arise directly from a narrative event: 'Hann var allra manna fríðastr ... hann var mikilleitr ok vel farinn í andliti, manna bezt eygðr ok ljóslitaðr; mikit hár hafði hann ok fagrt sem silki, ok fell með lokkum, mikill maðr ok sterkr' (He was the most handsome of all men ... he was striking to look at, with well-formed features, lovely eyes and a clear complexion. He had plenty of beautiful hair, as fine as silk, and falling in curls).[74] The saga author continues with a panegyric to his other qualities: he is outstanding in every physical way, better at fighting and swimming, and indeed all other skills, and yet humble, and so popular that even children loved him; he was also cheerful and generous.[75] This description functions as a definitive introduction to the adult Kjartan, and the narrator pauses the storytelling to focus the reader or listener's attention on the excellence of the hero.[76]

We might at first feel that this is a case of the narrator intervening in the narrative, telling his audience what to think. But significantly, the assessment of Kjartan is still rooted in popular opinion rather than the individual assessment of the narrator: 'allir undruðusk, þeir er sá hann' (everyone who saw him marvelled [at him]).[77] And in keeping with the family tradition, when Kjartan goes on a formal visit to his rival Bolli, he too relies on outward display. In terms which clearly echo those used to describe his father's successful attempts to impress the Irish soldiers and, later, Þorgerðr, Kjartan means to gain advantage with lavish and imposing attire: 'tekr hann nú upp skarlatsklæði sín, þau er Óláfr konungr gaf honum at skilnaði, ok bjó sik við skart; hann gyrði sik með sverðinu konungsnaut; hann hafði á höfði hjálm gullroðin ok skjöld á hlið rauðan, ok dreginn á með gulli krossinn helgi; hann hafði í hendi spjót, ok gullrekinn falrinn á' (now he gets the scarlet clothes which King Óláfr had given him when they parted and arrayed himself in finery; he put on the sword called 'Royal Gift'; he had on his head the helmet decorated with gold, and at his side, a red shield with a golden Cross; he had a spear in his hand, and it had a gold-inlaid socket).[78] Here we see another way in which the narrator avoids direct intervention: the description is turned into narrative as an account of Kjartan actually putting on the finery; the artificial placing of a passage of straight description is sidestepped. The description serves the function of a dramatic pause, but true to the habits of family saga style does not technically constitute one.

While the author of *Laxdœla saga* develops the theme of outward show in the narrative, as we have seen, the author of *Eyrbyggja saga* is concerned with issues of settlement, and the coming together of a community. The author is also noted for an interest in period detail. This is all evident in the lengthy description of the pagan temple which Þorólfr Mostrarskeggi had built when he first settled at Þórsnes. At this point, as elsewhere in the saga, the narrator clearly steps outside his role as the conduit of the story and offers his audience some learned information.[79] This is a technique I shall discuss in detail in Chapter 4. For the moment, the description stands as a passage of narrative in which nothing happens. However germane it may be to the concerns of the saga as a whole, it constitutes a descriptive pause in the account of the settlement of Þórsnes. The distinct sense that the saga author is instructing us, passing on information in connection with the story, rather than just telling it, also informs his introductory descriptions of Snorri goði and Þórgunna in which their physical attributes are apparently realistic, rather than panegyric and therefore value-laden.[80] We can contrast this clear narratorial intervention with the more nuanced case of the description of Steinþórr of Eyrr, as he proudly marches up to his enemies' farmhouse in order to pay compensation for the killing of a slave. This scene echoes in both content and narrative technique the dramatic portraits in *Laxdœla saga*.

The circumstances are extremely tense, because it is rumoured that the murdered slave had been sent by Steinþórr's enemies, advised by Snorri goði, to make a murderous attack himself on someone from Steinþórr's faction. Steinþórr is nevertheless following proper legal procedure in offering compensation for the dead slave, and he takes the risk of trusting Snorri goði, the leader of his enemies, to follow a legal route and accept the compensation, rather than simply attacking him. Snorri's men are edgily pacing the floor inside the farmhouse as Steinþórr approaches. At this crucial juncture, the narrator describes Steinþórr's attire: 'hann væri í rauðum kyrtli ... hann hafði fagran skjöld ok hjálm ok gyrðr sverði; þat var forkunnliga búit; hjöltin váru hvít fyrir silfri ok vafiðr silfri meðalkaflinn ok gyldar listur á' (he had on a red tunic ... he had a fine shield and helmet, and was wearing a sword; that was beautifully decorated; the guard and pommel were shining with silver, and there was silver wrapped around the grip, artfully gilded).[81] This arresting figure is partly dazzling, partly threatening and wholly imposing. As it happens, Steinþórr's visual display is almost counterproductive: a woman tactlessly praising his appearance sparks an attack from the men inside the farmhouse, but Snorri goði manages to put a temporary stop to the hostilities.

While halting the narrative to give a description in this way does clearly add to the suspense at what is already a tense moment, the description itself is not simply framed as a narratorial intervention: like Óláfr pái in both of the examples from *Laxdœla saga* above, Steinþórr has armed and dressed himself so as to look as imposing as possible in the circumstances, and the narrator recounts this tactic as part of the story. Although a short pause is created, the description is not a free-standing, extra-diegetic narratorial intervention but a necessary element in a narrative event. Furthermore, Steinþórr's imposing appearance goes on to play an active part in the diegesis, as is evident because the woman responds directly to it.

Elsewhere in saga narrative, passages of description may clearly function as a literary technique to halt the narrative and thus increase the tension of an approaching conflict – and yet the saga author is still careful to absorb them into the diegesis, even though this may cause a certain awkwardness in the narrative. In *Laxdœla saga*, for instance, when revenge is about to be taken on Helgi Harðbeinsson, long after his killing of Bolli Þorleiksson, we are told that Helgi has had bad dreams and asks a young shepherd to spy out the land around where he is staying. The shepherd reports that a group of men have gathered a short distance away. He describes each one in turn, and in great detail: their physical appearance, their bearing and what they are wearing. From the descriptions, Helgi is able to identify each individual and recognizes them as enemies on their way to kill him. He quickly plans to distract his attackers by sending the women of the household to ride away, dressed in men's clothing, but his enemies see through the ruse and attack and kill him.[82]

The lengthy descriptions of all ten attackers certainly pause the narrative and increase the tension, although the need for description is carefully, if perfunctorily, motivated. It is, however, slightly troubling that the pause itself is too long: that the time taken by the shepherd to recount his descriptions is – in terms of the storyworld time, *erzählte Zeit* – wasted when Helgi might have been preparing his escape. This alone might point to the essential implausibility, and by extension, the fictionality, of the scene, even apart from the conspicuous construction of narrative suspense.

Integrating this sort of description also proves problematic in *Hrafnkels saga*. When Hrafnkell is in deadly pursuit of Sámr's brother Eyvindr, a boy in Eyvindr's company reports that they are being followed. The description the boy gives of the group's leader is minimal: 'Er þar mikill maðr á baki í blám klæðum, ok sýnisk mér líkt Hrafnkeli goða' (There is a big man there on horseback, in dark clothes, and he looks like Hrafnkell the chieftain to me).[83] But the boy's reason for describing Eyvindr's attacker is poorly motivated in the saga narrative: as if subconsciously recognizing this problem, the saga author has the boy add that he is not sure of his identification because he has not seen Hrafnkell for a long time. In fact, he has been away from Iceland with Eyvindr, so there is no reason for him to be able to see or identify the pursuers any better than Eyvindr might have.[84] There is a more successful example of this trope in *Bjarnar saga Hítdælakappa*, in which the eponymous hero Björn is said to be short-sighted, giving the boy in that saga better reason to describe the attackers to him, and thus the saga author a more natural reason to include the descriptive passage. As in *Hrafnkels saga*, the tension is increased even further as Björn, like Eyvindr, wonders – or pretends to – whether the approaching armed men may be on a peaceful errand, rather than being on their way to kill him, thus delaying the account of the inevitable attack still further.[85]

The repeated and ramified description of the appearance of Skarpheðinn Njálsson as he and his father's close ally, Ásgrímr Elliða-Grímsson, go around the Alþing attempting to rally support for their impending court case constitutes one of the most dramatic and effective uses of descriptive pause anywhere in saga literature. At first, a series of unflattering descriptions of Skarpheðinn are incorporated into the diegesis, rather than being presented directly by the narrator – that is, a character in the storyworld does the describing. Again, as we shall see, this causes some minor implausibilities in the narrative line.

Ásgrímr and Njáll's sons have met with a mixed response in their canvass. Some of those approached agree to lend support; others refuse, and some remain neutral. But the tension builds as Skarpheðinn responds aggressively and insultingly to those who are not willing to help. The whole scene is based almost entirely on the exchanges between Ásgrímr and his would-be supporters, in each case capped by Skarpheðinn's inflammatory responses. Each person approached makes an allusion to Skarpheðinn's appearance, briefly describing him – ostensibly, in order to ask who he is. This is an intriguing version of the way a third party describes attackers approaching their intended victim, who may then identify them. And in the same way, there are evident difficulties in incorporating the act of description into the diegesis – here, because of the implication that the describer, improbably, implies that he does not recognize Skarpheðinn.[86] Thus, when Ásgrímr asks Skapti Þóroddson (who was to become a well-regarded lawspeaker) for support, Skapti refuses and Ásgrímr snaps back at him with an insulting retort. Skapti then asks, 'Hverr er sá maðr … er fjórir menn ganga fyrri, mikill maðr ok fölleitr ok ógæfusamligr, harðligr ok tröllsligr?' (Who is the fifth man in your company, a big man and pale-faced, with an unlucky look, but fierce and like a troll?).[87] Skarpheðinn points out that Skapti must know perfectly well who he is and turns the oddly otiose question – really, I would argue, the result of a piece of rhetorical fiction – into a joke: 'en vera mun ek því vitrari en þú, at ek þarf eigi at spyrja þik, hvat þú heitir' (but I must be cleverer than you because I don't need to ask who you are).[88] He follows this up with an offensive insult.[89] This pattern is repeated a number of times, and a half-comic tension builds steadily. Snorri goði does not dismiss out of hand Ásgrímr's request for support, but still asks who the fifth man is, with a similarly unflattering description: 'Hverr er sá maðr er fjórir ganga fyrri, fölleitr ok skarpleitr ok glottir við tönn ok hefir øxi reidda um öxl?' (Who is the man behind the first four, pale-faced and sharp-featured, scowling, and with an axe carried on his shoulder?).[90] Again, this provokes an insult from Skarpheðinn. Hafr inn auðgi (the wealthy) asks who it is who is 'svá illiligr sem genginn sé út ór sjávahömrum' (so ugly that [he] might have emerged from a sea cliff [that is, troll-like]).[91] As above, Skarpheðinn trades the unflattering description for a fierce insult, which ends the encounter, and of course puts paid to any possibility of support. When Ásgrímr and his company approach Guðmundr inn ríki (the powerful) the same pattern is repeated, but Guðmundr is not implacably opposed to helping them. Even his description of Skarpheðinn is less negative: Guðmundr says he is 'jarpr á hárslit ok föllitaðr, mikill vöxtum ok drengiligr ok svá skjótligr til karlmennsku, at heldr vilda ek hans fylgi hafa en tíu annarra' (auburn-haired, with a pale face, large in stature and valiant, and so adept at manly things that I'd rather have him as a follower than ten others). And yet, adds Guðmundr, 'er … maðrinn ógæfusamligr' (the man is unlucky).[92] Skarpheðinn makes an offensive retort – mocking Guðmundr for allowing himself to be slandered by the man who is to be their next interlocutor, in fact – and the encounter is over.

By the time of Ásgríms's final attempt to rally support, the pattern is firmly established and the tension is high. Ásgrímr begs Skarpheðinn to keep quiet this time, and their interlocutor Þorkell hákr (the bully) is introduced as a formidable fighter who 'eirði hvárki í orðum né verkum, við hvern sem hann átti' (spared no one with whom he had dealings in words or deeds), and is thus, implicitly, a match for Skarpheðinn.[93] Ásgrímr cautions all his followers to proceed very carefully and warns Skarpheðinn not to say anything. It is at this crucial moment that the narrator pauses the narrative with a description of Skarpheðinn: he 'var svá búinn, at hann var í blám kyrtli ok í blárendum brókum, ok uppháva svarta skúa; hann hafði silfrbelti um sik ok øxi þá í hendi, er hann hafði drepit Þráin með ok kallaði Rimmugýgi, ok törgubuklara ok silkihlað um höfuð ok greitt hárit aptr um eyrun' (was dressed in this way: in a dark tunic and dark striped trousers, and high dark shoes; he had a silver belt around him, and in his hand the axe with which he had killed Þráinn, which was called Rimmugýgi [battle-ogress], and a small shield, and a silk headband, and his hair pulled back behind his ears).[94]

This description is not voiced by a character in the storyworld but presented as a direct intervention by the narrator, although there is no explicit acknowledgement that this is the case; the narrator does not draw attention to the placing of the description. However, it certainly constitutes a dramatic narrative pause, increasing the established tension, and strictly speaking, it constitutes a sort of anachrony – a disruption to narrative chronology – since Skarpheðinn has presumably fitted the description given since the very beginning of the scene, and its placing at this relatively late stage is purely for dramatic effect. Furthermore, the description includes some information which the narrator is addressing directly to the audience: the name of Skarpheðinn's axe, and what he had previously used it for. The axe has not been named before, although it plays a prominent part in the subsequent narrative. Following the descriptive passage, the encounter at first follows the same pattern as previous ones: Þorkell refuses to help and then frames a description of Skarpheðinn as a rhetorical question by asking his identity. Skarpheðinn insults him – perhaps even more offensively than he insulted previous chieftains. This time, however, Skarpheðinn provokes a response: Þorkell rushes at him, but Skarpheðinn faces him down, gaining the grudging respect of Ásgrímr, in spite of having derailed his plea for support.[95] Indeed, as it turns out, Guðmundr inn ríki is so impressed when he hears of Skarpheðinn's action that he agrees to lend Ásgrímr his support after all.[96]

The above description of Skarpheðinn constitutes a distinct pause in the narrative, and it has been purposefully placed for dramatic effect. It is important to reiterate, however, that though the mode may be contrived, this does not necessarily mean that the description is fictional – that is, that Skarpheðinn was *not* dressed as described. And although, as I have noted, every element in and feature of the narrative is inevitably a result of authorial choice or manipulation, in cases like this particular passage of description, the specific and purposeful nature of the placing is especially evident. We have moved some way from the apparently artless reporting of 'what happened'. Nonetheless, we are still a long way from hearing the voice of our silent narrator, the subject of Chapter 4, even if we can discern narratorial intrusion.

At this point, I would like to consider briefly another kind of narratorial manipulation of the narrative pause: the placing of skaldic verses in family saga narrative.[97] I have explored the poetics of stanza placement at some length elsewhere, and I do not want to repeat here what I said there.[98] But a key distinction in the way verses are incorporated into the narrative needs to be revisited and restated: the distinction between verses presented as the direct speech of characters in the narrative and those which are presented as corroborative material – a distinction conveniently evident in introductory phrases such as 'þá kvað X' (then X said ...) as opposed to 'svá kvað X ... ' (as X said).[99] In *Skaldic Verse and the Poetics of Saga Narrative*, my primary interest in this distinction was to do with the appearance of fictionality versus historicity, based on the fictional strategy of showing characters (wholly improbably) moving smoothly from lucid and colloquial prose to heavily metrical and metaphorically cryptic skaldic verse, versus the impression of historicity produced by the corroborative quotation of a stanza. What I was not especially concerned with there – but am very much concerned with here – is the distinction between a verse ostensibly spoken within the diegesis and one proffered directly to an audience (readers or listeners) by the saga author.[100] This is precisely analogous to the distinction between the descriptive pause which is created when a character in the diegesis does the describing, and the descriptive pause narrated directly to the audience, as, for instance, with the deftly placed final description of Skarpheðinn as opposed to the preceding ones voiced by the chieftains in the storyworld. I argued in *Skaldic Verse and Saga Narrative* that the corroborative verses were diagnostic of historicity, and the direct speech verses – with the exception of some instances of staged recitation – of fictionality. Here, I am arguing that descriptive passages displaced on to characters in the diegesis are no more or less fictional than descriptions in the narrative voice; the key issue is rather the preservation of the integrity of the storyworld as against the manifest intervention in it by the narrator.

Analysis of the descriptive pause in family saga narrative concludes my exploration of Gérard Genette's categories of what he terms *duration* – the ratio of *erzählte Zeit* to *Erzählzeit*, that is, the time events would have taken to occur versus the time it takes to relate them. As we have seen, it has sometimes been necessary to anticipate some analysis of the role and voice of the narrator, as for example where the relatively slow *Erzählzeit* of scenic narrative allows scope for some aspects of the rhetoric of fiction, or where the descriptive pause is produced directly by the narrative voice rather than being incorporated in the diegesis. But before moving on to a fuller exploration of the ways in which the narrator may explicitly intervene in the narrative, we need to consider the second of Genette's major categories of how narrative time is manipulated: *order.*

3

The management of narrative time: Order

What Gérard Genette terms *order* concerns the sequence in which events are narrated, as opposed to the sequence in which they would have occurred had they actually happened. This, as I noted in the introduction, is one of the most basic features of the rhetoric of fiction and is usually figured as the fundamental distinction between *fabula* and *sjuzhet*, or story and discourse. Genette terms the disturbance of naturalistic chronology *anachrony*, defining it as 'all forms of discordance between the two temporal orders of story and narrative'.[1] He distinguishes two basic forms of anachrony: *prolepsis*, in which an event which is not due to take place until some point in the narrative future is narrated or alluded to in advance; and *analepsis*, in which an event which occurred at an earlier point in the story or discourse than the present moment of the narrative is not narrated or alluded to at the time at which it took place, but at a later point in the narrative. Perhaps more familiar terms, especially for filmgoers, are flashforward and flashback, and both are indications of marked interventions on the part of the author of the narrative. In addition, Genette considers *reach*, that is, how far backwards or forwards the anachrony stretches, and whether the anachrony refers to events within the extent of the primary narrative, or to events completely outside it. He warns that analepses and prolepses which do relate to the matter of the main story run the risk of repeating, or 'interfering with' it.[2] In relation to saga narrative, Vésteinn Ólason is very clear about the avoidance of repeated narration which may arise with anachrony, declaring that saga narrators 'never state in advance what will happen later, and never describe the same events more than once'.[3]

Anachrony implies a purposeful re-ordering of the sequence of events in the discourse, rather than the narrative voice simply relating events in the order in which they might have happened. In fact, a common misconception about the relationship between *fabula* and *sjuzhet* is to suppose that the *fabula* is in some sense the originary story, lying behind and prior to the *sjuzhet*, and that the *sjuzhet* is an artful manipulation and re-ordering of it. Of course with fiction, it's actually the other way round. It may seem simply intuitive to understand the series of underlying events – the *fabula*, or story – as somehow preceding the *sjuzhet*, or discourse, which apparently rearranges the pre-existing chronology to create the discourse. But as Peter Brooks (following Jonathan Culler) has pointed out, in fiction 'the apparent priority of *fabula* to *sjužet* is in the nature of a mimetic illusion, in that the *fabula* – "what really happened" – is in fact a mental construction that the reader derives from the *sjužet*, which is all that [she or he] ever directly knows'.[4] We as audience in fact construct the *fabula* from the *sjuzhet*.

Such theoretical problems have very little place in the analysis of family saga narratives. For one thing, as we have seen, the naturalistic background of real historical time in family sagas gives the impression of some historical basis to the *fabula*, and indeed some of what is related might have happened in historical actuality, and thus actually would pre-date the discourse. But most importantly, events in family sagas are by and large related in the chronological order in which they might have happened in actuality, and so the distinction between *sjuzhet* and *fabula* is minimal. However, this does not mean that anachrony is absent from family sagas. As is sometimes the case with the deployment of the descriptive pause, references to the past and the future of the narrative's present moment are typically displaced on to the characters, thus firmly situating any anachrony within the diegesis.[5]

In temporal terms, then, the anachrony in saga narrative seems not to issue from a narrator's lofty *totum simul* perspective – knowing and seeing the past, present and future of the narrative as a whole and at once, and rearranging events at will for dramatic effect – but is presented from the perspective of characters in the storyworld. Their experience of anticipating the future and remembering the past is not conveyed to the reader or listener through interiority, either, but almost always in speech, as spoken recall or as prophecy. Wayne C. Booth notes that it can actually be 'unrealistic' to avoid anachrony altogether: 'to begin at the beginning and plod methodically through to the end'.[6] And indeed, although family saga narratives do relate events chronologically, this 'plodding' effect is powerfully mitigated by diegetic anachrony, that is, the attribution of prophecy and recall to the characters themselves. By framing these instances of anachrony as direct speech acts, occurring as they would have, or might have, in their proper place in the flow of events, the heterodiegetic narrative voice preserves the illusion that what is being related is simply the succession of events as they happened, in due chronological order, without a narrator rearranging things.

I shall also explore the various means by which the saga author avoids the repetition of material which Gérard Genette warns about, and whose absence from saga narrative Vésteinn Ólason so categorically asserts.

Prolepsis

Genette defines prolepsis as 'any narrative maneuver that consists of narrating or evoking in advance an event that will take place later'.[7] But in fact, he seems in practice to restrict narrative prolepsis to direct intervention by the narrator. Alluding to a proleptic remark in Proust's *Á la Recherche du Temps Perdu*, he argues that 'such [a] notification cannot be the hero's doing, but must of course be the narrator's – like, more generally, all forms of prolepsis, which (except for an intervention of the supernatural, as in prophetic dreams) always exceed a hero's capacities for knowledge'.[8] But the most striking form of allusion to the future in saga narrative is in fact the prophetic dream. Genette's restriction of prolepsis to narratorial intervention rests on the belief that characters cannot know their own futures, as is the case with people in the real world. But characters can – and do – predict the future in saga narrative, either through prophetic dreams, Genette's exception, or through the wise interpretation of what is likely to happen, or even as an expression of generalized gloom or (much less often) optimism about what the future holds. Furthermore, the distinction between a curse, a threat or a promise on the one hand, and prophecy on the other, is a very fine one. When these allusions to the future are accurate, I would argue that what we have is narratorial prolepsis displaced on to a character and located in the diegesis: diegetic anachrony. Occasionally, such future evocations turn out to be wrong or unfulfilled. This, then, is a rather unusual form of prolepsis, if indeed it can strictly be termed prolepsis at all, but I shall nevertheless discuss some striking instances of it, just as I will consider some intriguing instances of imperfect or deliberately distorted recall in my analysis of saga analepsis, or flashback. Such cases are incidentally very obvious examples of how repetition of material is avoided. In all this, I make no attempt to be exhaustive in my lists of examples; I concern myself with particularly interesting or representative cases, with the aim of alerting readers to the technique, rather than documenting every example.

I will begin with predictions which are associated with supernatural figures, before moving on to the teasing proximity of apparent clairvoyance to mere wisdom about the course of events based on experience or intuition about human nature. I will also consider some predictions which clearly do not require special powers. Next, I will explore more generalized expressions of pessimism about future events, often centring on misgivings about the luck or otherwise of another character. This will lead on to a consideration of one specific category of intimation about the future: a character's presentiment of his or her own death, or the death of someone close. I will move on then to visions and prophetic dreams, which are presented as in some sense visited on characters, and I will finish with a few examples of portents which are evident as such to several characters in the storyworld and are not attached to one particular perspective. Throughout, we shall see how clairvoyance or prescience is presented as part of the storyworld, as a character trait, but at the same time functions as one of the saga author's ways of managing the narrative. Furthermore, we shall see that the narration of a 'passed past' means that everything in the narrative actually *is* pre-ordained; that nothing could have been different, and that the characters' fatalistic intimations of this match our – and the saga author's – actual extradiegetic knowledge. The *totum simul* perspective of author and reader on the one hand, and the lived time experience of the characters, which we share in as we read or listen, on the other – what Ricœur calls the 'double temporality' of narrative – coincide when characters fatalistically acknowledge, implicitly or explicitly, that the future is predictable and, therefore, fixed.

Prophecy associated with supernatural voices occurs in a number of family sagas, but as one might expect, two sagas in which the supernatural figures prominently – *Eyrbyggja saga* and *Grettis saga* – offer striking examples. In *Eyrbyggja saga*, we have a large number of supernatural manifestations, which I shall discuss towards the end of this section as portents, and one character – Katla – is not only labelled a witch, but also shown performing magic spells to shape-shift her son Oddr in order to disguise him from their enemies.[9] Oddr Kötluson is eventually hanged for his misdeeds, and the chieftain Arnkell condemns his mother as the cause of his evil end. Katla responds with a curse, predicting that she will be the cause of an evil end for Arnkell in his turn, 'en þat væri vili minn' (and that is what I intend), adding 'vænti ek ok, at þat mun svá vera' (and I predict that it will be so).[10] Specifically, she continues, 'þat vilda ek at mín ákvæði stœðisk, at þú hlytir því verra af feðr þínum … vænti ek ok, at þat sé mælt áðr lýkr, at þú eigir illan föður' (I want my curse to be realized such that your father will be an (even) worse cause of evil for you … and I predict that it will be said before long that you have an evil father).[11] This elaborate blend of curse and prophecy, echoing key phrases and throwing them back at Arnkell, fits well with Katla's identity as a spell-casting witch, and indeed her curse/prophecy about

Arnkell and his father is fulfilled in the saga narrative. Similarly, in a celebrated scene from *Grettis saga*, mentioned in the previous chapter, the revenant Glámr curses Grettir: he is never to become any stronger than he is now (though he is already very strong); outlawry and killings are destined to be his fate; and finally, that he will be haunted by Glámr's gaze, and so find it burdensome to be alone, a particularly difficult fate for an outlaw.[12] One may say both that his prophecies come true and that his curses are effective. In Glámr's speech, curse and prophecy are conflated.

Njáls saga contains a very considerable number of allusions to the future of the narrative. Not only Njáll himself, but also his son, Helgi, and even Gunnarr's dog, Sámr, and Gunnarr's halberd are presented as prophetic: the dog can tell if someone means to harm Gunnarr, and the halberd makes a ringing noise in anticipation of action.[13] Sámr's second sight is (just about) plausible, given the widely held belief that dogs can sense incipient hostility, but the sentience of the halberd is unequivocally supernatural. However, to turn now to non-magical, or real-world clairvoyance: Njáll himself is by far the most frequently predictive character. His introduction into the saga narrative as a prophet seems to be quite clear: he is described as both 'langsýnn ok langminnigr' (far-sighted and long-memoried), which puts him in the same category as the formidable mythical sibyl of *Völuspá*, who could remember a time before the world was created, and see forwards to a time beyond its end.[14] But Njáll's clairvoyance is not completely unequivocal. One manuscript tradition does not include these epithets; and, as we shall see, Njáll's prescience as demonstrated in the course of the narrative is never completely divorced from real-world plausibility.[15]

From the outset, Njáll's many predictions hover between the prophetic and the plausibly shrewd. He sees that his friend Gunnarr is much envied and reasonably predicts that this will cause him difficulties.[16] He predicts trouble from Gunnarr's intended wife, Hallgerðr, but since Gunnarr is not her first (or even second) husband, and both her previous marriages ended in her husbands' deaths, his anxiety is perfectly reasonable.[17] In the accelerating series of reciprocal killings instigated by Bergþóra and Hallgerðr, Njáll correctly predicts that his own sons will soon be involved. However, given the rising tensions and his sons' volatile temperaments, which are explicitly noted before Njáll makes this prediction, their involvement is almost inevitable.[18] More specific, and thus more uncannily prophetic, is Njáll's famous advice to Gunnarr never to kill twice in the same family.[19] This otherwise perfectly sensible counsel is wrapped around with prophecy: firstly, that Gunnarr's honour will only be increased by his recent killings of Otkell and Skamkell and, secondly, that if he does not follow Njáll's advice he will not have long to live. This raises the possibility of an alternative: if Gunnarr *does* follow the advice, he will live on into old age, and contradicts the view, expressed by Njáll and others, that events are largely preordained – 'mjök á kveðit' (much is predetermined).[20] In addition, we also have an intriguing case of a self-fulfilling prophecy, for Gunnarr's enemies hear of Njáll's stipulation and manoeuvre Gunnarr into the double killing. The advice not to kill twice in the same kin group might be seen as practical shrewdness rather than second sight. Nevertheless, within the storyworld, Gunnarr is completely persuaded by Njáll's prophetic powers and asks him – wonderingly, it seems – if he is able to predict the cause of his own death. Njáll replies that he is. When Gunnarr presses him to say what it will be, Njáll responds: 'Þat, sem allir munu sízt ætla' (Something that everyone would consider the least likely).[21] Only towards the end of the saga is this prophecy fulfilled, although perhaps few listeners or readers would or will be ignorant of the eventual fate of Brennu-Njáll (Burnt Njáll). So, at this point in the narrative, what Njáll's prescience predicts is evident to us, but not, crucially, to Gunnarr. Had Njáll specified the cause of his death, this would simply have been an instance of prophetic prolepsis. But here we are as close as we can get to full-blown proleptic, that is, dramatic, irony, in which audience and one character know more than other characters.

A number of other characters in family sagas are explicitly identified as having second sight. In *Njáls saga* itself, as I have mentioned, Njáll's son Helgi is credited with clairvoyance: although he makes a modest disclaimer in response to Earl Sigurðr of Orkney's question 'Ertú forspár maðr?' (Are you a man who can prophesy the future?), his brother-in-law Kári speaks up for him, significantly, from within the diegesis: 'mun hann satt til segja, því at faðir hans er forspár' (what he says will come true, because his father can prophesy the future).[22] Helgi's uncanny prediction that one of the earl's men in Scotland will have been killed proves true.[23] Similarly, Gestr Oddleifsson is introduced into *Njáls saga* as 'manna vitastr, svá at hann sá fyrir ørlög manna' (the wisest of men, such that he knew people's destiny).[24] In *Eyrbyggja saga*, a character aptly nicknamed Spá-Gils (prophecy-Gils) is said to be 'framsýnn' (far-sighted) and is consulted about the disappearance of some horses because he was, usefully enough, 'eptirrýningamaðr mikill um stuldi' (a good investigator of theft).[25] However, none of these second-sighted characters are shown as sufficiently engaged in prophecy for us to be able to judge whether their gift is a shrewd understanding of human nature and the workings of society, or uncanny prescience.

Perhaps the most striking example of a protracted narrative episode which takes place in the future of the saga's present moment is Njáll's advice to Gunnarr about how to reclaim his kinswoman Unnr's dowry from her ex-husband Hrútr. This is a good example of plan as prolepsis: Njáll sets out in detail a strategy for Gunnarr to arrive at Hrútr's farmstead disguised as a pedlar. He directs Gunnarr how to dress, how to behave, what to say and how to respond to his unwelcoming hosts in a way which will allow him to deliver an oral summons as if he were only pretending to. The detail is wrapped up in a kind of extended resultant prophecy: if Gunnarr says or does a particular thing, others will respond in predictable ways – predictable to Njáll at least. Njáll warns Gunnarr that the plan will only work if Gunnarr follows it to the letter, and Gunnarr promises to do so.[26] This injunction converts the plan into an example of actual prolepsis: an account in the narrative present of something which is still to take place in the narrative future – not hypothetically, but as definitely as possible. This is not the only such case in *Njáls saga*. Earlier in the narrative, Unnr's father Mörðr lays out for her a plan for divorcing Hrútr. Again, the strategy is set out in detail and involves a number of predictions about how people will act and speak in response. And again, the author of the plan – Mörðr, in this instance – takes care to demand, in the storyworld, that it is followed precisely.[27] Mörðr checks this after the plan has been put into operation: he asks Unnr if she has followed his advice, and she responds 'Hvergi hefi ek af brugði' (I haven't deviated from it in any way), a very close echo of Gunnarr's promise to Njáll: 'Hvergi skal ek af bregða' (I will not deviate from it in any way).[28] These two assurances confirm perfect consonance between the plan, as proleptically outlined, and the episodes as they are duly played out; the narrative does not need to repeat itself by recounting the (successful) enactment of the plans.

Clearly these two episodes are fictional constructs, bravura elaborations on and celebrations of the power of cunning operators like Mörðr and Njáll to manipulate the future on the basis of shrewd prediction. They do not depend on supernatural effects, even though with their elaborate detail they are not wholly realistic either. Less extended predictions about the future which also do not depend on the supernatural are relatively common in saga narrative. Sometimes, like Njáll's more elaborate plans, they are based on some sort of privileged knowledge. Thus, in *Laxdœla saga*, the chieftain Snorri rightly predicts that vengeance for the death of Bolli Þorleiksson will not be long coming, but it soon emerges that he himself has a plan in mind to hasten it.[29] More straighforwardly commonsensical is Þórólfr bægifótr's surmise in *Eyrbyggja saga* that his enemy Úlfarr will be loaded with gifts, since he's on his way back from a lavish feast. Þórólfr uses this simple inference to persuade his ally Spá-Gils (the prophet) to attack Úlfarr.[30] As it happens, Úlfarr himself is presented as a skilled weather-forecaster, and Þórólfr consults him closely about the chances of a dry summer that year. Úlfarr's prediction of a rainy spell followed by a fortnight's dry weather proves to be accurate.[31] Later in the same saga, Snorri plans an attack on his enemy Björn on the simple surmise that, on a fine day, he will be outside – and therefore vulnerable to attack – drying hay.[32] These weather and farming details, incidentally, are entirely consonant with what I have already noted as the underlying concerns of the whole saga: the settlement of the land. And weather forecasting has always fallen somewhere between an art and a science.

Sometimes in saga narrative, characters themselves point out that predictions may depend more on common sense than on clairvoyance. In *Eyrbyggja saga*, Björn Breiðvíkingakappi rightly predicts that Snorri goði will get the better of Steinþórr Þorláksson, who is leading the opposition. In this instance, Björn himself draws attention to the fact that this is a prediction that anyone with any sense could make, adding 'en eigi em ek framsýnn' (not that I'm clairvoyant).[33] Moreover, predictions themselves may be less significant in the narrative than what they may tell us about characters who are able – or not – to make them. In *Njáls saga*, for instance, Glúmr Óleifsson arrives at the farm of Höskuldr Dala-Kollsson with his brother Þórarinn and a large company of men. They stay overnight. In the morning, Höskuldr asks his brother Hrútr to come over for support. He tells Hrútr – perhaps a little nervously – that he doesn't know what his unexpected visitors want, because they haven't broached their business with him so far. Hrútr at once rightly predicts that they have come to ask Höskuldr if Glúmr can marry Höskuldr's daughter Hallgerðr, and shortly afterwards Þórarinn requests precisely this on behalf of his brother.[34] Here, the prediction throws light on the character of Hrútr, down to earth and sensible, and his relationship with Höskuldr, who is more needy and nervous in spite of his attempts at bluster.

A final example demonstrates how the privileged knowledge of one character and the wise common sense of another may produce the same prediction. Towards the end of *Njáls saga*, after Njáll and his family have been burned in their farm, the leader of the burners, Flosi, tries to identify a suitable lawyer to defend him. His friend Bjarni dismisses Flosi's first suggested candidate – a kinsman of Bjarni's – on grounds that he wouldn't wish such a controversial case on a kinsman, adding 'En segja mun ek þér, at þat verðr þess manns bani, er vörn fœrir fram fyrir brennumálit' (And I can tell you that taking on the defence for the burning will be the death of the man who does it).[35] This prediction is underscored by Snorri goði, who spots that Eyjólfr Bölverksson, who has by this stage been secretly employed by Flosi and the burners, is wearing a valuable ring which Flosi has given him. Snorri, always alert to conspiracy and intrigue, at once recognizes it as a bribe and adds 'skyldi þessi hringr eigi verða þér at höfuðbana' (may this ring not be the death of you).[36] Bjarni's prophecy and Snorri's ironic warning are both proleptic; Eyjólfr is killed by Njáll's son-in-law Kári.

Somewhere between these commonsensical or shrewd predictions and purported clairvoyance is the sense expressed by many characters in family sagas that some unspecified bad thing is in the offing. For instance, in *Njáls saga,* after Gunnarr has killed one of his enemies, his wife Hallgerðr is pleased, but his mother Rannveig gloomily remarks 'Vera má, at gott sé verkit, en verra varð mér við en ek ætla, at gott muni af leiða' (It may be that something good has been done, but I think that something worse rather than good will come of it).[37] In *Gísla saga,* Gísli gives his brother-in-law Vésteinn one half of a token to be used as a warning device, predicting 'En mér segir svá hugr um, at vit munim þurfa at sendask á milli' (And something tells me that we two will need to send [it] to each other).[38] Gísli feels the need to warn off Vésteinn only a few chapters further on, and he is murdered shortly after. On occasion, a saga character even makes it clear that he or she wants to distinguish this generalized feeling of doom from an actual prophecy. This is the case in *Laxdœla saga* with Óláfr pái's reservations about his son Kjartan's developing relationship with Guðrún from Laugar. As Óláfr tells Kjartan, 'Nú er þat hugboð mitt, en eigi vil ek þess spá, at vér frændr ok Laugamenn berim eigiallsendis gæfu til um vár skipti' (Now I have a feeling – but I don't want to [actually] predict this – that we kinsmen and the people of Laugar will not enjoy altogether good luck in our dealings with each other).[39] Here we have a hint of the sense that to make a prophecy may be to bring about its fulfilment, but Óláfr's caution is futile: Guðrún is to be the direct cause of Kjartan's death. Such intimations of misfortune do not so much reflect on characters' prescience or shrewdness as contribute to a more general air of narrative fatalism. The characters act as the mouthpieces of narratorial prolepsis.

There is also a set of minor predictions characteristic of saga narrative, in which one character declares that he or she is seeing the other for the last time. When the speaker is a Scandinavian ruler, and his interlocutor a visitor from Iceland, the prediction need have no ominous dimension. Thus, for example, in *Laxdœla saga,* King Hákon tells Höskuldr Dala-Kollsson 'ok nær er þat minni ætlan, at þú siglir nú it síðasta sinn af Noregi' (and my guess is that you are now sailing [home] from Norway for the last time).[40] This seems rather to indicate a gift-giving moment than to be occasion of sadness or foreboding. Similarly, in *Njáls saga,* King Haraldr Gormsson tries to persuade Gunnarr to stay in Denmark, but Gunnarr insists he want to return to Iceland. Haraldr responds,

'Þá munt þú aldri aptr koma til vár' (Then you will never come back to us).⁴¹ Both predictions prove to be true. Such signals may be understood as the equivalent of a discreet kind of narrative management common in sagas, though technically it might be termed 'narratorial prolepsis': when narrators themselves tell us that some character or other is from this point 'out of the saga'. In *Laxdœla saga*, for instance, we are advised about a character called Ásgautr that 'endir þar sögu frá honum' (there ends the story about him), or about Þorleikr Höskuldsson that 'lúku vér þar sögu frá Þorleiki' (there we finish the story of Þorleikr).⁴² Similarly, in *Eyrbyggja saga* we are told that Björn Breiðvíkingakappi 'kemr síðar við þessa sögu' (will come into this story later on), and that when Börkr inn digri (the fat) is divorced by Þordís, he moved away and eventually settled in Glerárskógar, 'ok bjó þar til elli' (and lived there until old age).⁴³

The narrator of *Grettis saga* often informs us of something which happened at a point in advance of the present moment of the narrative: that the mother of Grettir's grandfather 'giptisk síðan norðr í Víðidal' (was later married in Víðidalr, in the north); or that one of his son's neighbours was the father of a woman who was the wife of Ísleifr, 'er siðan var byskup í Skálaholti' (who later became the bishop of Skálholt); or that, although Þorgeirr Hávarsson had an aggressive encounter with a character called Gautr, '[v]arð ekki at með þeim Þorgeiri at því sinni, en þó reis af þessu sundrþykki með þeim, sem síðar bar raun á' (nothing occurred between him and Þorgeirr on that occasion, but there arose from this a quarrel between them, as was later evidenced).⁴⁴ These minor textual nudges are again in the narratorial voice, and so here I am again anticipating the next chapter, but as with the analysis of descriptive pauses, I do this in order to highlight at this point the difference between diegetic prolepsis – when the characters do the predicting – and extra-diegetic, or narratorial prolepsis – when we can almost hear the voice of the narrator directing us, although this voice is not in any way characterized. As I have suggested, in *Njáls saga* insistent diegetic prolepsis reinforces the impression that the past has passed, along with all the people in it, but we are being shown what the future looks like from their point of view. In *Grettis saga*, rather differently, the narrator, from outside the storyworld, is informing the audience of people and events which seem to have an objective existence, whether in actuality or in tradition.

Another vehicle for predicting the future is the recognition by one character that another character is an 'ógæfumaðr' (unlucky person). In saga narrative, 'luck' is not so much an individual, unexpected or undeserved piece of good fortune, but the more extended likelihood of being generally fortunate in one's life; to be unlucky, by contrast, indicates that bad things – undeserved or not –

will tend to happen to a person, or to those associated with them.⁴⁵ In *Grettis saga*, many figures recognize this quality in Grettir himself and allude to the unhappy future it portends. The Norwegian King Óláfr makes the most explicit statement about it: 'en miklu ertu meiri ógæfumaðr en þú megir fyrir þat með oss vera' (but you are far too much of an unlucky person to stay [here] with us).⁴⁶ However, Grettir's mother and father, for example, and Jarl Sveinn of Norway, his uncle Jökull Bárðarson and the chieftain Vermundr all predict a poor future or a bad end for Grettir, implicitly on the basis of his somehow evident unluckiness, although actually, of course, it's an aspect of narratorial prolepsis.⁴⁷

But the prediction of future ill-luck may be soundly based on past history. In *Njáls saga*, for instance, the Norwegian chieftain Guðbrandr í Dölum is explicit about the miscreant Hrappr: 'Ekki lízk mér svá á þik sem þú munir gæfumaðr vera' (You don't look to me as if you will be a lucky person).⁴⁸ Hrappr had sought a passage to Norway with a merchant called Kolbeinn, who himself had predicted bad fortune for anyone who helps Hrappr: 'Þess get ek … at sá hafi verr, er þik flytr' (I reckon that it will be the worse for anyone who offers you a passage).⁴⁹ Since Hrappr has just told Kolbeinn that he is on the run from powerful men seeking redress for a killing he has committed, Kolbeinn's assessment of Hrappr is not especially prescient, and both his and Guðmundr's predictions prove to be accurate. By contrast, in one of the most celebrated *ad feminam* predictions of bad fortune, as we have seen, Hrútr Herjólfsson claims to see 'þjófsaugu' (the eyes of a thief) in the young girl Hallgerðr's face at the very beginning of *Njáls saga*.⁵⁰ Even in a saga with so much emphasis on prophecy, as a diegetic event this is uncanny, and even implausibly prescient; Hrútr has had no evidence on which to base his prediction, unless we assume that he is basing his negative assessment on some sort of unstated folk physiognomy – that thieves have eyes of a distinctive shape or quality, or a discernible 'look' to them. It is more likely a bold example of narrative prolepsis, characteristically displaced on to a character in the storyworld. Throughout the saga, however, other characters repeatedly predict that Hallgerðr will cause trouble. Hrútr himself predicts the unhappiness and fatal failure of Hallgerðr's first marriage, and her first husband's brother warns the new husband – in a delicately but ominously comic exchange – that Hallgerðr's laughter at him is not necessarily a sign of wifely affection.⁵¹ But their predictions are evidence-based. And Njáll's grim prediction about Hallgerðr to her husband-to-be Gunnarr later in the saga – 'Af henni mun standa allt it illa' (She will be the source of every bad thing [that happens]) – is, as we have seen, a clear example of foresight based on a reasonable assumption.⁵² Njáll elaborates his prediction about Hallgerðr a little beyond what Hallgerðr's past could have taught him: he warns Gunnarr that Hallgerðr will be a serious threat to their friendship, but that Gunnarr will always compensate for her ill will. Nevertheless, the probability remains that Njáll is basing his forecast on his past knowledge not only of Hallgerðr's behaviour, but also of his loyal friend Gunnarr.

Prophecies may be fulfilled in spite of warnings attached to them because the warnings are wilfully disregarded. In *Njáls saga*, a widow called Steinvör begs Þorgrímr, a Norwegian whom her husband had employed, to stay in Iceland to guard her and her property.[53] A little earlier in the saga, Þorgrímr's comrade and Steinvör's husband were both killed in an attack on Gunnarr. Þorgrímr now recalls a prophecy his comrade made before attacking Gunnarr: that he would join Steinvör's husband in that attack, but 'mun hvárrgi okkarr aptr koma' (neither of the two of us will return).[54] This prophecy has been fulfilled, but Þorgrímr recalls another of his comrade's predictions: that Þorgrímr would himself be killed by Gunnarr if he stayed in Iceland. However, Steinvör now offers Þorgrímr her daughter's hand in marriage, and all the family property, if he will stay and help out. Tempted by the offer, Þorgrímr marries the daughter that summer and is the first to be killed during the subsequent attack on Gunnarr.[55] Somewhat similarly, in *Eyrbyggja saga* the Hebridean woman Þórgunna makes a failed attempt to control the future: having predicted her approaching death, she bequeaths her possessions to the farmer and his wife where she is employed. However, she insists that the luxurious bedclothes and bed hangings she has brought to Iceland with her should be burnt.[56] When Þórgunna dies, the farmer's wife refuses to obey her wishes, although her husband warns her that no good will come of it. They compromise and she keeps the sheets and a quilt, but the prophecy Þórgunna made before she died – 'at menn hljóti svá mikil þyngsl af mér, sem ek veit at verða mun, ef af er brugðit því, sem ek segi fyrir' (that people will be visited with great troubles, which I know will come about, if what I have decreed is not adhered to) – is fulfilled.[57]

Presentiments of death – either one's own or that of another character – are common in saga narrative. Gunnarr, for example, hears the death howl of his dog Sámr and predicts that his death will follow very shortly, as indeed it does.[58] When Gunnarr decides against leaving Iceland, his brother Kolskeggr vows to abide by the terms of their outlawry and grimly instructs Gunnarr to tell their mother and relatives he will never return from his exile abroad, because 'ek mun spyrja þik látinn, frændi, ok heldr mik þá ekki til útferðar' (I will hear that you have been killed, brother, and then nothing will draw me to return).[59] Of course, Gunnarr's breach of the terms of his outlawry makes this outcome likely enough. Similarly, in the midst of the series of reciprocal killings sparked by the hostilities between Bergþóra and Hallgerðr, Bergþóra's servant Atli is ambushed by Hallgerðr's man Brynjólfr. Atli predicts that because of the head wound Brynjólfr has just given him, death is very close, and that Hallgerðr will be pleased to hear this. But he adds a second prediction: that Brynjólfr's own death will not be long coming.[60] Both predictions are entirely reasonable. Similarly, Njáll predicts the death of one of his sons as the eventual entailment of the violent encounter in which Skarpheðinn dramatically kills Þráinn Sigfússon on a frozen river; given the tensions and level of violence in the area, this is quite likely to happen.[61] In cases such as these, the saga author is not simply using the character's prediction to inform the reader or listener of something that would otherwise not be known, nor even to plant a suggestion or confirm a fear, but further, to deepen the sense of predestination around the characters, as with the set of expressions of impending misfortune discussed above. But Njáll's next prediction is different. Having agreed to foster Höskuldr, Þráinn Sigfússon's son, in an attempt to placate the inevitable continuance of the violence, Njáll praises the boy for his peaceable instincts and makes a prediction: 'munt þú verða góðr maðr' (you will become a good man). Höskuldr is pleased with this prediction, declaring his belief that Njáll is both 'forspár ok ólyginn' (clairvoyant and truthful).[62] If Njáll were indeed clairvoyant, then he is being somewhat economical with the truth here, for Höskuldr is destined before too long to be the innocent victim of Njáll's own sons. For those readers or listeners who do not know the story, the good intentions expressed in this touching scene keep open the hopeful possibility of a peaceful future. Those who do know the story will feel its poignancy all the more. Predictions of good fortune are extremely rare in saga narrative; even this exceptional example is compromised by what Njáll does *not* say.

The presentiment of approaching violence may sometimes take the form of a vision. In *Eyrbyggja saga*, the old woman Geirríðr, who is teaching magic to a young man, provokes the jealousy of the witch Katla. Geirríðr, in a markedly stylized, alliterative and almost incantatory utterance, warns Gunnlaugr against going out that night, because 'margir eru marlíðendr; eru ok opt flögð í fögru skinni' (many are the sea-sliders; and also ogresses are often in seductive shapes).[63] Geirríðr concludes that Gunnlaugr does not look to her to be 'hamingjusamligast' (altogether lucky-looking), perhaps making reference to the concept of the *hamingja* or guardian spirit, whose out-of-body appearance, however, is sometimes in saga narrative a herald of death. In fact, although Gunnlaugr is indeed attacked by the other witch Katla, he does not die of his injuries. But in *Víga-Glúms saga*, for example, Glúmr describes in one of his verses his vision of the advance of an enormous spirit woman who bestrides a whole fjord such that her shoulders touched the mountains on either side.[64] The saga author implies that Glúmr recounts this vision publicly as a dream he has had and interprets it himself: the monstrous woman is identified as the *hamingja* of his grandfather, who, as Glúmr correctly interprets as the reason for the vision, has just died in Norway. In *Njáls saga*, Þórðr leysingjason (freedman's son), who has fostered Njáll's sons, suddenly tells Njáll that he can see the farm's tame goat lying in a hollow and 'alblóðugr allr' (all covered in blood).[65] Njáll at once interprets the vision – which, significantly, he himself cannot see – as a sighting of a *fylgja*, or fetch, a concept very closely related to the *hamingja*, and predicts that Þórðr is doomed to die. He tells Þórðr that he must be on his guard, but Þórðr points out that taking care will be useless if he is indeed fated to die.

In *Njáls saga*, there is an unusual example of a vision of *fylgjur* presaging not doom, but a more positive set of events. Njáll sees what he understands to be the *fylgjur*, or personal spirits, of his friend Gunnarr's enemies. But this is not a sign that they are massing in order to attack Gunnarr; quite the opposite. Although they are 'grimmligar' (fierce), Njáll sees that they 'láta ólmliga ok fara þó ráðlausliga' (are behaving as if they are savage, and yet roving around without any plan).[66] No one, not even Njáll, hazards an interpretation of this strange behaviour, but as the narrative goes on to relate, Gunnarr's enemies are half-heartedly gathering for an attack which is very easily averted by Njáll – this is evidently the meaning of the vision, and as it turns out, the cowardice of the attackers is almost comic. Njáll's vision reinforces our belief in his engagement with the future.

Njáll has another vision later in the saga, but this time a very bloody one: 'þykki mér sem undan sé gaflveggirnir báðir, en blóðugt allt borðit ok matrinn' (I seem to see both gable walls fallen, and the table and the food all bloody).[67] This vision comes in the context of Bergþóra's own prediction that this will be the last food she will ever prepare for her household. She adds that as a sign that her prediction is well-founded, their sons Grímr and Helgi will arrive home unexpectedly, which of course they do.[68] But their unexpected decision to return to the family home is not itself based on their own second sight: they have been informed that their enemies are gathering and rightly see this as evidence that an attack is being mounted, and that they will be needed.

The distinction between a waking vision and a dream is not always a clear one. In *Laxdœla saga*, for instance, Óláfr pái slaughters an ox, and the next night dreams that a woman – 'mikil ok reiðulig' (large and angry) – appears to him.[69] She asks him if he is asleep. He claims to be awake, but she corrects him: 'Þér er svefns, en þó mun fyrir hit ganga' (You are asleep, but the outcome will be the same either way).⁷⁰ She predicts – correctly – that he will live to see his son Kjartan come to a bloody end, claiming that she has witnessed Óláfr killing *her* son – presumably, the ox. Óláfr wakes up but thinks he can still see an image of her. He recounts his dream to friends, but no one interprets it in a way that pleases him, and he likes to believe people who call it a 'draumskrök' (false or fictitious dream).⁷¹ Here, the dream woman inhabits both sleeping and waking worlds, and the distinction is carefully blurred.

In accounts of visions, as well as of prophetic dreams, the same introductory terms are typically used: 'ek þykkjumk sjá' (I seem to see); 'hann þóttisk sjá' (it seemed to him [that] he saw). Sometimes, the explicit verb *dreyma* (to dream) is also used, though we often find the impersonal form – 'mik dreymði' (a dream came to me) – thus reinforcing the sense that the dream is more objective than subjective.⁷² And crucially, although one might categorize visions and dreams together as clear components of a character's interiority, in saga narrative access to such mental experience is almost always realized in the diegesis – as in the examples above – by having the dreamer recount the experience.

One striking exception to this rule is the sequence in *Gísla saga* in which Gísli has a series of dreams in which dream women predict his death and produce visions of an afterlife. This stretch of narrative is a complex and extended example of prosimetrum which I have discussed in detail elsewhere.⁷³ It seems likely that the skaldic stanzas have provided the substance of the prose narrative, and they often repeat it, even though the match between the two is not perfect. For instance, the existence of a contrasting pair of dream women, one benevolent and one malevolent, is a creation of the prose narrative; the visions are sometimes ominous, and sometimes seductive, but nothing in the verses themselves suggests two different dream women.⁷⁴ But what I am interested in here is not so much how the verses relate to the narrative, as how the dreams themselves relate to it, in terms of their diegetic status and their proleptic value.

Gísli's experience of dreaming is initially fully realized in the storyworld. Firstly, the saga author characterizes Gísli as 'draumamaðr mikill ok berdreymr' (a man who often had dreams, and prophetic ones).⁷⁵ On this particular occasion, his wife Auðr sees that he is sleeping restlessly and asks him what he has dreamed. In his prose reply – which, as I have said, is repeated when the verses themselves are quoted – he describes a vision of an afterlife: a hall in which his kinsmen are sitting by the fire and drinking. The good dream woman tells him that the seven fires he can see are an indication of how many years he has left to live, and she exhorts him to give up pagan customs. In the sense that this dream vision is predictive – of Gísli's impending death – it is just about proleptic, but there is no indication of the manner of that death; and the dream itself, being about the afterlife, does not prefigure any actual event in the storyworld beyond the timing of Gísli's death. A little later, with the longer autumn nights, Gísli's dreams are said to become more frequent, and more troubling: Gísli dreams of being drenched in blood by a dream woman. He again describes these nightmares to Auðr, and even, in one of the verses, states that he has reported them, though to unspecified 'warriors' ('viðir oddflaums' – trees of the flood of the weapon point), not his wife.[76] However, in the lead up to the next set of dreams, the saga narrator does not specifically state that Gísli has recounted his dreams to anyone; their occurrence and substance are simply related as part of the narrative. The previous prophecy of seven remaining years is smoothly incorporated into the saga's chronology as actuality: we are told that only two years of the original seven now remain. His dreams are reported as narrative events: 'koma aptr draumar hans allir ok harðar svefnfarar' (all his dreams and troubled nights return).[77] Finally, the substance of the dream is reported as if part of the narrative – strictly, of course, a substance which the narrator could not know unless it had been reported: 'Gísla dreymir, at konan sú in betri kom at honum' (Gísli dreams, that the better of the two women came to him).[78] I have argued that the seductive image of a luxurious afterlife attended by Valkyrie-like women would be an awkward vision for Gísli to report to his loyal wife Auðr, as she is presented in the saga.[79] So it may simply be a tactful strategy on the saga author's part to omit specific reference to the dream being reported to Auðr. Nevertheless, the effect is that the narrator seems to demonstrate privileged access to a dream, which is a classic element of interiority and a clear mark of fictionality. Family saga authors elsewhere in the corpus invariably take care to present the substance of dreams as they are recalled by the dreamer, rather than as privileged narratorial knowledge.

Gísli's dreams continue, bloodier and more ominous than ever, and are duly reported to Auðr. As they reach a pitch of intensity, and the time remaining to Gísli has almost run out, Gísli reports a different kind of dream to Auðr: this is a more obviously proleptic dream of his last battle with his enemy Eyjólfr, who nevertheless appears in the dream in almost berserk form, 'grenjandi mjök' (howling loudly) and 'á honum vargs höfuð' (a wolf's head on him).[80] The subsequent verses which Gísli recites – though coded through the cryptic lexis of skaldic verse – predict the actual progress of Gísli's last stand against Eyjólfr and his men. This is a different category of dream from the ominous visions of blood and an afterlife which Gísli has so far experienced.

The most obvious distinction between a prophetic dream and a vision is the more extended narrative dimension to dreams: they prefigure an actual event or set of events in the saga narrative, rather like the vehicle of an allegory, with the tenor as the actual future event in the narrative.[81] The dreamed episode is not, however, necessarily a precise prolepsis of what is to come, but is usually coded, or figuratively related. This avoids repetition, which Genette warned about, and confirms Vésteinn Ólason's assertion that the narrator never repeats material. The dream is interpreted by a character in the narrative as alluding to an episode in the future of that narrative. However, the experience of dreaming and the action of recounting and interpreting the dream usually take place in the present moment of the narrative, so that the chronological order of events is not violated. Sometimes the content of the dream mirrors the events it predicts very closely and is genuinely proleptic in that it includes specific details in the narrative which could not have been predicted simply through reasonable assumption or generalized pessimism. Thus, in *Njáls saga*, Gunnarr dreams that he is attacked by wolves in a place called Knafahólar; one wolf tears open his brother Hjörtr's chest and eats his heart. The saga author brings this dream – as an event – very firmly into the diegesis by showing Gunnarr's brothers observing his restless sleep and debating whether or not to wake him. Gunnarr publicly recounts his dream, which is so transparent that it needs no formal interpretation; both Gunnarr and Hjörtr at once recognize that it foretells the latter's death, although Hjörtr fatalistically rejects Gunnarr's advice to ride home.[82] As is invariably the case, when the dream prophecy is fulfilled, no one mentions it again.[83]

We might contrast this with a less prominent dream, also from *Njáls saga*. Flosi, having led the burning of Njáll in his house, is riding round the district gathering support for the approaching case at the Alþing. Flosi enlists the support of two brothers, but their mother Yngvildr weeps when she hears them pledge to ride to the Alþing with Flosi and tells one of the brothers: 'mik dreymði, at Þorvaldr, bróðir þinn, væri í rauðum kyrtli, ok þótti mér svá þröngr vera sem saumaðr væri at honum; mér þótti hann ok vera í rauðum hosum undir ok vafit at vándum dreglum. Mér þótti illt á at sjá, at honum var svá óhœgt, en ek mátta ekki at gera' (I had a dream, that your brother Þorvaldr was dressed in a red tunic, and it seemed to me so tight that it was as if he had been sewn into it. And it seemed to me as if his leggings were also red, and laced up terribly tightly. It seemed distressing to me that he was in such pain, and I couldn't do anything about it).[84] We have no more of the dream than this static depiction of Þorvaldr, but his wretched situation is plainly a coded reference to his coming death, which again might have been a predictable result of siding with Flosi. There is no need for an explicit interpretation of it. What is significant is that the experience of the dream is itself narrated analeptically – that is, Yngvildr states that she has already had the dream, at some unspecified earlier point in the narrative, but is recounting it now prompted by hearing that her sons have decided to go to the Alþing in support of Flosi. Yngvildr's emotional distress is the focus of the scene, vividly conveyed in the vision of her son's physical torment. The predictive force of the dream is still powerful, however, and perversely reinforced by the sons' fate-tempting dismissal of the dream as 'loklaus[s]' (meaningless), and 'geip' (nonsense); a first-time reader or listener will be warned rather than reassured.[85] There is a similar analepsis earlier in the saga, when Hallgerðr orders her slave Kolr to kill Bergþóra's servant Svartr. Kolr predicts that such a killing will prove to be the death of him. But Hallgerðr insists, and he duly kills Svartr. Hallgerðr assures him that she will protect him, but Kolr now claims to have had a dream which has suggested the opposite.[86] There is very little emotional intensity in the scene: the conventional slave names of the two servants – literally, 'charcoal' and 'black' – underline their function as little more than ciphers in the narrative, and Hallgerðr clearly cares nothing for her man, whom she evidently regards as expendable. And crucially, we are not told anything about the actual content of the dream. But the predictive force of the dream gives Kolr the authority to contradict Hallgerðr.

Perhaps the most celebrated, and extended, prophetic dream sequence in saga narrative is that of the young Guðrún Ósvífrsdóttir in *Laxdœla saga*. Guðrún has four dreams: that she threw a headdress which she felt did not suit her into a stream; that she lost a beloved silver ring, which disappeared into a lake; that she accidentally broke a gold ring, which bled where it broke; and that a heavy headdress fell from her head into Hvammsfjörðr.[87] Guðrún recounts her dreams when she is entertaining the celebrated Gestr Oddleifsson, described in the saga as 'höfðingi mikill ok spekingr at viti, frammsýnn um marga hluti' (a great chieftain and wise in thought, clairvoyant about many things).[88] Gestr interprets the dream as predicting the events and character of Guðrún's four marriages, which form the backbone of the whole saga henceforth. The allegorical explication of each of the dreams is perfectly judged: to predict the future marriage it refers to and yet to remain sufficiently coded as not to be a straightforward narrative re-telling. The effect of prolepsis is created by both characters in tandem. Guðrún's dreams are the vehicle for the prophecy; Gestr's contribution is simply to interpret them, as she explicitly points out: 'Hitta myndir þú fegri spár í þessu máli, ef svá væri í hendr þér búit af mér' (You would have made pleasanter prophecies in this matter, if I had given you the appropriate material).[89] However, the key elements in Guðrún's life – her love for Kjartan, her failure to marry him and her part in bringing about his death – have no part in this prophecy, and are notable, in retrospect, by their absence. The dreams are thus remarkable for what they do not predict. These dreams are plainly a literary fiction. They cannot be absolutely categorized as fictional, of course, since there is no absolute bar on the possibility of a prophetic dream. But four dreams which prove to match so neatly and elegantly the succession of Guðrún's husbands are beyond any reasonable plausibility. As such, they are no less authorially proleptic for having been expressed diegetically, in the voices of characters in the storyworld.

I have stressed here that the prolepsis is inherent in the dreams themselves, and not the simple result of Gestr's prophetic interpretations of them, even though Guðrún herself claims not to know what they might prefigure. It is hard to imagine how Gestr or anybody else might have interpreted them other than the way described in the saga. But a dream reported in the saga by Guðrún's fourth husband Þorkell is shown to have more than one possible interpretation. Þorkell recounts it to Guðrún as follows: 'Þat dreymði mik ... at ek þóttumk eiga skegg svá mikt, at tœki um allan Breiðafjörð' (A dream came to me ... that I seemed to have a beard so large that it stretched over all Breiðafjörðr).[90] He asks Guðrún to interpret the dream, but she throws the challenge back to him. Revealing his ambitious and power-hungry nature, he supposes that it means that his influence will eventually be felt all over the district. Guðrún interprets the dream very differently: she thinks it will mean that sometime in the future, his beard will be dipped into the fjord.[91] She is proved right when he is drowned there.[92] The contrasting interpretations of this dream reflect Þorkell's character as well as alerting us to the narrative future.

Of course, prophetic dreams are not peculiar to family saga narrative, but are common in many classical and medieval traditions. Towards the end of *Njáls saga* there is an example of a dream episode which has been identified as a borrowing from patristic tradition – in this case, Gregory's *Dialogues*.[93] The episode begins with a familiar diegetic event: Flosi, the leader of the burners, is observed to be sleeping badly. His companion Glúmr tries to wake him up, but finds it hard to do so.[94] The impression given is that Flosi is in the grip of an external force. When he is finally awoken, Flosi relates his dream using familiar formulae: 'Mik dreymði þat ... at ek þóttumsk vera at Lómagnúpi' (A dream came to me ... that I thought I was at Lómagnúpr).[95] Flosi says that he saw the rocky face of the mountain open up to reveal a man dressed in a goatskin, holding an iron staff in his hand. This figure then calls out a long list of names – the names of

Flosi's followers in the order and groupings in which we later learn that they will die.⁹⁶ The dream speaker then describes how his plan is to clear the way for a battle at the Alþing, which takes place – as predicted – a few chapters later.⁹⁷ Flosi is advised not to tell anyone else about the prophecy, so that dramatic irony comes into play as readers and listeners and some of the characters know more about what is to come than the doomed characters themselves. And again, as with Guðrún's dreams about her future husbands, the most significant name is notable by its absence: Flosi's own name is not on the list.

These prophetic dreams are represented as being to some degree objective, either because of the formulae introducing them, or because of the need for them to be interpreted; the prophecy is the property of the interpreter(s) as much as of the dreamer, who may only be the unknowing medium. There is another vehicle for prolepsis I want to mention, a wholly objective one within the storyworld, in that it comprises a significant event which is in theory accessible to any character in the storyworld: the portent.

As might be expected from a saga in which supernatural events play a very large part, there are a number of portents in *Eyrbyggja saga*. In the midst of a celebrated accumulation of supernatural events at the farm at Fróðá – including the animation of the corpse of the Hebridean woman Þórgunna, a shower of blood rain which I shall discuss very shortly and a series of what the saga author calls 'reimleikar miklir' (major hauntings) – a half-moon appears one evening and seems to make its way all around the main room in the farmhouse.⁹⁸ This is not a personal vision: the saga author stresses that 'þat máttu allir menn sjá' (everyone could see it).⁹⁹ Its sinister circling is said to be in the opposite direction to the path of the sun, and it persists for a long time that evening, and every evening for the next week. The farmer, Þóroddr, asks what the apparition means, and Þórir viðleggr (wooden leg) recognizes it as an *urðarmáni* – literally, a fate-moon, signifying someone's death. Not long afterwards, Þórir himself is found dead, and indeed comes back to haunt the farm.¹⁰⁰ And after a series of further deaths, the farmer Þóroddr is drowned, but returns to haunt Fróðá with his whole lost crew.¹⁰¹ The portentous half-moon is a wholly supernatural apparition. Similarly, earlier in the saga, a man called Freysteinn sees a severed head speaking a half stanza which predicts the approaching Battle of Alptafjörðr. He tells his fosterfather what he has seen, and it is pronounced 'tíðenda-vænligt' (likely to result in something newsworthy).¹⁰² This too is a wholly supernatural occurrence, though confined to the vision of one character. But immediately prior to this, Freysteinn's foster-father's slave Egill claims to have witnessed an eagle swooping down and carrying off a large dog. This is also pronounced to be an omen – 'fyrir tíðendum' (a precursor of something newsworthy).[103] One might argue that the encounter between the eagle and the hound is an exceptional but not absolutely impossible event in the natural world. But it is interpreted in the storyworld as a portent because the eagle flies off in the direction of the gravemound of Þorólfr bægifótr, whose malevolent living presence seems remain active after his death.

Later in the saga, another Þóroddr has a frighteningly aggressive bull calf, and an old woman at his farm, hearing the calf bellow, urges that it should be slaughtered, calling it 'vábeið[a]' (a creature portending evil).[104] Þóroddr is unwilling to kill such a fine beast, but the old woman persists: 'láttu skera kálfinn, því at vér munum illt af honum hljóta' (have the calf slaughtered, because we will get nothing but evil from him).[105] This animal is also connected with Þorólfr bægifótr, for the cow which gave birth to it is said to have been seen licking the ashes where Þorólfr's unquiet corpse was finally cremated.[106] As it happens, Þóroddr is still unwilling to slaughter the bull calf, and lies to the old woman about it; she continues to maintain that it will mean bad luck to them. Finally, Þóroddr promises the old woman that the bull will be slaughtered in the autumn, but the old woman predicts that it will then be too late: she next speaks two verses which may well be the ultimate source of the whole incident, and both stanzas predict that the bull will be the death of a man – as indeed proves to be the case, when Þóroddr is attacked and killed by the rogue bull that summer.[107]

Just as the eagle attacking a dog contains just a kernel of plausibility as an event in the natural world, it remains within the bounds of plausibility that the recognized unpredictability of rogue bulls might occasion a wise old woman's warning. However, the saga author has presented these two events in such an uncanny context that it seems obvious from the perspective of those both outside and inside the storyworld to interpret them as supernatural occurrences. The vision of the moving half-moon is rather different, though, and it is significant that the saga author takes pains to stress that the weird vision was seen by everyone present.

The appearance of 'blood rain' is also interpreted as portentous in family saga narrative, as we see in *Eyrbyggja saga* and *Njáls saga*. Blood rain is a widespread classical and medieval topos.[108] In *Eyrbyggja saga*, it is yet another supernatural event associated with Þórgunna, and although she foresees an unspecific doom – 'en þat þykkir mér líkligast ... at þetta muni furða nökkurs þess manns, er hér er' (and it seems most likely to me ... that this is a fateful sign for someone here) – the blood rain presages not only her own death, but also the series of deaths afflicting the farm at Fróðá.[109] As with the interpretation of dreams, the significant aspect of these visions is that the saga author has a character articulate the interpretation, in response to a prompting question, rather than articulating the prediction in the narrative voice. In *Njáls saga* there is a fascinating example of even further distancing. When blood appears on Gunnarr's halberd – which, as we have seen, is also granted the prophetic quality of sounding out before action – Gunnarr's brother Kolskeggr asks what that might signify. Gunnarr replies that 'þat væri kallat í öðrum löndum benregn; – "ok sagði svá Ölvir bóndi, at þat væri fyrir stórfundum"' (that was called wound rain in other countries; – 'and Ölvir the farmer said that it was a precursor of great battles'), here attributing the interpretation to a Norwegian he had met while in Norway.[110] Gunnarr articulates the interpretation, but only at second hand, and the origin of the whole phenomenon is carefully situated outside Iceland itself.[111]

In *Njáls saga*, a whole series of portents – including three further occurrences of blood rain – are associated with the Battle of Clontarf, in Ireland. Oddly, these portents are all reported *after* the battle has been recounted. In this sense, they constitute, confusingly, analeptic prolepsis, that is, they are omens which, it is now reported, had previously occurred in the narrative past. The first involves the celebrated vision of a man called Dörruðr, who sees mysterious women chanting a poem, now known as 'Darraðarljóð' (the song of Dörruðr), which is quoted in the narrative, and which is presented as relating to the battle itself, although its actual connection with Clontarf has been questioned.[112] The women are weaving a textile made up from the intestines of warriors, with their heads acting as loom weights, and it rains blood over the ensuing battle. This episode and poem constitute a weird variation on an episode earlier in the saga, in which Hildigunnr holds above Flosi the cloak in which her late husband was murdered, causing a sort of blood rain – in this case, clots of dried blood – to fall on him.[113] Both falls of blood from cloth are harbingers of approaching and momentous slaughter: the burning of Njáll and the Battle of Clontarf.

Having constructed the elaborate prosimetical account of Dörruðr and the weird women, the saga author then abandons a discursive narrative in favour of a perfunctory collection of similar portents. The next one is not described at all: 'Slíkan atburð bar fyrir Brand Gneistason í Færeyjum' (A similar event happened to Brandr Gneistason in the Faroe Islands) – Brandr is otherwise unknown in saga literature.[114] There follows a minimally described fall of blood rain: 'Á Ísland at Svínafelli kom blóð ofan á messuhökul prests föstudaginn langa' (In Iceland at Svínafell blood fell on a priest's mass garment on Good Friday).[115] Next, a priest at Þváttá had a vision of the sea next to his altar on Good Friday, and 'sá þar í ógnir margar' (saw in it many frightening things). The specific references to Good Friday reinforce the chronological place of these events, although they are related in the saga after the battle. Two more oddities are briefly summarized: a follower of Sigurðr jarl, who had been killed in the battle, has a vision of Sigurðr and rides off with him, never to be seen again; and finally, a Hebridean earl, Gilli, who is Sigurðr's brother-in-law, has a dream in which a man speaks a verse describing Sigurðr's bloody death in battle.[116] These last two episodes are not clearly timed, and could be understood as having taken place after the battle, not before it, though no distinction between them and the portents is made by the narrator. The temporal 'reach', as Genette terms it, of these four events is within the scope of the saga's primary narrative, but they either occur, or relate to, events outside Iceland. As such, I would argue that the saga author has not woven them into the texture of his narrative, but has assembled them as snippets of external tradition. Only the story of Dörruðr and the Valkyrie women has been integrated into the primary saga narrative, and again, not chronologically, but metaphorically.[117]

So far, prophetic dreams and visions have been limited in their temporal 'reach': they are fulfilled within the timescale of the saga itself. But a character's apparent gift of prophecy is powerfully magnified when their predictions extend beyond that. Thus, the Hebridean woman Þórgunna asks to be buried at Skálholt, 'því at mér segir svá hugr um, at sá staðr muni nökkura hríð verða mest dýrkaðr á þessi landi' (because something tells me that this place is destined to be the most venerated in this country).[118] As we know, and crucially, every member of any original saga audience would have known, Skálholt was to become the site of the first bishopric in Iceland. Here, Þórgunna is shown to know more than any other character in the storyworld, an instance of clear proleptic irony from within the diegesis. Even more strikingly, Njáll famously declares that 'með lögum skal land várt byggja, en með ólögum eyða' (with laws shall our land be built up, but with lawlessness laid waste), which has obvious proleptic relevance to later periods – even including our own – although Njáll is still ostensibly making reference to the topical situation in the saga narrative.[119] Similarly, with his famous last words to his household that they should commit themselves to God's mercy because 'mun hann oss bæði láta brenna þessa heims ok annars' (he will not let us burn in both this world and the next) – Njáll reaches right outside the world of the narrative itself and into divine time, which neither saga author nor any saga audience can know.[120]

Saga characters regularly remark fatalistically that the future is unalterably laid out. For instance, Njáll remarks of the killing of Lýtingr that 'slíkt er mjök á kveðit' (such things are largely preordained).[121] Gunnarr too resigns himself to what fate has allotted him: 'Koma mun til mín feigðin ... hvar sem ek em staddr, ef mér verðr þess auðit' (Death will come to me ... wherever I am, if that's what fate has decreed for me).[122] In *Gísla saga*, Gísli too acknowledges the immutability of what is fated to happen, as, for example, near the beginning of the saga, when he insists that 'þat mun fram koma, sem auðit verðr' (that will come to pass, just as has been decreed).[123] Later in the saga, Vésteinn resigns himself to what he believes will be his fate even though he could have avoided it. Having been warned just in time to abort his visit to Gísli, he goes anyway, drawn, illogically and mysteriously, to what he sees as his destiny, as if caught up in a current there is no point trying to swim against: 'en nú falla vötn öll til Dýrafjarðar, ok mun ek þangat ríða' (and now all rivers flow towards Dýrafjörðr, and I will ride there).[124] Both fatalism and prescience in saga narrative are the vehicle for our understanding that the past – whether an actual historical past or an account of it – has passed, and having happened, or been related, could not have happened otherwise, or been otherwise related, whatever the future looks like to those living in the narrative present.

Analepsis

As with the use of prolepsis in saga narrative, analepsis, or flashback, is not normally expressed in the narrative voice in family sagas, but is similarly shifted into the storyworld as the recall of saga characters. This recall is presented as an event – a speech act – in the narrative, and like prophecy occurs in its due chronological place. At the outset, I want to distinguish this from a rather different kind of recall, which occurs when either the saga narrator or one of the characters sets the scene for an event which is about to be narrated by presenting a necessary brief backstory, or historical context. Material from the past is brought in to the narrative present, but it is material not already concerned with or arising from the primary narrative. A very clear example occurs in *Grettis saga* when, one evening, Grettir sees a mysterious light shoot up from a headland in Norway. He asks about the light, suspecting that it indicates treasure buried in a gravemound. He is then told the story of Kárr inn gamli (the old) who is buried in a mound on the headland, and has since haunted the place. Grettir determines to break into the mound and retrieve the treasure, although he is warned of the danger.[125] The backstory of Kárr inn gamli contributes to the primary narrative, but comes from outside of it; Kárr himself has not been part of the narrative hitherto. We might contrast this with the story of the Irish slave princess Melkorka in *Laxdœla saga*. When Höskuldr hears her speaking to their son Óláfr, he asks about her origins, and she tells him that she is the daughter of the Irish King Myrkjartan, and was taken into slavery as a girl.[126] Although Melkorka has already featured in the saga narrative, her backstory is outside the ambit of the primary narrative, both spatially and temporally. Nevertheless, this new information about her has been carefully withheld, as a literary strategy, and is revealed at a dramatic point in the narrative; her origins have been kept mysterious. I shall discuss further this and other episodes, in which the emphasis is on the holding back of information until some significant revelatory moment in the narrative, in Chapter 5, when I come to consider the deliberate withholding of significant information, which, I will argue, is an aspect of plot.

It might seem at first glance that prolepsis and analepsis are mirror images of one another. But in fact there is a very major asymmetry between the two in saga narrative, an asymmetry which arises precisely out of the saga author's policy of displacing anachrony on to the characters and into the diegesis. For while characters in the storyworld – like people in real life – cannot be shown actually to know the future, both we and they can have some recall of their past. Thus, with prolepsis we have a spectrum of ways in which characters may be shown as predicting the future, from non-specific pessimism, through wise knowledge of human nature and the likely course of events, right through to the overtly supernatural cast of prophecies and portents. Recall, on the other hand, need have no relation at all to the supernatural or the uncanny.

Both analepsis and prolepsis may reach backwards or forwards within the confines of the saga narrative. But if the predictions and recalls are made by characters in the diegesis, then their reach, as Genette terms it, is necessarily different. Prolepsis can refer to events right outside the third time of saga narrative, and even reach into the real time – the time of our world or the saga author's – which encloses the narrative. Þórgunna's prediction about Skálholt, for example, achieves this. However, the saga author cannot show characters having personal memories of a time before their own existence, although they may be shown to remember events which preceded the beginning of the saga as we receive it.[127]

In saga narrative, as in life, the past can be shown to exert a powerful influence on the present, most often malign, but sometimes affirmative. Thus, for instance, when Gunnarr is attacked by his enemies, he asks his wife Hallgerðr for help. At this dramatic moment in the narrative, she brings up the past: 'Þá skal ek nú ... muna þér kinnhestinn, ok hirði ek aldri, hvárt þú verr þik lengr eða skemr' (Now I shall remind you of the slap [you gave me], and I don't care whether you defend yourself for a long or a short time).[128] Gunnarr did indeed slap her earlier in the saga (as did also the two husbands before him), and at that time she vowed to pay him back. This long-borne grudge against Gunnarr is articulated in an extended stretch of narrative exploring context of memory, recall and prediction: Gunnarr's mother Rannveig castigates Hallgerðr and predicts that she will have long-lasting shame from this; a skaldic verse composed in celebration – and, of course, memorialization – of Gunnarr's brave last defence is quoted in the narrative; and Gizurr Teitsson, one of his attackers, declares of Gunnarr that 'mun hans vörn uppi, meðan landit er byggt' (his defence will be spoken of as long as this country is inhabited).[129] The help which Gunnar had requested from Hallgerðr is decidedly fanciful – almost fairy tale – and wholly impractical: strands of her hair which his mother could twist into a string for his bow. The whole episode is clearly a set of variations on the theme of past and present.

Elsewhere in saga narrative, malicious taunts about a past failure or humiliation are shown to act powerfully and directly on present circumstances. In *Grettis saga*, for instance, Grettir tangles with a fellow traveller to the Alþing, who brings up an incident from Grettir's youth, when an older boy got the better of him at a ball game: 'Of fjarri er nú Auðunn at kyrkja þik, sem við knattleikinn' (Auðunn is now too far away to throttle you like he did at the ball game).[130] Grettir kills his challenger. And I have already discussed in the context of descriptive pauses the way Skarpheðinn in *Njáls saga* taunts a series of potential supporters at the Alþing with scandalous accusations about their past conduct. In these cases, the past behaviour Skarpheðinn brings up has not been previously related in the saga narrative, unlike the incidents above involving Gunnarrr and Grettir. The narrative force of the analepsis in *Njáls saga* is contained in the timing of the taunts – 'blasts from the past' which are shocking and effective for being unexpected and unverifiable.[131] In *Gísla saga*, women talking about past love affairs are overheard by the husband of one of them, and even though their flirtations apparently did not continue once they were married, the husband – Gísli's brother Þorkell – feels humiliated.[132] This overheard discussion of past relationships opens up the division between Gísli, his wife Auðr, and her brother Vésteinn on the one hand, and Þorkell, his and Gísli's sister Þordís, and her husband Þorgrímr on the other – a rift which runs right through the whole saga. Here, no malice was intended, and the conversation was perhaps even light-hearted. But the consequences of recounting events from the past prove fatal.

Although there are many instances of such potently destructive recall in saga narrative, there are also some examples of recourse to the past as providing a positive model for present behaviour. Even the notoriously obstreperous Skarpheðinn agrees to help Gunnarr's son Högni to avenge the death of his father, after recalling how Gunnarr did not immediately pursue vengeance against him when he killed one of Gunnarr's kinsmen, an episode which is recounted earlier in the saga.[133] Perhaps most movingly, Bergþóra, refusing Flosi's offer of safe passage from her and Njáll's farmhouse, in which they are about to be burnt alive, recalls a promise she made at the very beginning of their marriage, when she was young, 'at eitt skyldi ganga yfir okkr bæði' (that one [fate] should befall us both).[134] Had the saga narrative begun as early in saga time as the marriage of Njáll and Bergþóra, and had her promise been articulated at that time, we would have had an example of a vow as a sort of coded prolepsis. Instead, we have its temporal opposite: a vow from the past recalled at a crucial moment in the narrative present.

There are even some rare instances in which the past is not recounted, but reported to have been internally recollected – episodes of a character's thoughts being made known, as if the saga author had privileged access to their interiority. When Guðrún is attempting to incite her husband Bolli to kill his foster-brother Kjartan, she accuses him of forgetting how badly Kjartan has treated him in the past – though she does not cite any actual examples. Bolli responds by recalling 'hversu ástsamliga Óláfr hafði hann upp fœddan' (how lovingly Óláfr [his foster-father, and Kjartan's father] had brought him up).[135] But when Guðrún threatens Bolli with divorce, prompted by what Guðrún has said, he summons up the past in his own head, and then goes a step further: 'miklaði Bolli fyrir sér fjándskap allan á hendr Kjartani' (Bolli magnified to himself all Kjartan's enmity towards him).[136] It is hard to imagine how Bolli might have been shown to articulate this response in dialogue, and therefore easy to understand why the narrator – unusually – reports his thought processes, but still leaves scope for the audience to speculate further.

There is considerable variation between the degree to which allusions to past events repeat those events, either in summary or fully, or allude to otherwise unknown ones. Clearly the effect of the analepsis is different in each case. If the material is repeated, the audience is given the opportunity to compare and contrast past and present contexts: as Genette puts it, 'the future has become the present but does not resemble the idea of it that one had in the past'.[137] Or the allusion may be a surprising or shocking revelation articulated at a dramatic point in the narrative, forcing us to reconsider our view of the narrative so far – the 'blast from the past'. There is an intriguing example of this kind of allusion to the past again in *Gísla saga*, and again concerning previous romantic attachments; the saga is as a whole notable for its play of speech and silence, and many things are left unsaid only to be recalled later. In this case, at the very beginning of the saga, we have what I have called an oblique prefiguration of the events in the body of the saga, as a story about Gísli's forebears in Norway is recounted.[138] Ari Þorkelsson, the uncle of the saga's eponymous hero, is killed in a duel with a berserk, who then claims Ari's wife, Ingibjörg, as his prize. Ari's brother Gísli takes on the berserk, and Ingibjörg offers him a sword, along with a remarkable revelation: 'Eigi var ek af því Ara gipt, at ek vilda þik eigi heldr at hafa' (I was not married to Ari because I wouldn't rather have been married to you).[139] This enigmatic admission implies a sexually charged backstory which is absent from the opening narrative of *Gísla saga* as it stands. One might imagine that it would have been suppressed even if that backstoryworld had been related, to be revealed at an opportune moment.

If episodes from the past are retold in the present moment of the narrative, as the dialogue of one of the characters, then we can measure how close the two versions of the same event are: whether a character has distorted, misremembered or perhaps exaggerated what happened, as we are told Bolli did, although his actual thoughts are not articulated. I will consider this issue in greater detail shortly, when I come to consider what I will call imperfect anachronies, both proleptic and analeptic. But before that, I want to consider briefly the part played by skaldic verse as an enduring memorialization of the past.

The quotation of a verse – by a saga author, not a character – which appears to match what has already been recounted in the saga prose is a characteristic feature of historical narrative in Old Norse, or of episodes in family sagas to which saga authors seem to want to add an additional air of actual historicity. This is still a form of analepsis, or allusion to the narrative past in the narrative present, but its function is corroborative, rather than rhetorically literary. But the authors of family sagas could also exploit the status of skaldic stanzas as time-resistant texts which might allow characters themselves to bring the past into the narrative present. In a verse which Gísli recites after the burial of his rival Þorgrímr, he appears to confess to having killed Þorgrímr: 'Gauts þess 's geig of veittak | gunnbliks' (I gave a death blow to the god of the light of battle [sword > warrior]).[140] Gísli's sister Þórdís hears the verse, commits it to memory, and though she says nothing at the time, she later reveals it to her husband Börkr, the dead man's brother.[141] Although Gísli's guilt is now clear, and he is in due course outlawed for the killing, the moment for Börkr to take violent vengeance for his brother's death passed by while Þórdís kept the verse to herself. But she is shown able to recall the admission of guilt perfectly, and not just allude to it, when the right time comes.

The final category of recourse to the past I want to discuss is the inevitable recall involved in legal proceedings: the appeal to precedent and the retrospective testimony of witnesses. In *Grettis saga*, for instance, after a violent dispute about rights to a beached whale, the warring parties ask the lawspeaker to make a ruling. Just as one might expect, he relies on previous case law. He refers in fact to an agreement made between his grandfather – Ingólfr Arnason, traditionally held to be Iceland's first settler – and a female neighbour, who had divided up land and driftage without formal payment, thus setting a precedent for the present case.[142] Similarly, later in the saga, there is another whale dispute, and the lawspeaker is again called upon to make a ruling. This time, he alludes to a pertinent fact which has been already recounted in the narrative – that an offer to give away some part of the whale had previously been made, suggesting that a requirement to share the whale had been conceded.[143] Since the derivation of the word *lög* (laws) is that which has been *laid* down, or established, such recourse to past events is to be expected. And, as with the first example, the case law may refer to events outside the scope of the primary narrative.

Certain legal procedures also necessitate recalling past events – most obviously, witness statements and any judicial summing up – and this is duly reflected in saga narrative. So, for example, in *Njáls saga*, Mörðr Valgarðsson opens legal proceedings with a formal statement of the grounds of the case he is bringing against Flosi: 'nefni ek í þat vætti ... at ek lýsi lögmætu frumhlaupi á hönd Flosa Þórðarsyni, er hann hljóp til Helga Njálssonar á þeim vættvangi, er Flosi Þórðarson hljóp til Helga Njálssonar ok veitti honum holundar sár eða heilundar éða mergundar, þat er at ben gerðisk, en Helgi fekk bana af' (I call witness to the fact that I am giving notice of an assault as is legally fitting against Flosi Þórðarson, that he attacked Helgi Njálsson, in that place where the attack happened, and [that he] inflicted an internal wound, a head wound or a marrow wound, which turned out to be a wound which Helgi died of).[144] This of course repeats the circumstances of Helgi's death, though the formulaic legal language allows some details – in this instance, the precise kind of wound – to be left open. In fact, as the case progresses, witness testimonies about the assault are not related; the case turns instead on the technicalities of which witnesses are legally eligible to take part. Witness statements are not a usual component of saga narrative, even those sagas, like *Njáls saga*, in which legal proceedings play a large part. In *Hrafnkels saga*, for example, Sámr's eloquent and expert prosecution of his case against the chieftain Hrafnkell is praised but not related. And we never get a chance to hear Hrafnkell's defence because he is physically prevented from addressing the court.[145] We can only presume that Sámr's testimony was an accurate reflection of what the saga narrator has already related and will not repeat. Similarly, when Þorbjörn tries to persuade his nephew Sámr to take on the case in the first place, he 'sagði allt it sanna, hversu farit hafði með þeim Hrafnkeli' (told the whole truth about what has happened between him and Hrafnkell).[146] Without simple repetition of that story to compare with what the narrative has recounted, we must assume that Þorbjörn did in fact report the circumstances fully and accurately. By contrast, although we are told of his intention to intimidate his prosecutors, the substance of what Hrafnkell's legal defence might have been remains a matter of highly fascinating speculation: he killed a shepherd who violated a solemn vow which Hrafnkell explicitly declared to him. Would Hrafnkell have had any legal defence? One imagines that a medieval saga audience, well versed in contemporary legal niceties, would find plenty here to chew over.

If a character demonstrates an accurate recall of an event already narrated, repetition is inevitable. It is, however, a very different matter when the accuracy of recall is either uncertain or actually disputed. This brings me to the final aspect of a saga author's practice of displacing anachrony on to the characters and into the storyworld. I shall call this *imperfect anachrony*: prophecies which are not fulfilled, and explicit recall which does not accurately reflect what the narrative has previously reported. This proves to be a rich source of characterization, without recourse to either interiority or explicit intervention from the voice of the narrator.

Imperfect anachrony

As Gérard Genette pointed out, in a naturalistic narrative, characters in the diegesis cannot actually predict the future, any more than those of us living in the real world can.[147] If the narrator alludes to an event ahead of the present moment of the narrative, this betrays the *totum simul* perspective of the narrative voice, and we must assume that the prophecy will come true, since it emanates from privileged knowledge. But we need not assume the accuracy of a prophecy put in the mouth of one of the characters, even if the prediction is the result of some supernatural intervention. The inherent fallibility of a prophecy articulated in the storyworld allows for a range of effects from which we can infer a great deal about motive and disposition.

A striking example is the bold self-assurance of Kjartan in *Laxdœla saga*, when he refuses to take advantage of help offered by his companions who fear that he is in danger: 'Eigi mun Bolli, frændi minn, slá banaráðum við mik' (My kinsman Bolli will never be behind my death).[148] Kjartan's characteristic over-confidence is misplaced, and the effect of the mistaken prophecy is both to create pathos and to underline how forcibly Bolli has had to be coerced by Guðrún to plan a lethal attack. In *Eyrbyggja saga*, a quite different and close to comical effect arises comes from Vermundr's misplaced prediction that taking back to Iceland a pair of berserks he has chosen as a gift from Earl Hákon of Norway will increase his standing at home, especially in the face of his successful brother Styrr's status. In fact, as the earl correctly predicts, Vermundr cannot control his prize, and has to swallow his pride and appeal to his brother for help, even though he at first tries to make Styrr believe that he is passing them on as a generous favour. Again, the disposition of both brothers is vividly conveyed: Vermundr's foolishly misguided and failed attempt to gain status, and Styrr's shrewdness in recognizing the trick and coming out on top, again.[149]

These are telling examples of rather touching failures to read the future. I will end with another perhaps rather poignant naïveté about what one's behaviour may entail in the future: the shepherd Einarr's failure to foresee the consequences of breaching Hrafnkell's taboo on riding the sacred horse Freyfaxi in *Hrafnkels saga*. The saga author here violates saga narrative convention by revealing what was in Einarr's mind when he determined to ride the horse, and I shall discuss further this use of interiority in Chapter 4. What is at issue just now is Einarr's inability to read future events: he is said to suppose that Hrafnkell will not find out even if he does ride the horse, thus not allowing for the quasi-supernatural actions of the beast as it at once races down to Hrafnkell's farmhouse to make known that it has been ridden.[150] But Einarr's first response to Hrafnkell's stipulation that the horse must never be ridden is expressed not as a prophecy, but obliquely as a question: why would he ride the horse specifically forbidden to him, given that there are plenty of others available?[151] The effect on readers and listeners has the force of prophecy: as experienced receivers of narrative we know intuitively that this breach – however unlikely – is bound to happen. So we are not in quite the same position as Einarr, who cannot foresee any circumstances in which it might come to pass. In fact, the author of *Hrafnkels saga* is persistently concerned with the inability of some of the saga's characters to predict the future. The old man Þorbjörn, for example, refuses even to speculate on what his actions may entail, noting simply 'Verðr at þar, sem má' (What will be, will be), and throughout the saga there is a play on this lack of foresight, as for instance when Þorbjörn has to act the part of a short-sighted old man for reasons he ironically cannot discern.[152] We might at this point think back to the way some saga characters declare that they have presentiments of their own death: they can predict the future sufficiently to foresee a bad outcome, but not how to prevent or sidestep that outcome. In *Grettis saga*, Grettir is persuaded against his better judgement to fetch fire from across a stretch of water, and expresses his foreboding: 'en eigi segir mér vænt hugr um, at ek hafa gott at sök hér fyrir' (but my sense is that it's not likely that I will do well out of this).[153] Nevertheless, he does what they urge, and though it does not result immediately in his death, catastrophe ensues. Here again, Grettir's foreboding is the equivalent of narratorial prolepsis.

Imperfect analepsis in saga narrative is not so often the result of a character's fallibility of recall as it is the direct result of a desire to mislead. A false report is produced about the past: a lie is told. As with imperfect prolepsis, imperfect analepsis – in the absence of a narrative voice manipulating the order of events – allows us to infer a great deal about those who produce the distorted recall.

In *Grettis saga*, for example, Þorbjörn ferðalangr (far traveller) recalls in front of an eager audience a fight Grettir had had the previous summer with Kormákr, who was Grettir's opponent in a horsefight. One participant tells the story in Grettir's favour, presenting it as a lucky escape for Kormákr that the warring groups were forced to separate by a third party. Þorbjörn ferðalangr tells the story somewhat differently: he reports that Grettir was not only unimpressive in the fighting, but in addition that he 'skyti skelk í bringu' (felt fear in his heart) and was relieved when the groups were separated.[154] Significantly, this does not precisely contradict what has already been related in the narrative. But although that narrative characteristically did not make Grettir's feeling known to us, the accusation of cowardice is both unrepresentative of what we know about Grettir (especially since the story of his encounter with the fearsome revenant Glámr has just been narrated) and offensively slanderous. Shortly afterwards in the saga, Þorbjörn updates the crew of the ship he is about to travel on with news from his part of Iceland. He reports the death of Grettir's father, but in shockingly disrespectful terms: 'Lítit lagðisk nú fyrir kappann, at hann kafnaði í stofureyk sem hundr, en eigi var skaði at honum, því at hann gerðisk nú gamalœrr' (This wasn't a heroic end, because he choked like a dog on the smoke beside the fire, but he was no loss, because he had by now become senile).[155] Again, the substance of the report is true, because Grettir's father, as the narrative has already reported, did indeed die at home, bedridden. But the slant of the account is deeply offensive to Grettir, who makes the grimly witty riposte that at least Þorbjörn will not choke on smoke from his own fireside, a prophecy which comes true when Grettir kills him on the spot. And the narrator slyly joins in the exchange, noting that in the view of those present, Þorbjörn's death was no loss either.[156]

Right at the end of the saga, we have another example of a slanderous report, this time against Grettir himself. Grettir has at last been overcome, and the leader of his enemies Þorbjörn öngull (hook) is regaling a grand assembly in Constantinople about his own great deeds. He boasts that he has killed a hero 'er Grettir hét inn sterki, er þar hefir mestr garpr verit ok fullhugi' (who was called Grettir the Strong, the greatest champion and a fearless one).[157] This praise of Grettir is designed to throw into relief Þorbjörn's own triumph in having killed him, and his account matches the narrative account of Grettir's demise in broad outline. But Þorbjörn drifts into outright misrepresentation, claiming that Grettir 'hafði ... mörg mín öfl' (was many times my strength).[158] As the narrative has already recounted, in fact, Grettir was fatally weakened before his encounter with Þorbjörn, having dealt himself an accidental leg-wound which became severely infected.[159] This time, Grettir's brother steps up to kill the liar.[160]

In *Njáls saga*, Gunnarr Lambason, one of the burners, tells Sigtryggr, earl of Orkney, that Skarpheðinn wept in the burning farmhouse.[161] Again, this is slanderous, but again it is not random fabrication, but is based on an exchange he and Skarpheðinn are reported in the saga narrative as having had: Gunnarr accuses him of crying, and Skarpheðinn angrily denies this, claiming that smoke is getting in his eyes.[162] But the slander is avenged by Njáll's son-in-law Kári, who kills Gunnarr in front of Earl Sigurðr.[163] In all these examples, we can see a common pattern: a dead man is openly slandered, his reputation put at risk and the damage shown to be significant enough to be avenged by a killing. Moreover, the slander is not simply articulated in public, but is in each case produced in a formal, public setting as news – as the equivalent of an official record of events. And in each case, the slander is the result of distortion, and the actual content of the slander has some, even if slight, basis in what the narrative has already recounted. The author of the distorted report is silenced, and by implication, the slander along with him.

It is particularly interesting that the saga author makes a careful distinction between distortion and outright lying: of Gunnarr's account, it is said '[u]m allar sagnir hallaði hann mjök til ok ló fra víða' (he distorted everything that was recounted, and lied about many details).[164] The slander about the crying is not itself explicitly included as one of the lies, although the audience may infer this. For outright lies with no basis in events we can turn to the story of Mörðr Valgarðson in *Njáls saga*. The situation here is different: Mörðr is trying to drive a wedge between Njáll's foster-son Höskuldr and his other sons. His tactic is to re-interpret as malicious those actions which have already been described in the saga narrative as friendly. He reminds Höskuldr that the Njálssons gave him a gift of a young horse, 'ok gerðu þat til spotts við þik, því at þeim þóttir þú ok óreyndr' (and they did that to make fun of you, because they think you are untried as well).[165] Mörðr goes on to claim that Skarpheðinn usurped Höskuldr's status as chieftain, 'ok aldri laust at láta goðorðit' (and will never give the chieftainship back), but Höskuldr counters this outright lie easily enough, pointing out that it has already been given back. Mörðr next tries to claim that the Njálssons broke a legal agreement with the killer of their half-brother, but Höskuldr refutes that too. Mörðr's last attempt is to suggest that Skarpheðinn was planning to kill Höskuldr with an axe hidden under his belt.[166] Höskuldr roundly rebuts the claim, and declares that Mörðr will never succeed in his slanders: 'þú segir aldri svá illt frá Njálssonum, at ek muna því trúa' (there is nothing bad you could say about the Njálssons that I would believe).[167] Mörðr gives up, and turns instead to the Njálssons themselves. This time, he lies about his conversation with Höskuldr, so fully recounted in the saga narrative, accusing Höskuldr of making the very accusations he has just attributed to the Njálssons: that it was Höskuldr who accused the Njálssons of breaking the legal agreement and that it was Höskuldr who believed that Skarpheðinn was planning to kill him. He then adds two further lies: an account of a failed plan to burn them in their house (itself disturbingly proleptic of the burning of Njáll) and a plan to attack them which failed when two of the company dropped out.[168] Accounts of hostile plans which failed are of course very hard to refute, in life as in literature. However, the Njálssons are more susceptible to Mörðr's lies: 'þá mæltu þeir fyrst í móti. En þar kom, at þeir trúðu' (they first challenged [Mörðr's lies]. But eventually they believed [them]).[169] An already fragile friendship is destroyed. This whole episode illustrates very vividly the dangerous power of the false report, but it is also a mini-drama of three kinds of disposition: the malicious liar, the loyal truth-teller and the susceptible receivers of slander who were, perhaps, always ready to hear ill of a favourite son.

I want to finish this section on deceptive recall of the past with an episode of non-verbal recall. As we have seen, *Njáls saga* begins with the story of Hrútr's failed marriage to Unnr. Unnr claims that the marriage cannot be consummated because Hrútr's erect penis is too large to penetrate her, and she eventually enlists her father Mörðr in divorce proceedings. Hrútr challenges Mörðr to a fight, but Mörðr backs out.[170] And then one evening Hrútr and his brother are staying overnight with a neighbour on the way back from the Alþing. A boy and two girls are playing together on the hall floor, and they are acting out the circumstances of the divorce: 'Annarr þeira mælti, "Ek skal þér Mörðr vera of stefna þér af konunni ok finna þat til foráttu, at þú hafir ekki sorðit hana." Annarr svaraði, "Ek skal þér Hrútr vera; tel ek þik af allri fjárheimtunni, ef þú þorir eigi at berjask við mik'" (One of them said, 'I'll play Mörðr to you and summons back your wife, because you haven't fucked her.' The other replied, 'I'll play Hrútr to you; I will lay claim to all your property if you dare not fight with me').[171] This little charade is of course highly slanderous and offensive to both parties. And it seems that it faithfully enough re-enacts what the saga narrative has previously recounted. But there may be a subtle but crucial misrepresentation of events in the children's re-enactment. An unconsummated marriage would perhaps usually be the result of the husband's impotence, and it is tempting to speculate that this is what the saga author represents as popular opinion about the cause of the divorce, reflected in the children's play. As we know, the problem has rather been an unusual excess of male potency in the marital relationship. But Hrútr himself manages to prevent the children's account of his problem from determining his reputation. While his brother Höskuldr, in embarrassment and anger, hits one of the children with a stick, Hrútr paradoxically demonstrates his manliness by giving the boy a gold ring, and warning him to be more careful in future. That this is a successful counter to the damaging drama is confirmed by the boy's response: 'Þínum drengskap skal ek við bregða æ siðan' (I will never forget your manliness), and the response of the assembled company: 'Af þessu fekk Hrútr gott orð' (Hrútr got a good reputation from this).[172]

Unsuccessful anachrony

In conclusion, I want to look at some less successful examples of anachrony in saga narrative. As we have seen in the course of this chapter, prolepsis can produce a grim sense of foreboding, can induce suspense, and can allow both audience and characters to imagine the future in the context of the narrative present, whether or not it actually influences the behaviour of those characters, or even whether or not what is predicted actually comes to pass. It also reinforces our sense of the passed past producing a predestined future for those living through the narrative present, and we as audience situate ourselves in a time outside the third time of narrative, looking down, or back, on it. Analepsis can also allow us and the characters to see the narrative past in the context of the narrative present, and to compare two versions of events. Displacing both analepsis and prolepsis on to the characters also adds to our understanding of their natures and dispositions. But the crucial difference between the two is that prolepsis in narrative is always a proactive and considered strategy – it doesn't come about by accident. The risk with analepsis is that it can be hard to distinguish analepsis for literary effect from simple authorial oversight: something the narrator should have revealed earlier, or more clearly.

This is easier to illustrate than to describe. In *Laxdœla saga,* when Óláfr pái travels to Ireland to meet his royal grandfather, his mother Melkorka gives him a 'fingrgull mikit' (large gold ring) which she describes as having been given to her by her father as a teething gift.[173] In Ireland, that ring plays a major part in identifying Óláfr as the genuine grandson of Mýrkjartan. As a token of identity, it resembles a common enough trope in folklore and romance literature, for instance.[174] And yet it is not at all plausible that Melkorka could have kept possession of the ring all through her abduction and slavery. When Höskuldr buys her, she is destitute, and poorly dressed. If the saga author produces the token analeptically, just in time for Óláfr's trip to Ireland to seek out his roots, some explanation of how Melkorka managed to keep it hidden is necessary for the analepsis to be convincing.

In *Njáls saga,* in another implausible analepsis, Gunnarr acts out Njáll's plan for him to reclaim his kinswoman Unnr's dowry from her ex-husband Hrútr, involving disguising himself as a pedlar, as I discussed earlier in this chapter. Afterwards, when the household is asleep, Gunnarr and his men sneak out of Hrútr's farmhouse and ride away. But the same night, Hrútr's half-brother Höskuldr dreams that Hrútr's farm was visited by a bear, and this leads him to suspect a trick. He questions his household about a tall man they had seen earlier in the day. One of them replies, 'Þat sá ek, at fram undan erminni kom eitt gullhlað ok rautt klæði; á hœgri hendi hafði hann gullhring' (I saw that [coming] out from under his sleeve there was gold decoration, and red cloth; and on his right hand he wore a gold ring).[175] Höskuldr immediately realizes that his dream of a bear was a vision of Gunnarr's *fylgja,* and that the tall man must have been Gunnarr himself. He rides at once to Hrútsstaðir, but it's too late; the pedlar, who was Gunnarr in disguise, has gone. Hrútr has been outwitted. But there are problems with the coherence of this episode. We are not told, for instance, that the men who encountered Gunnarr in disguise earlier in the day were members of Höskuldr's household, or indeed that they told Höskuldr about the encounter, so it's not clear why he questions his household. And, more to the point, it seems highly unlikely that first, Gunnarr would make such an elementary blunder with his disguise, and second, that having spotted the giveaway rich clothing hidden under the rough garment of a pedlar, the man who speaks up now would not have spoken up earlier.

I finish with examples of analepsis in which the narrator seems to recognize the omission and steps in to spell out what should have been made clear earlier.

In *Gísla saga*, Gísli is helped by a man called Ingjaldr, who lives on an island called Hergilsey. We have already been told that a magician has cast a spell to the effect that even if anyone tries to help Gísli, their efforts will fail.[176] But Ingjaldr is a great help to Gísli. The narrator suddenly steps in with an explanation: the spell, we are told, referred only to those living on the mainland of Iceland, and 'þat kom honum eigi í hug at skilja til um úteyjar' (it did not occur to him [the magician] to specify islands).[177] Ingjaldr, as an islander, was overlooked, and therefore exempt from the spell. This was not mentioned when the spell itself was cast. The narrator disguises the direct intervention by introducing the accidental exemption as popular opinion – 'ok þat er sagt' (and it is said) – but here we have a clear example of a narratorial rationalization, an attempt to sort out retrospectively an inconsistency in the narrative.

We have already seen how legal proceedings in sagas both impose specific timings on events and produce analepsis in accounts of legal cases when speakers recall what happened. In *Laxdœla saga*, we have a striking example of how a legal issue depends on the accuracy or truthfulness of an oral report of events. When a boat sinks and there is only one survivor, a man called Guðmundr, his account of the order of the drownings is crucial in determining who is to inherit the property of boat's owner. Guðmundr declares publicly that the boat's owner, Þorsteinn, was the first to drown, and then his son-in-law Þórarinn, followed by Þórarinn's three-year-old daughter. The last person to drown was the child's mother, Ósk, who would have inherited all the property from her little daughter. The property therefore falls to Ósk's husband, Þorkell trefill (fringe), not Þorsteinn's powerful kinsmen, as would have happened if Þorsteinn had been the last and not the first to drown.[178] But we have been told that Ósk's husband had made a deal with Guðmundr to recount the order of the drownings in this particular way. When Guðmundr's story spreads, the plan would seem to have been a success. At this point, however, the narrator steps in, claiming that 'Guðmundr hafði áðr nökkut öðruvísa sagt' (Guðmundr had previously said something rather different).[179] Suspicions are aroused, and Þorsteinn's kinsmen demand half of the inheritance. Þorkell trefill proposes that the issue be decided by ordeal, but at the last minute, Þorkell loses his nerve, fearing that the ordeal will expose his duplicity rather than confirming his (false) right to inherit Þorsteinn's wealth, and fixes the outcome through chicanery.[180]

The fascinating connexion between these last two passages is that, in both instances, the narrator not only steps in to fill in something we would and should have been told earlier if strict chronological order had been observed, but also intervenes elsewhere in the same short section of the narrative to pass comment on the diegesis. The magician who cast the spell on anyone helping Gísli, but forgot to specify islands, is explicitly denigrated as practising magic with 'allri ergi ok skelmiskap' (every perversity and devilry) – a very unusual example of explicit narratorial judgement.[181] Somewhat similarly, when Þorkell trefill worries about whether the ordeal will in fact expose his double-dealing, the narrator unexpectedly adds 'Ekki þóttusk heiðnir men minna eiga í atbyrgð, þá er slíka hluti skyldi fremja, en nú þykkjask eiga kristnir men' (heathen men did not consider their responsibility any less, when such things [as ordeals] were performed, than Christians do now).[182] Interventions such as these will be the subject of my next chapter.

4

The voice of the silent narrator

Paul Ricœur describes the narrative voice as 'the silent speech that presents the world of the text to the reader'.[1] This definition of course belongs to the world of reader and written text; if we are thinking of an original context of oral delivery, with an audible narrative voice, and an audience physically present at a recital, rather than an individual reader, silent speech is very much not the issue. And in a performed recitation of a saga, the narrator's voice is embodied in an actual person speaking. But what might be the relationship between that actual speaker and the written text which has come down to us? We surely cannot imagine that the saga text is a verbatim record of an actual recitation, although perhaps we could envisage a creative author dictating to a scribe.[2] Might the saga author have deliberately produced a text which actual performers could recite as if in their own words – that is, a text styled to be narrated aloud? Or might a long-standing tradition of orally performed sagas, or, more likely, shorter saga episodes, have influenced the style of a literate author? There is no obvious answer to the questions these issues raise. But whatever the circumstances of a saga's composition or recitation, what we now have to deal with is a written text, and Ricœur's formulation is a valuable starting point, especially given the particular character of the family sagas' 'silent speech' – that is, a discourse which is not only silent by being written rather than spoken, but also with the narrator's individuality effaced – a silent narrative voice, but also a silent narrator.

Family saga narrators are always heterodiegetic – that is, they are not themselves part of the storyworld, which is set long before their own time.[3] Moreover, narrators very rarely engage directly with their readers or listeners from their situation above and beyond the diegesis to comment on it. Family saga narrators are often described as simply recording what happened (or what might have happened), objectively and without interventions which might give them individuality or personality.[4] We are very far from narrators invented by authors either as authorial *alter egos*, or as characters in their own right, whose personal and sometimes idiosyncratic attitude towards the events and characters in the storyworld is part of the whole narrative experience. The narrative voice in family sagas is largely effaced in terms of expressing a distinctive moral standpoint, or adopting an individual stylistic mode.[5] In general, saga author and saga narrator are fused as producers of the text, the equivalent of what Wayne C. Booth termed the 'implied author' who is the 'organizing principle of the text' as distinct from the biographical, or flesh and blood author of the text.[6] And on the rare occasions when a narrator's voice seems to be heard passing extra-diegetic comment on the substance of the text, especially when the intervention is in the form of a brief subjective reaction to the narrative, there is another text producer to be taken into consideration: the scribe.

In what follows, I shall pursue a somewhat self-contradictory course, initially analysing and reaffirming the conventional concept of the self-effacing narrator, but then moving on to draw attention to moments when saga narrators do reveal something of their attitude towards their subject matter – in other words, when we do hear an otherwise effaced voice. So in the first half of this chapter I shall look at instances in which narrators notably fail to comment on surprising or shocking events, and in which the language used to describe such events is strikingly impassive. I will next explore the use of what I will term 'displaced comments' – when the narrator, instead of making a comment in the narratorial voice, relates how other people in the storyworld speculated on, judged or interpreted the action. This will be followed by a brief account of what I have called 'conventional judgements', which, though strictly speaking qualify as narratorial comment, serve as economical and uncontroversial introductions or valedictions to certain characters.

In the second half of this chapter, I turn to a set of examples which show narrators intervening to make comments on the narrative, not on its action or characters, but on the organization and scope of the narrative they are recounting, as if viewing it as a pre-existing – or at least 'immanent' – text which they are making their own, and mediating to an audience.[7] This hypothetical pre-existing narrative acts as a buffer between the narrator of the saga as we have it and any historical reality, because the narrator's engagement is with this *story* of the past, not the imagined past itself. I then explore more familiar examples of a narrator's explicit interventions in the narrative, looking first at comments providing extra-diegetic information about what is being related. Such comments have the effect of situating the narrator outside the temporal scope – though, crucially, not the geographical location – of the saga. I will then move on to explanatory or interpretational comments, in which the narrator clarifies or speculates on the action. Both these kinds of comment – offering either information or interpretation – reaffirm our sense that the narrative has a prior, independent existence (as a narrative, not merely as unformed history), and that it is independent of the narrator, who is helpfully recounting it to the audience from a *totum simul* vantage point.

Finally, I will look at those relatively rare but extremely significant instances in which saga narrators assume a sort of omniscience over their characters, and presume to tell readers or listeners what these characters are thinking – a clear indication of creative fictionality. In such cases, the narrator seems to be engaging directly with the saga's characters, not with a narrative about them, and to be directly revealing their unspoken responses to events.

The effacement of an individual narratorial voice shapes our own experience in the third time of narrative, as we make our way through the story – as if through life itself – with little in the way of either moral guidance or privileged epistemic access as we go. This is akin to another narrative experience, that of watching a drama with no chorus, or a film without a voice-over. It constitutes part of what Ricœur calls imperfect knowledge – here, an imperfect knowledge of how to respond to characters and events along the way, which arises from the effacement of the narrative voice.

The silent narrator

No comment

Selecting narrative moments when one might expect a narrator to make a comment on the action but no comment is forthcoming is of course a very speculative and even paradoxical procedure. The felt need for some sort of comment is plainly a subjective matter. However, I offer here some examples in which a narrator describes a surprising or shocking event without comment; or relates a puzzling event without offering further explanation; or presents an event which an audience, medieval or post-medieval, might find morally questionable without making any judgement on it. But I begin by citing Vésteinn Ólason's analysis of a narrative section in *Eyrbyggja saga*, which demonstrates very illuminatingly how narratorial impassivity, and avoidance of omniscience and overt comment can all work together to produce a satisfying narrative episode. Vésteinn begins by describing the 'neutrality' with which the narrator relates the killing of the chieftain Arnkell at the hands of Snorri goði.[8] Noting that the narrative 'has the objective manner of an official report', he goes on to say that the narrator 'gives no hint as to the state of mind of Arnkell or of Snorri the Chieftain [his adversary] and his men, not to mention [his] own view of the events'.[9] Nevertheless, he argues, the reader's sympathies are always with Arnkell, and this is due in part to fact that hitherto in the saga he has been portrayed as a man of courage and honour – although one might add that the dispute between Arnkell and Snorri is not a simple matter of a good character versus a wicked one. Vésteinn adds that 'the reasons for the attack are perfectly clear, and there is no need to give voice to the thoughts of pursuers and pursued'.[10] Finally, he draws attention to the tribute to Arnkell which closes this episode: 'The narrator at this point emerges from the shadows and his voice suddenly becomes more personal, even though the verdict on Arnkell should be taken as representing a commonly acknowledged truth.'[11] The narrative is so skilfully constructed that we hardly need any comment from the narrator to help us understand what has led up to the killing, or to judge the rights and wrongs of it. Moreover, the concluding tribute – just like, as I shall suggest in due course, the character sketches with which figures in the narrative are introduced – is not the privileged judgement of a narrator but an accepted popular opinion. But of course, 'need' is the key word here: what is strictly necessary for making sense of a narrative is not normally a criterion we apply to a fictional text. The creation of a storyworld usually includes much more of Wayne C. Booth's 'rhetoric of fiction' – thoughts, comment, description, point of view and so on – than the mere establishment of an intelligible narrative line. I want now to explore how self-effacing narrators nevertheless engage us in psychologically complex and engaging narrative episodes.

In *Njáls saga*, the young Hallgerðr Höskuldsdóttir is married off without her consent to a husband she believes to be beneath her. When he slaps her, her complaint about him to her foster-father, a man with whom she has an oddly charged and perhaps even sexualized relationship, provokes him to murder the husband.[12] Hallgerðr is consulted about her next marriage, and is pleased with the match. Their marriage is a happy one. However, in spite of their otherwise harmonious relationship, this second husband slaps her too, and the sexual jealousy and vengefulness of her foster-father kick in again; he murders the second husband in turn.[13] When he reports the murder to Hallgerðr, 'hon hló at' (she laughed in response).[14]

Sif Ríkharðsdóttir has offered a perceptive and persuasive reading of these two episodes, linking them together and bringing them into focus with other scenes of inappropriate laughter in Old Norse literature.[15] Sif's primary interest in Hallgerðr's inappropriate response is with how some expressions of emotion are suppressed or distorted in saga narratives. My own focus is the lack of guidance the narrator offers about this response. Sif's interpretation is both psychologically and rhetorically subtle, but she also cites William Ian Miller, who supposes that Hallgerðr's laughter is an involuntary, nervous reaction.[16] Without comment from a narrator, either reading is plausible. I think that Sif is certainly right to see the laughter as being 'staged as a literary device ... to actively engage the reader (or audience) in the interpretation'.[17] But there are indications in the narrative about how the reader or listener might respond. For one thing, we are told that Hallgerðr loved her second husband, so we can at least be confident that the response is inappropriate.[18] But following the strange laughter, Hallgerðr tells the murderer to seek help from her uncle Hrútr – thus sending him to certain death.[19] One obvious interpretation is thus that Hallgerðr – with almost superhuman self-control – has lulled the murderer into a sense of false security, behaving as if she approved of the killing and is giving him good advice – as, indeed, she did when he killed her first husband. Perhaps there was no need to spell out Hallgerðr's self-possessed strategy; the saga author is making the audience work.

But there are other instances in which it is harder to decide what's going on without narratorial guidance. Later in *Njáls saga*, Hallgerðr's third husband, Gunnarr, is sentenced to three years' outlawry after a killing. Gunnarr decides at the last moment not to leave Iceland and returns to his farmstead at Hlíðarendi. We are told that Gunnarr's mother was not pleased by his return – or at least, we can infer this from her tight-lipped response: 'lagði fátt til' (she said little about it). But Hallgerðr is explicitly shown to welcome it: she 'varð fegin Gunnari, er hann kom heim' (was glad to see Gunnarr when he came home).[20] It is evident from the story so far that Gunnarr's mother is more reliable and trustworthy than Hallgerðr, so we do not need explicit guidance that Gunnarr's return is not a good thing. And of course, this becomes evident as we move through the time of the narrative. But why exactly is Hallgerðr pleased to see him return? Is she being presented as too impercipient to realize that staying in Iceland will be his downfall, and is simply glad to have him back? Or is she being presented as so cold-heartedly prescient that she welcomes his fatal decision to return precisely because it will be the death of him? This little episode is another striking example of the saga author's technique of actively engaging the audience in speculation, although Hallgerðr's motivation in this second instance is harder to assess. Here, the two interpretations of Hallgerðr's behaviour are mutually exclusive but equally plausible.

One final example, again from *Njáls saga*, is not so emotionally charged, but still involves a conspicuous absence of narratorial explanation. A man called Atli is taken on to work on Njáll's farm by Njáll's wife Bergþóra. He describes himself as 'skapharðr' (ruthless) and ominously adds 'hefir margir hlotit um sárt at binda fyrir mér' (many have had to bandage [their] wounds on my account).[21] It will not be long before Bergþóra orders him to kill one of Hallgerðr's servants. But when he is hired, while Njáll expresses reservations about him, we are told – without comment – that Njáll's formidable son Skarpheðinn 'var vel við Atla' (got on well with Atli).[22] Skarpheðinn's liking for Atli does not have any consequences in the narrative. When he hears that Atli has killed one of Hallgerðr's servants, he remarks drily that thralls are now into serious violence, and when Hallgerðr arranges for Atli himself to be killed, in revenge, Skarpheðinn jokes '[e]kki lætr Hallgerðr verða ellidauða húskarla vára' (Hallgerðr does not let our servants die of old age).[23] Are we simply to understand that Skarpheðinn recognizes Atli as another violent and ruthless man, and that there is fellow-feeling between them? Or is it a subtly proleptic narrative strategy, hinting that Skarpheðinn recognizes Atli as a potential hired killer, who may come in useful in due course? Without any explicit guidance from a narrator, we can only speculate, although it is significant that a little later in the same episode, Skarpheðinn notes that the money his father Njáll accepted from Gunnarr the previous summer in recompense for the killing of their servant may also be about to come in useful – as if he is indeed prescient about imminent violence. But his remark is left hanging. The absence of explicit narratorial comment in this whole episode, as in the others I have discussed, serves to engage an audience, perhaps even prompting discussion about the narrative, and throughout the next two chapters we shall see so many examples of conspicuous ambivalence that we can conclude that leaving judgement open to the audience is a major and purposeful literary strategy in saga narrative.

Saga narrators may also leave us to draw our own conclusions when there are rivalries between two characters, or two opposing factions. Thus, for example, in *Laxdœla saga*, there is long-standing enmity between Hrútr Herjólfsson and his nephew, Þorleikr Höskuldsson. But when a third party tries to rob Þorleikr of some valuable horses, Hrútr defends his nephew's interests and ends up killing the thief. Hrútr tells Þorleikr what has happened, but Þorleikr, far from being grateful, feels humiliated, and employs two of his tenants to humiliate Hrútr in revenge.[24] This is plainly unjust, though psychologically convincing. So far in the saga Hrútr has been presented, through his actions, as a wise and honourable man, always generous and helpful, and is widely regarded as such. But the saga author makes no direct comment on Þorleikr's unfair behaviour. His action in employing sorcerers to cast spells on Hrútr's household – which results in the death of Hrútr's young son Kári – is even more evidently wrong, but still the narrator makes no comment; instead Þorleikr is condemned by his brother Óláfr, who succeeds in persuading him to leave Iceland.[25] Far from coming to a bad end, however, he is accorded respect for the rest of his days: 'Þat er flestra manna sögn, at Þorleikr ætti lítt við elli at fásk, ok þótti þó mikils verðr, meðan hann var uppi' (Most people say that Þorleikr did not have to struggle much against old age [i.e. did not survive to old age], but was nevertheless regarded as a worthy man for as long as he lived).[26]

The narrator of *Laxdœla saga* also consistently maintains impartiality in the account of Hrútr's difficult relationship with his half-brother Höskuldr. From the outset, we are told that when their mother died in Iceland, Hrútr was living in Norway. As a result, Höskuldr took over the inheritance, 'en Hrútr, bróðir hans, átti hálft' (although his brother Hrútr was due half of it).[27] This is simply a statement of legal fact – no explicit judgement is passed on Höskuldr's unfair appropriation of the estate, although we anticipate the inevitable confrontation which occurs when Hrútr comes to Iceland to claim his fair share.

The impassive narrator

A rather similar effect is produced when shocking events are recounted impassively by the narrator.[28] I give only two examples of many. The first is a somewhat problematic one from *Grettis saga*. Grettir is himself a morally ambivalent character who often resorts to violence. In chapter 48 of the saga, Grettir seeks out Þorbjörn øxnamegin (oxen-might), who has killed Grettir's brother Atli, and so might reasonably be seen as an obvious target for lethal violence in revenge. But Þorbjörn is praised in the saga as a hard-working man, and he is tying up bundles of hay with his sixteen-year-old son when Grettir launches his attack, which he faces with commendable courage. In fact, Grettir's first victim is the boy, Arnórr, and the killing is described entirely dispassionately: 'þá reiddi [Grettir] hátt saxit; laust hann bakkanum saxins í höfuð Arnóri svá hart, at haussin brotnaði, ok var þat hans bani' (then Grettir lifted his short sword up high, and struck Arnórr's head with the blunt edge of the short sword so hard that [his] skull was smashed, and that was the death of him).[29] The narrator makes no comment at all on this killing of a teenage boy, and nothing in the description betrays disapproval. Grettir's violence is not presented as an especially heroic act, and Grettir shows no regret. In fact, Grettir's mother is said to be pleased about what Grettir has done, because it sends a clear message to his enemies. However, we may here be dealing with our own anachronistic response to the violence. For one thing, as Matthew Roby has pointed out, as understood in medieval Iceland, sixteen-year-old boys were not regarded as children but as being on the cusp of full adulthood.[30] And the boy's father also seems to have no scruples about involving his son in this violence, instructing the young Arnórr to creep up behind Grettir and, effectively, deal him the death blow.

A dispassionate stance with regard to a more unequivocally horrible act of violence may be cited from *Hrafnkels saga*. The chieftain Hrafnkell has been defeated in the lawsuit over the killing of his shepherd. The dead boy's cousin, Sámr, with support from other chieftains from outside the district, makes a surprise attack on Hrafnkell, and he and his men are very viciously tortured by being strung upside down from a clothes beam. Hrafnkell himself points out that there is no reason for his men to be killed and, while he does not plead for his own life to be spared, he asks not to be tortured: 'Er yðr engi sœmð í því' (There is no honour for you in that).[31] Nevertheless, the torture goes ahead while a court of confiscation, to dispossess Hrafnkell of his goods and property, is held. Sámr then proposes that Hrafnkell be exiled from the district, rather than killed outright. The powerful chieftain supporting him is taken aback by Sámr's leniency: 'Eigi veit ek, hví þú gerir þetta. Muntu þessa mest iðrask sjálfr, ef þú gefr honum líf' (I can't understand why you are doing this. You'll be the one to regret it most, letting him live).[32] And so it proves: in due course Hrafnkell takes vengeance on Sámr and regains his authority and property. But the narrator makes no comment on the torture, to either deprecate or excuse it. Like Grettir's killing of the boy Arnórr, it is described without rhetorical colouring. And crucially, Sámr pays the price for his leniency. Without narratorial guidance, a saga audience may feel at a loss about how to respond to this episode.

It may be that we have to acknowledge that ethics – especially those associated with violence and killing – may be historically contingent, that is, that values change over time, and what seems shocking to us might not have been regarded as such in earlier, harsher times, as with the account of Grettir killing the teenager Arnórr. Less emotively, in *Njáls saga*, Njáll's complex but successful strategy to deadlock lawsuits in order to pave the way towards providing his foster-son with a chieftainship, and thereby improve his marriage prospects, might seem sharp practice in some societies, and admirable cleverness in others.[33] The saga narrator, of course, makes no comment either way. But there are certain fundamental human values which seem to transcend social or historical contingency. Is the lesson to be drawn from *Hrafnkels saga* that it's wise to kill one's enemies if one has the chance? The author of the saga was almost certainly a Christian, writing for a Christian audience; this makes the lack of comment on the bleak import of the story even more conspicuous.

Displacement

In the absence of overt narratorial interventions, citing the opinion of other people is a very common method of delivering comment on the action of family sagas. Technically, this preserves the narrator's detachment from the narrative, but allows the expression of an independent and often (but not always, as we shall see) authoritative comment. I will begin with some examples of popular opinion which may simply indicate that the community took an interest in the affairs of others. For example, in *Laxdœla saga* we are told that the name which Óláfr pái gave to his new and very imposing farmstead – Hjarðarholt (Herd's wood) – was generally considered a very fitting one.[34] Óláfr, as his nickname suggests, is given to ostentation, and his farmstead has naturally made an impact on the local community. We might well compare Óláfr's grand announcement about a lavish memorial feast for his late father Höskuldr shortly afterwards in the saga: his speech inviting the whole neighbourhood is received with 'góðr rómr' (great approval) and 'þótti þetta ørendi stórum sköruligt' (this offer was felt to be extremely magnanimous).[35] Similarly, in the same saga, a favourable assessment of Óláfr's wife displaced on to popular opinion – 'Auðsætt var þat öllum mönnum, at hon var skörungr mikill' (It was evident to everyone that she was an impressive woman) – reaffirms our impression that he and his wife are the object of local interest and even scrutiny.[36]

Another area in which public opinion may simply be a narrative fact, rather than substituting for a judgement made in the narrative voice, is legal process. In this sphere, public acclamation is a key issue, and the assessment of a speech – whether for the defence or the prosecution – is often reported in the narrative. In the most straightforward cases, a speech from the winning side is admired and welcomed by those listening to the proceedings. In *Njáls saga*, for instance, in which so much of the narrative action is driven by or ends up with lawsuits, there are numerous examples. In the climactic legal battle between the sons of Njáll and Flosi's supporters, for example, arbitrators are appointed between the two sides, and we are told 'allr þingheimr yrði þessu feginn' (everyone at the þing was pleased about this).[37] When Snorri goði speaks on their behalf, declaring that they have decided to call for an unprecedentedly large settlement, 'Hans orð mæltusk vel fyrir' (His words were warmly welcomed), and when Hallr of Síðá announces the agreed sum, 'allir svöruðu vel' (everyone responded positively).[38] All this general approval is related as part of the narrative of the legal proceedings, and does not necessarily substitute for the opinion of the narrator, but when the settlement fails, its failure does seem all the more regrettable given the popular backing it is said to have attracted.

As Vésteinn Ólason rightly noted with regard to the concluding tribute praising Arnkell in *Eyrbyggja saga*, the overall assessment of celebrated or notorious saga characters may be traditional and uncontroversial and, in such cases, the narrator does not always trouble to displace the judgement. I would argue that this is the rationale behind the openly judgemental character sketches with which certain characters are introduced. Especially in family saga narratives, in which we are often introduced to a huge cast of characters, there is simply no scope for each character to prove the assessments of their worth expressed in these introductions, which are often formulaic, whether admiring or deprecatory. Nevertheless, even generally recognized appraisals are given added weight if they are attributed to popular opinion. For example, at the beginning of *Laxdæla saga*, the great matriarch Unnr in djúpúðga secretly and successfully moves her whole household from Scotland when her son is betrayed by the Scots, and killed. The narrator notes: 'ok þykkjask menn varla dœmi til finna, at einn kvenmaðr hafi komizk í brott ór þvílíkum ófriði með jafnmiklu fé ok föruneyti' (and men can hardly think of another example of a woman escaping from such perils with such wealth and such a retinue).[39] Coming so close to the beginning of the saga, Unnr's story is distanced from both audience and narrator, and takes on the form of an accepted summary of the past, part of the long lead in to the main body of the saga.[40] A learned narrator knows these facts, but does not presume to make a judgement about Unnr's position in a roll call of impressive women.

There are also very many examples of summary post-mortem judgements about figures who play a minor role in the body of the narrative. Such appraisals are typically not delivered in the voice of the narrator, but displaced on to public opinion. They too are often formulaic, and serve neatly and politely to seal the departure of the figure in question from the saga narrative. In *Njáls saga*, for instance, the death after illness of Mörðr gígja, with whom the whole saga opens, is reported, and 'þótti þat skaði mikill' (it was thought a great loss).[41] Mörðr's narrative legacy is simply that his daughter Unnr inherits his estate; he has no lasting influence and, apart from engineering Unnr's divorce at the beginning of the saga, he makes no great impression. The impersonal nature of this minimal formula recurs often in saga narrative: in *Eyrbyggja saga*, the death by drowning of the settler Þorsteinn þorskabítr is also respectfully and impersonally noted as being thought 'mikill skaði' (a great loss).[42] In exactly the same way, in *Laxdæla saga*, when Herjólfr, the father of Hrútr, dies, 'þat þótti mönnum mikill skaði' (people thought it a great loss).[43]

But a classic example of how popular opinion can stand in for narratorial judgement occurs in *Grettis saga*. Grettir is a complex amalgam of good and bad traits: a violent sociopath who is capable of heroic good deeds but who is often – to use a familiar euphemism – misunderstood. In general, the saga narrator does not pass direct comment on judgement on Grettir's behaviour, good or bad. One of Grettir's enemies, Þórir of Garðr, presses to have him outlawed from Iceland, even though, at the time, Grettir is away in Norway. The case is a complicated one. Þórir's sons were killed in Norway in a fire accidentally started by Grettir, and the narrator, without judging the matter either way, tells us that Þórir was enraged, and that 'þóttisk hann þar at sonarhefndum sjá eiga' (it seemed to him that he should be responsible for exacting vengeance on behalf of his sons).[44] The lawspeaker in Iceland, Skapti Þóroddson, is less sure about the case, and unhappy that Grettir is not in Iceland to defend himself, remarking proverbially 'jafnan er hálfsögð saga, ef einn segir' (a story is always half-told, if only one person tells it).[45] But Þórir persists and Grettir is outlawed. The narrator makes no final judgement on the justice of the sentence of outlawry, but purports to quote popular opinion: 'Margir mæltu, at þetta væri meir gört af kappi en eptir lögum' (Many people said that this had been done more because it had been forced through than that it was in accordance with the law).[46] Popular opinion – and not the narrator – confirms what may have been our suspicions.

When Grettir himself kills a character called Þorbjörn, who has insulted him, we are told: 'ok ekki þótti þeim skaði at, þótt Þorbjörn væri drepinn' (and no one thought it any loss, that Þorbjörn had been killed).[47] Here, public opinion serves to deprecate the slanders, and implicitly to excuse Grettir's violence. The deaths of witches and sorcerers are similarly celebrated. When the witch Katla is stoned to death in *Eyrbyggja saga*, public opinion is at the very least unmoved: 'spurðusk nú þessi tíðendi öll jafnsaman ok var engum harmsaga í' (now this news spread all over, and no one was sorry about it).[48] And in *Laxdæla saga*, when a family of sorcerers is believed to have caused the death of Guðrún's second husband with their spells, popular opinion is cited again: 'þóttu þat ólífismenn, er slíka fjölkynngi frömðu' (people who perpetrated such magic were thought not worthy to live).[49] Such displaced judgements as these serve to indicate where an audience's sympathies should lie, if indication were felt to be necessary, that is.

When comments relate to material or ostensibly factual details in the narrative, rather than being morally judgemental, displacement often lends a measure of added and apparently objective authority. Narrators may emphasize the unanimity of such judgements, or the particular authority the sources. Again in *Laxdœla saga* – which is rich in displaced comment, perhaps because status and show are such dominant themes in the saga – we are told that the controversial headdress which was originally destined for Kjartan's betrothed, Guðrún, but which is given instead to his wife Hrefna, had as much as eight ounces of gold woven into it, 'en þat er hygginna manns frásögn' (and that is according to clever people).[50] Here, the narrator backs up the calculation of how remarkably splendid the item was by citing more reliable sources than mere popular opinion, but does not make a personal assessment. In *Gísla saga*, unanimity and authority are linked: the final tally of Gísli's years as an outlaw is displaced on to the agreed reckoning of 'öllum vitrum mönnum' (all wise men).[51] In *Eyrbyggja saga*, when Þorgunna arrives in Iceland from the Hebrides, the narrator describes her appearance, but gives us no clues about her origins or intent in coming to Iceland. Her publicly observable habits – she is a daily mass-goer, and polite to others – are noted, and the fact that she is neither cheerful nor chatty. But the saga narrator does not presume to know her age: 'Þat var áhugi manna, at Þorgunna myndi sótt hafa inn sétta tøg' (People estimated that she was in her fifties).[52] The narrator does not claim to know more about her age than the other characters in the saga do. Similarly, we are told that her bed hangings are so fine 'at menn þóttusk eigi slíkan sét hafa þess kyns' (that people thought that they had never seen their like).[53] The assessment is displaced into the storyworld; the narrator does not imply any direct knowledge – or direct authorship – of how good the hangings were.

Two areas in which the narrator displaces judgement or comment in particularly interesting ways are those involving sexual relations, and the supernatural. In cases of sexual intrigue, the displacement of judgement on to popular opinion may be the result of the narrator's delicacy in not taking principled stand on sexual matters. Alternatively, and perhaps more likely, it may be a strategy to avoid betraying privileged knowledge about matters which would normally be clandestine to some degree, and in the naturalistically depicted storyworld, the subject of gossip but not necessarily openly discussed. Displacement of judgement about supernatural matters is harder to explain, but very frequent in family sagas narratives. It is almost as if the narrator is not willing personally to credit supernatural events – especially when associated with pagan beliefs – or to commit to reporting them as fact.

Perhaps simply because sexual liaisons in small communities are inevitably the subject of gossip, there are a number of instances in family sagas in which notice of an extra-marital affair is conveyed to us in the form of rumour. Thus, for example, in *Laxdœla saga*, we are told that, not long into Guðrún's first, unhappy marriage, 'fell þar mörg umrœða á um kærleika þeira Þórðar ok Guðrúnar' (there arose a lot of talk about a love affair between Þórðr [Ingunnarson] and Guðrún).[54] At this point, Þórðr, who is presenting himself as a friend of the married couple, is also himself married. The narrator makes no comment on the reliability of the rumour. The explicitly reciprocal nature of the affair between Guðrún and Þórðr is notable, and most likely due to the power and agency accorded to women in general and Guðrún in particular in the saga. More usually, however, the rumour is that a male suitor is seducing a woman: the verb *fífla* (to seduce) or some derivative of it is commonly used. For example, in *Njáls saga*, we hear of a disreputable and violent character called Hrappr, who is rumoured to be seducing the daughter of a man with whom he is staying in Norway. Because they are often seen talking together, 'margir töluðu, at hann myndi fífla hana' (many people said that he must be seducing her).[55] We are told that her father warns her not to talk to Hrappr in private any more, but she continues talking, and shortly afterwards Hrappr and the woman are found *in flagrante delicto*.[56] Again, rumour has alerted us to a possibility which duly transpires. In *Gísla saga*, there is an interesting twist on a rumoured affair: in the opening chapters of the saga, '[þ]at töluðu sumir men, at Bárðr fífldi Þórdísi Þorbjarnardóttir' (some people said that Bárðr was seducing Þórdís Þorbjarnardóttir) – Þórdís is Gísli's sister, and Bárðr is a neighbour.[57] But Bárðr roundly dismisses the gossip: he 'kvað ómæt ómaga orð' (said that the talk of nobodies was worthless).[58] The narrator offers us no guidance here about the truth of the rumours, but Gísli, offended by the gossip, kills Bárðr. Gísli's brother – a friend of Bárðr's – insists that Gísli has killed without just cause, and in fact, this difference between them marks the beginning of a sibling rift which echoes throughout the saga. But it is never made clear whether Bárðr was seducing Þórdís or not. We are left to draw our own conclusions – or even, perhaps, to leave the matter unresolved.

An example of how a narrator can guide the audience through an extended sequence of events by citing the judgement of popular opinion occurs in *Njáls saga*, when Hallgerðr is disastrously married off to her first husband. As we have seen already, as part of the background to Hallgerðr's unexplained laughter at the news of the death of her second husband, her foster-father Þjóstólfr was also responsible for the death of her first husband. The depiction of the relationship between Hallgerðr and her sinister and violent foster-father is remarkable for the narrator's mastery of the non-committal: the absence of comment and displacement of judgements. The first popular judgement we hear about Hallgerðr and Þjóstólfr is that he was in general bad influence on her: 'Þat var mælt, at hann væri engi skapbœtir Hallgerði' (It was said that he did not improve Hallgerðr's disposition).[59] The narrator holds back from direct comment on their relationship. When Hallgerðr marries her first husband, she is said to be perfectly happy – 'allkát' – during the wedding feast.[60] Although we later learn that her outward demeanour does not necessarily reflect her inner feelings, at this point in the narrative it is hard to understand why she seems so content, given that she was opposed to the match – except for the fact that when she complained about the marriage a little earlier to Þjóstólfr, he reassured her that she would be married a second time. Perhaps she is relying on her foster-father's prediction. Next, a popular judgement demonstrates typical uneasiness about private conversations in saga narrative. During the wedding celebrations, Þjóstólfr talks not only to Hallgerðr, but also to Hallgerðr's uncle, a man called Svanr, a new and minor character who is in fact openly criticized by the narrator as 'ódæll ok illr viðreignar' (a bully and difficult to deal with).[61] We are told, 'fannsk mönnum mikit um tal þeira' (people were very struck by [all] their talk).[62] This talk is seen as ominous – in a way the narrator never clarifies. And although the bride seems content, and the wedding feast is a success, we have been alerted to the possibility of trouble in store communicated through the open criticism of Svanr by the narrator and the unspecific unease of the audience within the diegesis. A final comic moment seals this ill-omened wedding. Hallgerðr's husband Þorvaldr seems not to be aware of the possibility of trouble, even though as they ride away, Þjóstólfr keeps close to Hallgerðr, and 'töluðu þau jafnan' (they never stopped talking).[63] Þorvaldr proudly tells his father that he knows that Hallgerðr likes him, because she laughs at his every word. We find out more about Hallgerðr's laughter in due course, but her father-in-law is already clear about what it means: 'Eigi ætla ek hlátr hennar jafngóðan sem þú … en þat mun þó síðar reynask' (I don't think her laughter is as good a sign as you think … but that will be borne out later).[64]

In *Eyrbyggja saga*, the love affair between Björn and Þuríðr is made quite overt in the narrative with the celebrated love verse which Björn is represented as speaking to Þuríðr: 'Guls mundum vit vilja | … | þenna dag lengstan' (We two would wish this day to be the longest ever).[65] Nevertheless, the saga narrator still represents their relationship as it is seen within the storyworld, as the object of local gossip: 'var þat alþýðumál, at með þeim Þuríði var fíflingar' (it was the talk of everyone, that Þuríðr and Björn were having an affair).[66] When Þuríðr gives birth to a baby boy, the narrator makes no comment whatever on the child's paternity, although placing the news of this birth immediately following the re-telling of Björn's trial and outlawry, a trial for the violence which has in fact arisen over this suspected affair, might imply that he is indeed the father.[67] Björn is outlawed and leaves Iceland, but when he returns, he is questioned closely about Þuríðr's son Kjartan. He notes – again in a skaldic verse – that the boy is 'iðglíki mér' (exactly like me).[68] His second verse makes the position even clearer: when asked directly what Þuríðr's husband thinks about the boy's paternity, Björn declares that the likeness proves the truth of what her husband has suspected – that he and Þuríðr had been lovers.[69] Throughout the whole scene, the narrator's own voice has been silent. Elsewhere in *Eyrbyggja saga*, we hear of a foster-son described as a 'kenningarsonr' (natural son), and this view is attributed to popular talk – 'því at þat var flestra manna sögn, at hann væri hans sonr, en ambátt var móðir hans' (because most people said that he was his son, but that his mother was a slave woman).[70] Here again, the narrator reflects what was being talked about in the district, in a perfectly naturalistic way, and disappears behind the gossip.

In family sagas, many supernatural events are related impassively, alongside conventionally naturalistic, mundane happenings. Any distinction between a supernatural and a natural event is, like the distinction between a good and a bad action, socially and historically contingent. This is nowhere more evident than in religious matters, in which supernatural events such as miracles, and supernatural figures such as angels or divinities, are actually articles of faith. Nevertheless, the saga author seems on occasion not to commit the narrator to recounting certain supernatural episodes without some reservation or displacement. This is particularly the case when the supernatural involves pagan belief. In *Gísla saga*, for instance, when Gísli's brother-in-law is killed and interred in a mound, it is noticed that the snow never lies on one side of the mound. One might argue that there are any number of rational explanations for such a phenomenon, especially in Iceland with its geothermal areas, and indeed any south-facing slope anywhere, but popular opinion supposes it to be a strange and novel occurrence: 'ok gátu menn þess til, at hann myndi Frey svá ávarðr fyrir blótin, at hann myndi eigi vilja, at frøri á milli þeira' (and people reckoned, that he was so favoured by [the god] Freyr because of the sacrifices he had made, that he [the god] did not want frost to come between them).[71] The narrator makes no comment.

In *Njáls saga*, there is another allusion to popular superstition when a character called Svanr is drowned. We are told that 'fiskimenn ... þóttusk sjá Svan ganga inn í fjallit Kaldbakshorn, ok var honum vel fagnat' (fishermen ... thought they saw

Svanr enter into the mountain Kaldbakshorn, and he was warmly welcomed).[72] This is presented as a report of what others claimed to see, not as a narrative fact, but the narrator further undermines the credibility of the report, adding 'en sumir mæltu því í móti ok kváðu engu gegna' (but some disagreed and said there was nothing in it), before concluding that everyone agreed that whatever happened, his body was never found.[73] Similarly, in *Eyrbyggja saga*, the narrator reports competing stories about the conception of a bull calf from a crippled cow which has licked the ashes from the newly burnt body of Þórólfr bægifótr, whose re-animated corpse has been terrorizing the district. We are told that 'er sumra manna sögn, at þá er eyjamenn fóru útan eptir firði með skreiðarfarma, at þá sæi þeir kúna upp í hlíðinni ok naut annat' (according to the account of some people, when islanders travelled along the fjord with a cargo of dried fish, they saw the cow up on the mountainside with a bull).[74] Note that this is double displacement: the account of some people is that some other people saw the cow. But even so, an opposing view is recorded: 'en þess átti engi maðr ván' (but no one thought this likely).[75]

In such cases as this, the element of pagan superstition may be the cause of the narrator's explicit displacement. Certainly, many supernatural events are related as narrative fact in family sagas, and this is particularly evident in *Eyrbyggja saga*. An exhaustive survey of which supernatural events in which sagas are held at arm's length by the narrator would yield interesting results, and go towards establishing a cultural hierarchy of socio-historical credibility or plausibility. That, of course, is way beyond the scope of this book. But at the risk of resting on anachronistic standards of believability, I conclude this section with one bizarre supernatural occurrence, carefully doubly displaced, from *Laxdœla saga*.

Þorgils Hölluson – the man who gained dubious renown by leading the fatal attack on Helgi Harðbeinsson, which he had been tricked into by an apparent promise of Guðrún's hand in marriage – has premonitions of his own death. At the Alþing, in an otherwise notably natural-seeming scene, people are spreading out their clothes on the walls of the booths to dry. Unspecified 'people' heard Þorgils's own cloak speak a verse boasting knowledge of two plots against Þorgils – first, the trickery which led him to attack Helgi, and the second, presumably, the imminent killing of Þorgils himself: 'Menn heyrðu, at heklan kvað … ' (People heard, that the cloak said …).[76] And popular opinion seals the uncanny event: 'Þetta þótti it mesta undr' (This was thought to be the most extraordinary thing).[77]

So far, the most obvious functions of comments displaced on to popular opinion have been to lend weight to a particular judgement, or to substitute for narratorial comment which would otherwise undermine the habitual objectivity or externality of the narrator, or betray access to privileged – that is, authorial – knowledge of the storyworld. But these functions demand that popular opinion be authoritative – or, more simply, right. And there are interesting occasions when popular opinion – reported by the narrator – misjudges the situation. In some cases, the effect of this mistaken assumption is to put the saga audience in the position of the characters themselves, to be as ignorant of the import and entailment of events as they are. Perhaps the most striking instance of an uncorrected mistaken assumption is the episode in *Eyrbyggja saga* in which the young man Gunnlaugr, having become the object of sexual rivalry between two witches, Katla and Geirríðr, is violently and almost certainly sexually assaulted on his way home late one night.[78] This assault shocks the neighbourhood: 'var margrœtt um hans vanheilsu' (there was a lot of talk about his injuries).[79] Katla's son Oddr openly blames Geirríðr for the attack, and 'þat hugðu flestir men, at svá væri' (and it was the opinion of most people, that [this] was so).[80] The narrator does not correct this opinion, but it is significant – and passes without narratorial comment – that the subsequent legal action against Geirríðr does not succeed.[81] Eventually, Katla is executed for witchcraft, and finally, before she dies, she defiantly claims responsibility for assaulting Gunnlaugr.[82] The narrative voice lets events play out in front of the audience without any direct intervention. We are made to wait for explicit confirmation of her guilt, although of course we may well have suspected Katla all along. As first-time listeners or readers, our perspective on the unfolding of events matches that of characters in the storyworld: like them, we may have suspicions but we do not know for certain. In *Grettis saga*, when the revenant Glámr does not appear for two nights in a row, we are told that the farmer believes that things may be improving, but shortly afterwards, the discovery of a brutal attack on Grettir's horse proves him wrong.[83] Again, in the same saga, popular opinion mocks an attempt by one of Grettir's enemies to enlist his elderly mother to curse Grettir and work magic against him: 'Mikinn hlátr gerðu menn' (People laughed a lot).[84] But her magic turns out to be no laughing matter.[85] With no corrective from the narrator, the audience coming to the episode for the first time technically shares time with (at least some of) the characters in the diegesis.

My final category of displaced comment involves the narrator presenting other characters in the diegesis as offering explanations and interpretations about motive and causation. Instead of leaving the audience to draw their own conclusions, the narrator guides our response, but not by direct comment. In *Gísla saga*, for instance, when Gísli's brother-in-law Vésteinn is killed, his young sons arrive looking for vengeance, and kill Gísli's brother Þorkell at a local assembly. On their way there, they are seen talking in secret to a man called Gestr. They arrive at the assembly incognito: we are told only that two poorly dressed strangers have appeared. Having killed Þorkell, they manage to escape, proudly identifying themselves as Vésteinn's sons. Þorkell's brother-in-law consults Gestr about how best to proceed with a case against them, and Gestr is discouraging, suggesting that if he were the killers, he would have used a false name, so that he could not be prosecuted.[86] By now, an attentive audience may suspect that Gestr has not only aided their mission, but also actually suggested the name change plan to them – a plan which they are revealed, much later in the saga, to have indeed adopted.[87] The saga narrator shares no inside knowledge on any of this. But there is a displaced explanation: 'Þat hafa men fyrir satt haft, at Gestr hafi verit í ráðum með sveinunum, því at hann var skyldr þeim at frændsemi' (People think that the truth of the matter is that Gestr had been advising the boys, because he was related to them).[88] The connexion between Vésteinn's sons and Gestr is not a close one.[89] So even if, alerted by Gestr's secret talk, we may suppose that he has been helping the young killers, we still need to know why and the narrator gives us an explanation via popular opinion.

Perhaps the most interesting element in this episode is what I will, in my final chapter, call the conspicuous silence – when the narrative voice draws attention to something significant being said (or sometimes done) but does not relate what. In the instance above, the Gestr's secret talk with the boys alerts the audience to an omission which the displaced explanation fills. There is a similar instance in *Eyrbyggja saga*. Here, an outlaw asks to be sheltered by Snorri goði but, although Snorri refuses to take him in, we are told that they had a secret talk.[90] The outlaw then moves on to Snorri's enemy Arnkell, whom he attempts to kill. We may not initially suspect Snorri of being behind this attack, because he had refused to give shelter to the outlaw, but the narrator helps us by displacing an explanation on to popular opinion: 'Sá orðrómr lagðisk á, at Snorri goði hefði þenna mann sendan til höfuðs Arnkatli' (The rumour began, that Snorri goði had sent that man to kill Arnkell).[91]

Conventional judgements

Before moving on to the second half of this chapter, in which I will explore interventions in the narrative by a clearly evident narratorial voice, I want briefly to consider two marked departures from the supposedly non-interventive family saga narrator which were apparently accepted as features of the conventional narratorial mode of family sagas: the introductory character sketch and the retrospective summary – effectively a eulogy – of an admirable character's achievements throughout the saga.

The summing-up of a major character's life after what is often a premature end is a notable feature of saga narrative. The most extended eulogy of this kind occurs after the death of the upstanding chieftain Arnkell in *Eyrbyggja saga*. We are told in detail about Arnkell's outstanding qualities, about his model disposition, his success in lawsuits and how his pre-eminence provoked envy. The narrator describes him, in sum, as 'allra manna bezt at sér um alla hluti í fornum sið' (the most accomplished of all men in all respects in times gone by).[92] The achievements of outlaws such as Gísli and Grettir are also celebrated: of Gísli, we are told that 'eigi hefir meiri atgörvimaðr verit en Gísli né fulllhugi' (there has never been a more proficient or courageous man than Gísli).[93] At the end of *Grettis saga*, the opinion of Sturla Þórðarson the lawspeaker is cited as the authority for a eulogistic summing-up: Sturla considers Grettir to have been the cleverest of men, since he was able to evade capture for so long, and the strongest man of his age in Iceland, as shown by the way he dealt with *aptrgöngur* (the walking dead) and other monsters.[94] It is notable that all these judgements situate their heroes above and beyond the saga narrative in question, locating them in the much larger context of Icelandic history. And the judgement passed on Grettir is only indirectly narratorial – it is ostensibly the considered opinion of a highly regarded and learned authority, offered to the audience by the narrator. The assessments of heroes' last stands are similarly formulated: it is reported about Gísli's last stand, for instance, that 'engi hafi hér frægri vörn veitt' (no one in the land has offered a more valiant defence), and Gunnarr in *Njáls saga* 'varði sik vel ok frœknliga' (defended himself well and bravely).[95] These judgements are matters of accepted tradition, of reputational fact, and not the narrator's individual view of a saga character in the midst of particular circumstances in the narrative.

The same is true of the introductory character sketches which feature so often in family saga narrative. Celebrated figures such as Kjartan, or the redoubtable Guðrún, in *Laxdœla saga*, are introduced in such a way that we are left in no doubt about their pre-eminence. And again, it is notable that this pre-eminence is set in a context of all Iceland, not just the saga narrative itself: Kjartan is described as 'allra manna fríðastr, þeira er fœzk hafa á Íslandi' (the handsomest man ever to have been born in Iceland); Gúðrún is 'kvenna vænst, er upp óxu á Íslandi' (the most beautiful woman to have grown up in Iceland).[96] This is not mere hyperbole, but indicates a wider assessment of excellence than simply that of the narrator, in a wider all-Iceland context than that of the saga at hand.

Such judgements, whether introductory or valedictory, are not uniformly approving. Like a number of other family saga characters, Hrafnkell is introduced to us as 'ójafnaðarmaðr mikill' (a terrible bully), although a very able man.[97] Many other characters are pre-judged in saga narrative: as cowardly, wise, legally adept or brave. Again, one could attribute this to established tradition, especially in the case of relatively major characters. But as noted earlier, in narratives which play out over a long time span, as family sagas do, and with a great many characters in the narrative, as family sagas have, it is not practicable to demonstrate an individual character's traits through their actions and interactions before the main events of the saga take place. Brief, incisive character sketches prime us to regard those characters in certain ways, and to interpret their actions in the coming narrative in the context of those pre-judgements. This is perhaps best understood in terms of narratorial distance – that is, how closely the narrator seems to be positioned in regard to the character, and as a consequence, how close we as audience feel to the character in question. Placed at the moment a character is introduced, these sketches do not bring us closer to the characters they describe, but have in fact the opposite effect of distancing and objectifying them. They are crucially different from narratorial comment offered in the thick of saga narrative, when narrators comment on the immediate and closely focused actions of their characters. We may experience the third time of saga narrative in a way analogous to the way we experience life in the real world, without a narrator to give us access to the thoughts and motives of those around us, but in that real world, we do often have some idea of what to expect from those around us, to anticipate how they might behave in certain circumstances, to form judgements about them based on what we know, however distantly, about them. In real life, our preconceptions are often wrong, and people surprise us. But in sagas, characters behave in the ways we have been led to expect. This, then, is the function and effect of the introductory character sketches in family saga narrative: briefly and efficiently, they prepare us for what we can expect of a character in the narrative future. Like the eulogies, they are summative, rather than offering judgement on a specific detail of a character's life.

The voice of the narrator

Managing the discourse

I begin the second half of this chapter on the voice of the narrator with instances in which the narrator does directly intervene in the narrative, from outside the storyworld, but primarily to make clearer the future course of the story. These interventions do not give us any sense of the narrator's individuality; they are simply a means of guiding readers or listeners through a complex and multi-stranded narrative, and do not involve directing our responses to events or characters. However, they do establish the voice of a narrator – impersonal though it may be – standing outside the narrative and commenting on its organization and structure. Hence, they constitute a mid-point between the self-effaced narrator of the first half of this chapter and the intervening narrator of the rest of this second half. I am concerned in the chapter as a whole with the way moving through a narrative – listening to or reading it – is analogous to Augustine's conception of living in time, with the past as recollection, the future as anticipation and the present moment of attention scarcely existing.[98] I have been relying on Ricœur's theory of imperfect knowledge in characterizing our passage through this analogous 'third time' of narrative, a knowledge which is imperfect firstly because a self-effacing saga narrator draws back from guiding or advising the audience directly, and secondly – the subject of my final chapter – because certain details may be withheld by the narrator to create something like a plot. But whether narrators directly address their audience or not, they are themselves nevertheless always outside the third time of the narrative. This means that they can see the past, present and future of their discourse from the Boethian *totum simul* perspective. Thus, in mediating a narrative to an audience, a narrator can allude not only to what has already taken place in the narrative, speaking, as it were, from the moment of attention, but also to the direction or shape the discourse will take in the narrative future. So a key distinction which needs to be made here is between this sort of allusion to the discourse itself, on the one hand, and narratorial prolepsis, when the narrator tells us what is going to happen in the storyworld, on the other. In the cases I am about to discuss, narrators allude not so much to the substance of the future within the diegesis, but to how and when the not-yet-related narrative will deal with it, that is, they allude self-reflexively to their own narration. As Carol Clover has put it, 'the narrator addresses the audience on the mechanics of composition' – and I would extend this to include the mechanics of recitation.[99] The subject is the course of the narrative itself, not the storyworld it describes.

Reminders of what has already been related are very common in some sagas, and virtually absent in others. They are mostly insignificant little tags, and do not add a great deal to our reading or listening experience. For instance, near the beginning of *Grettis saga*, the narrator names a number of young men living in the same district as Grettir. At a ball game, Grettir is picked to play against one of those young men: 'við Auðun, er fyrr var nefndr' (against Auðunn, who was named earlier).[100] Later in the saga, Auðunn reappears in the story, now an adult, and Grettir broods on the ball game, which he had lost to Auðunn. The narrator reminds us of this episode: 'sem áðr er sagt' (as is related earlier).[101] Grettir has been away in Norway in the meantime; perhaps the narrator – or even a scribe – felt the need to bridge that absence with a reminder tag. Similarly, when Grettir is travelling round Iceland as an outlaw, he arrives at a location where he hopes to find Grímr, another outlaw who killed his friend Hallmundr. But Grímr is long gone, and the narrator reminds us that we should know this, because it has already been related: 'sem fyrr var sagt' (as was told earlier).[102] *Laxdœla saga* has a particularly large number of such tags and, interestingly, they seem to allude to a written version of the saga: 'sem fyrr var ritat' (as was written earlier), and there is an identical instance in *Eyrbyggja saga*.[103] A number of these instances are absent in some manuscripts, or in some versions the past participle 'getit' (told) is used, rather than 'ritat' (written); these variations may be scribal.

More significant are the tags which alert us to the future direction of the narrative. In *Njáls saga*, for instance, we are several times alerted to the fact that certain characters are 'ór sögunni' (out of the saga).[104] This is of real practical help in a complex narrative such as *Njáls saga*, although it should be noted that the alerts are not always reliable: elsewhere in *Njála* we are told that a man called Högni 'er … ór þessu sögu' (is out of this story), only for him to turn up more than once in later chapters.[105] More helpfully, in *Laxdœla saga*, a slave called Ásgautr helps Vigdís to shelter a relative of hers, against the wishes of her greedy and cowardly husband. She behaves bravely and nobly, and frees Ásgautr as a reward for his help. Our continuing focus is on the contrast between Vigdís and her husband; it is useful to be told by the narrator that when Ásgautr goes to Denmark, 'endir þar sögu frá honum' (his story ends there).[106] In the same saga, Þuríðr, the daughter of Óláfr pái, marries a man called Geirmundr, and he deserts her and their baby. In a celebrated episode, Þuríðr leaves the child with Geirmundr, and takes in exchange Geirmundr's sword Fótbítr. But Geirmundr is drowned, and the narrator concludes 'ok lýkr þar frá Geirmundi at segja' (and that's where telling the story of Geirmundr ends).[107] Also in *Laxdœla saga*, the narrator takes up the story of Höskuldr's descendants, but notes that 'Dœtra Höskulds er hér eigi getit mjök' (Not much is related about Höskuldr's daughters here).[108] And again, in *Njáls saga*, we are told that Unnr, having been divorced from Hrútr, 'fór heim með föður sínum ok kom aldri vestr þar síðan' (went home with her father and never went west [i.e. to Hrútr's farm] again).[109]

Such tags as these provide invaluable cues for the readers and listeners of these complex texts. They permit an audience to put concluded storylines to the back of their minds, and allow them to focus on live story threads. Elsewhere, sagas contain similarly useful tags to inform audiences that although certain storylines or characters may temporarily fade into the background, they will reappear in due course. For example, in *Njáls saga*, Njáll's family is introduced early on, before they play a part in the narrative, but the narrator warns us to watch out for their reappearance: 'koma þeir allir við þessa sögu síðan' (they all come into this story later).[110] Rather differently, in *Grettis saga,* when Grettir and his brother part, the narrator's coda comes as a shock: 'Skilðu þeir brœðr með vináttu ok sáusk aldri síðan' (The brothers parted on good terms and never saw each other again).[111] We are inclined to believe that the brothers will continue their relationship precisely because of their warmth towards each other, even if they do live in different countries. To tell us differently, the narrator must betray the knowledge that the end of the saga is already in place.

There is a clear distinction between the saga narrator or author knowing what is going to happen in the already passed *söguöld,* and the knowledge of what is going to be told in the narrative. But there is a middle way: prior knowledge of *the story of what happened*, which the narrator purports to relate and which has an indeterminate relation to actuality. A large number of formulae act as signposting in the narrative, indicating that a new subject or narrative strand is to be taken up. They are all variants on the phrase 'Nú er at segja frá … ' (now [it's time] to tell about …). These insignificant reminding or notifying tags may imply the prior existence of a narrative, but not necessarily so, although they are consonant with it. They may simply signal the narrator's intention to move to a new subject. But there is one significant variation on the formula in a number of instances: 'Nú er *þar* frá at segja … ' (now [it's time] to tell about *where* …). References to picking up the story at a certain point – *where*' – prompt one to imagine a linear narrative, and variations on the formula, such as 'Nú er þar til at taka … ' (Now to pick up [the story] where …) or 'Nú er þar til máls at taka … ' (Now to pick up the story where …) reinforce this impression of a pre-existing arrangement of events.

Instances such as these are perhaps not enough to indicate with certainty a definite precursor, in whatever form, to the saga as it has come down to us. But the phrase 'svá er sagt' (thus it is said), and minor variations on it, is common in family sagas, and often implies an actual source, and not just an opinion. In *Grettis saga*, for instance, the narrator informs us that after two years' hiding out in Drangey, 'svá er sagt' (so [it] is said), that Grettir had slaughtered almost all of the sheep.[112] One is left wondering where the information came from. At least four instances in *Gísla saga* very clearly introduce neither opinion nor information, and are not retrieval phrases, but instead introduce a new narrative thread. Firstly, 'Frá því er sagt' (Concerning this [it] is said) that Gísli's sister Þórdís tells her husband Börkr that Gísli has confessed to the murder of Börkr's brother Þorgrímr.[113] Secondly, 'þat er nú sagt' (it is now said) that Börkr sends his two nephews to kill Gísli; Gísli kills one on the spot, and one later in the saga.[114] Thirdly, 'Frá því er sagt' (Concerning this, it is said) that, as autumn draws on, Gísli begins to have bad dreams.[115] And finally, 'Nú er sagt' (now [it] is said) that a man sent to track down Gísli in hiding discovers the hiding place and tells Börkr about it.[116] We could read all of these instances simply as way of introducing a new narrative, just like the first signposting phrases I discussed earlier, but there is nevertheless an insistent if faint sense that some prior source is being referenced. It is also perhaps significant that three of these four instances pertain to the pursuit of Gísli by Börkr, as if the narrator of *Gísla saga* were referring to another narrative about this, in whatever form.

In *Grettis saga*, there are repeated references to what the narrator cannot tell us because – ostensibly – there is no information or pre-existing story about it, the obvious implication being that other material in the narrative *does* rest on pre-existing sources. Thus, we are told that Grettir had no more dealings with his adversaries 'svá at þess sé getit' (insofar as this is related) or 'svá at getit sé' (insofar as is related).[117] Interestingly, another instance in the same saga picks up and negates the 'svá er sagt' (so [it] is said) formula: 'eigi er sagt, at þeir fyndisk Kormákr síðan, svá at þess sé getit' (it is not said, that he and Kormákr met again, insofar as this is related).[118] In *Laxdæla saga*, a similar effect is created: in summarizing the biography of Hrútr when his active part in the saga is over, the narrator tells us that he had a third wife, 'ok nefnu vér hana eigi' (but we don't name her) – the clear implication being that the narrator does not have the necessary information in this particular instance.[119]

All these examples imply at least to some degree the existence (or absence) of a source which the narrator might use in the creation of the narrative. The sense we have is that the narrator is self-reflexively mediating to us material which once existed somewhere, in some form, whether as the future of an as yet uncomposed – but imagined – narrative, or as material out of which the present narrative has been built, the so-called immanent saga. There is an intriguing reference in *Njáls saga* to what may depict, or perhaps even authentically reflect, the real-world genesis of such material: towards the end of the saga Kári, Njáll's son-in-law, and another relative of Njáll are vengefully pursuing Njáll's enemies after the burning. Against the odds, they kill five men and put the rest to flight. The narrator tells us that 'Höfðu menn mjök at minnum eptirreið þeira' (People preserved their pursuit in their memories); there is a clear implication that such memories might well have crystallized into a narrative tradition.[120]

I want to mention briefly a special case in *Grettis saga* in which the narrator makes specific and surprising reference to a named source of information: Grettir himself. On at least four occasions, the narrator purports to report what Grettir has himself said. As an outlaw, often living or travelling alone in Iceland, Grettir's view often cannot be expressed by articulating his thoughts to another character. I have explored in depth the use of skaldic verse to communicate such interiority, and I do not want to revisit that here.[121] However, on one occasion, the narrator reports Grettir's veiled boast that, while he would be happy to take on four opponents single-handed, he would draw the line at five or more with the introduction 'svá hefir Grettir sagt' (Grettir has said this).[122] In this instance, a skaldic stanza purportedly by Grettir which corroborates this claim is quoted in the narrative. On two occasions, the narrator reports that Grettir has himself commented on a situation in which there was no feasible witness who could have heard his words if they had been spoken at the time. For instance, taking refuge in an isolated valley, 'Svá hefir Grettir sagt, at fyrir dalnum hafi ráðit blendingr' (Grettir has said that the valley was ruled over by a half-troll).[123] Similarly, when he took on a troll-woman single-handed, the narrator tells us 'þetta er sögn Grettis, at trollkonan steypðisk í gljúfrin' (this is Grettir's account, that the troll-woman plunged down into the cleft).[124] Elsewhere in the saga, the narrator tells us that Grettir 'kvazk hann mest bundizk hafa at sínu skaplyndi, at hann sló þá eigi, er þeir hœldusk við hann' (said that it had been a great effort of self-control not to strike those who boasted over him).[125] There is here a strong sense that Grettir himself has somewhere, somehow, been recorded as evaluating with hindsight 'what happened' – either in a verse, which is not however quoted in the narrative, or in some other tradition which the narrator has had access to.

In the cases discussed above, the narrator is commenting on the narrative and addressing the audience, which is strictly the subject of the final part of this chapter. However, I have engaged with it here because all these comments are still confined to the process of narration, and do not to refer directly to the storyworld itself. I want to consider next a few instances in which narrators objectify their own narrative by characterizing it as a saga amongst other sagas, calling attention to its existence as a narrated text and thus part of the Icelandic literary tradition.

As we might expect from a relatively late family saga, *Grettis saga* contains a number of references to other narratives. For instance, when the settlement of Grettir's father Ásmundr is said to coincide with the arrival of the first Christian missionaries in Iceland, the narrator notes 'Mart bar til tíðenda um sameign þeira byskups ok Norðlendinga, þat er ekki kemr við þessa sögu' (there were many stories about dealings between Bishop [Friðrekr] and his fellow missionary [Þorvaldr][on the one hand] and the men of the north [on the other], which do not come into this saga).[126] Similarly, the narrator notes that not everything known about Grettir's childhood is related in the saga as we have it: 'Mörg bernskubrögð gerði Grettir, þau sem eigi eru í sögu sett' (Grettir played many other tricks in childhood, which are not related in the saga).[127] And when Grettir is taking refuge on Drangey, the narrator notes that one year not only did Snorri goði die, but also Grettir's staunch supporter, the lawspeaker Skapti Þóroddson, adding 'mart bar til tíðenda á þessum misserum, þat sem ekki kemr við þessu sögu' (there were many newsworthy events that year, which do not come into this saga).[128] In *Laxdœla saga*, we can find similar examples: for instance, we are told that Gellir Þorkelsson lived to be an old man, and that 'hann kemr ok við margar sögur, þótt hans sé hér lítt getit' (he also comes into many [other] sagas, although little is related about him here).[129] In such instances, the narrator presents the saga as we have it as a narrated entity distinct from other narratives. The saga is regarded as comprising a selection of material from a wider pool of pre-existing sources which, it is implied, exist already in narrative form.

From here, we can move on to comments from the narrator which refer to or even specifically name other sagas as literary narratives alongside the saga being narrated. Thus, for example, in *Eyrbyggja saga*, the narrator notes of Snorri goði that he also features in *Laxdœla saga* and *Heiðarvíga saga*, although we cannot be sure that the named sagas are precisely the same as the ones that have come down to us.[130] We are told in *Grettis saga* of a farmer called Grímr that 'er mikil saga frá honum sögð' (a big saga is told about him), although this text is not extant.[131] Other sagas which have not survived are sometimes alluded to by name, as when in *Laxdœla saga* the aftermath of the killing of Þorgils Hölluson is said to have been related in *Þorgils saga Höllusonar*, which has completely disappeared.[132] Such references can be extremely tantalizing, such as the mention of *Böðmóðs saga ok Grímólfs ok Gerpis* – now lost – in *Grettis saga*.[133] On one occasion the fact that a saga apparently never existed is recorded: the narrator of *Grettis saga* confidently informs us that there is no saga about Grettir's son.[134] We hear in *Njáls saga* of a tradition about a man called Þiðrandi 'þann er sagt er, at dísir vægi' (about whom it is told that he was killed by *dísir* [supernatural female creatures].) [135] There are also references to surviving poetic compositions: to *Grettisfœrsla,* an obscene poem about Grettir's sexual exploits, or Úlfr Uggason's complex skaldic poem *Húsdrápa.*[136]

I have so far discussed instances in which the narrator does directly address the audience, but only with regard to the self-reflexive process of narration itself: to remind us of what has been related already, or to alert us to what will or not be related in the narrative future, and how the narration as a whole is situated in a wider Icelandic literary tradition. Allusions to the course of the narrative emphasize the narrator's position outside the third time which the narrative is creating. They make it clear that the narrator can see the narrative – *sjuzhet* as well as *fabula* – as a whole, comprising future as well as past, from the Boethian *totum simul* perspective. The narrator knows not only what happened in the past, but also how the discourse recounts that. This creates the sense that the narrator is mediating a pre-existing narrative. But it is important to bear in mind here that this voice, though directly engaging the audience, is not in any way personalized or individual, although the references to other literary texts do at the very least mark out the narrator as someone well-versed in saga literature.

I turn at last to instances in which narrators do comment directly on narrative events or characters, speaking from outside the third time of narrative to address the audience, and at the same time reminding us that we too are outside that third time. We are aware of a voice engaging directly with us, not only self-reflexively to chart the direction of the narration, but also to provide information about, judge or explain what is going on in the storyworld. I will deal with these three strategies in turn. Firstly, given that family sagas are set in a distinct period of Icelandic history – from immigration and settlement to the decades following the conversion to Christianity – and probably separated from their composition by several centuries, it is perhaps only to be expected that a narrator will provide some historical context to the events and characters in the saga. I am not here concerned with the accuracy of the information provided, though that is a fascinating if challenging subject in its own right. My concern is rather with the action of the narrator in offering the information, and especially in the distinction between contextual information which is necessary to understand what is happening and information which simply sets the scene, or adds period detail. Secondly, a narrator's explicit responses to events and characters in this past storyworld, involving apparently personal judgement, may at last allow us to hear what seems to be an actual, individual voice articulating a distinct moral stance. Finally, narratorial explanations of what is going on may confirm our impression that the narrator is only mediating a pre-existing story, rather than being the author of what is being related – because if what is related needs added explanation, why not relate it more clearly in the first place? Furthermore, helpful explanation – 'this is what *really* happened' – may suggest privileged knowledge in the part of the narrator, who, as the voice of the saga author, is the only one who can presume to see beneath the surface of people and events.

Information

It is fundamental to our understanding of the Icelandic family saga that there is a significant distance between the time in which the saga is set – the *söguöld* – and the date of the composition of the saga as it has come down to us. Of course, the precise extent of this distance is uncertain because we know so very little of the oral prehistory of sagas – that is, in what sort of form they might have existed, in part or in whole, before they were set down in manuscript. Nevertheless, we can assume that the narrator and the original saga audience were separated in time, probably by several centuries, from the events and characters which are the subject of the narrative. As a contemporary audience, we ourselves are of course even further distanced, although we are on the same temporal continuum. It is thus not at all surprising that saga narrators step in to make observations about details specific to the *söguöld* which might be interesting or necessary for a reader or listener to know about. As I have said, I will be particularly concerned with the distinction between these two: what is simply interesting information and what is necessary to understand the story.[137] In family sagas, narrators offer different kinds of information about the past: about customs and legal matters, about pre-Christian beliefs, and about material culture. But all emphasize the gulf in time between the narrator and audience on one hand, and the events related on the other. Rather differently, comments on other literary texts, or on placenames or named topographical features, tend to emphasize the continuity between the *söguöld* and the present time of narrator and original audience.

As we have seen, there is very little 'scene-setting' description in family sagas, but narrators do on occasion offer explanations of material details which are needed to clarify what is happening in the narrative. Thus, for example, in *Eyrbyggja saga*, a slave called Egill is sent to kill a member of an opposing faction, but trips over his shoe laces as he enters the enemy hall, so that he is easily caught, forced to reveal the plan and then killed. The narrator carefully tells us that he 'hafði skúfaða skóþvengi, sem þá var siðr til' (had tasselled shoelaces, as was the fashion at that time) – one of the laces had come undone and he trod on the tassel which was dragging along the ground.[138] This is a very simple and plausible accident, but it is made clearer with the note about the change in fashion. A temporal gap is also evident in a small but striking group of such references to material details, though the details are not always crucial to understanding what is happening. This seems to be the case in a half-comical scene in *Laxdœla saga* in which Halldórr, the son of Óláfr pái, is being pressurized into agreeing to a land deal. The prospective buyers position themselves so closely on either side of him that they are pretty well sitting on his cloak. The narrator tells us that Halldórr's cloak is fastened with a long brooch, 'sem var þá títt' (as was customary then).[139] When Halldórr, outraged by their bullying, tries to jump up, the brooch is torn away from the cloak. The narrator focuses on the period detail of Halldórr's cloak fastening, emphasizing the difference in time between the characters' then and the contemporary audience's now, but the detail is not strictly crucial to an understanding of the narrative. Other examples of such period details relate to the layout of dwelling places: in *Grettis saga* the interior of Grettir's father's farmhouse, with its central fires, and the setting up of tables at mealtimes, is carefully described, although again an understanding of the narrative does not depend on this description.[140] Slightly differently, in *Laxdœla saga*, Kjartan's humiliation of his enemies by blocking access to the lavatories would be hard to envisage without the understanding that the lavatories were in an outhouse a fair distance from the farmhouse itself. But whether an original audience would actually need the narrator's helpful aside that this was the arrangement in those days is a moot point; in a cursory reference to a similar siege the author of *Íslendinga saga* does not bother to explain that the facilities were outdoors.[141] Once again, it seems that the detail is simply a marker of the 'pastness' of the setting.

It can be hard to determine the authenticity of the information about the past. If we know, or assume, that the detail is authentic, then one important implication – especially in cases in which clarification is crucial to envisaging what is happening – is that the story being recounted itself originated in that past. So, for example, the episode in *Grettis saga* in which Grettir is urged by the crew of his Norway-bound boat to lend a hand with the bailing buckets would make no sense without the narrator's clarification that at that time bailing had to be done by hand, even in ocean-going boats, a practice incidentally attested in other sagas. It could well be, therefore, that the episode originated in that early period.[142]

Differences in legal practices are also carefully drawn attention to, and again it can be hard to determine whether the references to old laws are reliably authentic or not. In *Gísla saga*, for example, when Vésteinn is murdered in his bed, his sister, Gísli's wife Auðr, calls for a slave, Þórðr inn huglausi, to pull the weapon out of Vésteinn's body. The narrator explains: 'Þat var þá mælt, at sá væri skyldr at hefna, er vápni kippði ór sári; en þat váru kölluð launvíg, en eigi morð' (It was then the case that whoever pulled a weapon from a wound would be obliged to avenge it; and that was termed a secret manslaughter, and not murder).[143] The narrator characteristically fails to explain why Auðr urges a cowardly slave to pull out the spear – perhaps because if the slave was forced to take vengeance, and was then killed in retaliation, he would be a dispensable person? In any event, Þórðr is so very cowardly that he is afraid to go near the dead body, and Gísli himself takes on the responsibility. Here we have comedy and tragedy closely intertwined in this farcical aftermath of Vésteinn's murder, but the distinction claimed between secret manslaughter and murder is not borne out anywhere else in the sources.[144]

Sometimes, the narrator seems to assume a lack of historical legal knowledge on the part of the audience. In *Hrafnkels saga*, for example, the chieftain who is helping Sámr in his case against Hrafnkell instructs Sámr what must happen by law after someone has had a judgement made against them at the Alþing: he explains – surely ventriloquizing legal formulae – that Hrafnkell's outlawry will not come into force until a *féránsdómr* (court of confiscation) is set up, and that this court must be held within fourteen days of the *vápnatak*. In a clear narratorial intervention, the narrator adds: 'En þat heitir vápnatak, er alþýða ríðr af þingi' (and it is called *vápnatak* [the taking up of weapons] when everyone rides away from the assembly).[145] This information seems to be an accurate reflection of early Icelandic law.[146] We can only presume that the narrator did not expect the audience to recognize the meaning of the term, and felt that glossing was necessary. The timing of the court of confiscation – information provided here as the chieftain's direct speech instructions to Sámr – is crucial in the narrative of events, but it is not crucial that the narrator should use and gloss the technical term *vápnatak*. It is of course possible that the narrator was simply showing off legal knowledge. This certainly seems to be the case in *Eyrbyggja saga*, when, after the death of the widely admired chieftain Arnkell, we are told that there was general dissatisfaction about the prosecution of his killers because he only had female heirs. The narrator adds that 'þá fœrðu landsstjórnarmenn lög á því, at aldri síðan skyldi kona vera vígsakarðili né yngri karlmaðr en sextán vetra, ok hefir þat haldizk jafnan síðan' (then the leading men in the country made it law that never afterward should a woman, or a man under the age of sixteen, prosecute a case for manslaughter, and that has been the law ever since).[147] This is simply learned information, with no bearing on the narrative at this point.[148] But we should note how continuity in time between the *söguöld* on the one hand and the time of the narrator and a contemporary audience on the other is established: not only was it different in the past, but also, having been changed then, it remains the same now.

Information about placenames and topographical features in family sagas also underlines the continuity between saga events and the actual world of the narrator and audience. Events and characters in the narrative are identified as having given rise to placenames which are said to be still current, though not all are still current nowadays. Thus, for example, the place where Sámr left behind the horses when he ambushed Hrafnkell's farm 'heita þar síðan Hrossageilar' (has been called Hrossageilar [horse glens] ever since).[149] Family sagas are full of such placename references. Whilst often the origin of the name is obvious and uncontroversial, simply deriving from the name of a saga character who lived (or died) there, occasionally it appears that the saga author, or one of his predecessors, has resorted to back derivation – that is, a story has been invented to explain a name. A set of good examples comes at the beginning of *Laxdœla saga*, as the settlement in Iceland of the great matriarch Unnr in djúpúðga is related. We are told that the headland in Breiðafjörðr where she and her fellow settlers stopped for a morning meal 'er síðan kallat Dögurðarnes' (has been called Dögurðarnes [Breakfast-Ness] ever since), and a headland where Unnr supposedly lost a comb 'heitir síðan Kambsnes' (has since been called Kambsnes [Comb-Ness]).[150] These look very much like back derivations. But the important point here is not the authenticity of the name and/or the story, but the emphasis on the unbroken linearity of time between the *söguöld* and the saga narrative.

References to topographical features also stress this continuity. The past may have been a foreign country to L. P. Hartley's narrator Leo, but for medieval Icelanders the past took place not just in their own locality, but in a physical setting sometimes barely changed from the *söguöld* itself. One of the commonest formulae repeated in connexion with man-made features in the landscape is that 'sér enn þess merki' (traces of this can still be seen).[151] Sometimes, more straightforwardly, the continuity is indicated simply by the use of the present tense: an event is said to have happened 'at a place which is called ... '. And, on occasion, the saga narrator will describe, again using the present tense, the natural topography: in *Hrafnkels saga*, for example, Fljotsdalsheiðr 'er ... grýtt mjök ok blaut' (is very stony and soft); and Bersagötur 'er svarðlauss mýrr' (is a grassless bog).[152] Three times in *Grettis saga* reference is made to large boulders which Grettir is said in the narrative to have lifted, proving his superhuman might.[153] Grettir is such a celebrated saga hero that it's perfectly likely that stories alluding to his strength became attached to certain landscape features between the *söguöld* and the composition of the saga as we have it. But one of the most startling examples of establishing continuity between past and (saga) present occurs in *Grettis saga* as an entailment of Grettir's killing of Þorbjörn and his teenage son, which I discussed earlier in this chapter as an example of narrative *impassibilité*. Grettir cannot find the spear he hurled at Þorbjörn, but towards the end of the chapter, we are told that it has since been found, and that the spot it was discovered is 'nú' (now) called Spjótsmýrr (Spear-Swamp).[154] But the time of finding is, remarkably, described as 'í þeira manna minnum, er nú lífa' (within living memory) – specifically, 'á ofanverðum dögum Sturlu lögmanns Þórðarsonar' (towards the end of lawspeaker Sturla Þórðarson's time) – and we know that Sturla died in 1284.[155] Here, the narrator's situation nearer the present time of the medieval audience than the time of the story is made entirely explicit, and that audience is invited to identify with that position and see events in the saga in relation to it, and themselves.

In contrast to narratorial comment on placenames underlining the unbroken flow of time from past – the *söguöld* – to the present of the original audience (and, of course, sometimes, to our own present, at least where Icelandic topography has not changed radically since that time), the major discontinuity between past and present in Icelandic history is the shift from pre-Christian to Christian Iceland.[156] This shift was not, of course, as sudden or as absolute as the sources seem to imply. There were Christians living in Iceland before the conversion, and after Christian laws were adopted, some pre-Christian practices were by law allowed to continue for a transitional period; no doubt these and other practices also continued illicitly, and unreported, for some time.[157] Nevertheless, by the time the family sagas came into being, their authors, in commenting on a pre-Christian past, are looking back a long way, and it can be hard to know whether their remarks on pre-Christian beliefs and practices are authentic representations of the past.

As has often been noted, the author of *Eyrbyggja saga* is unusually keen to make reference to conditions and beliefs in the *söguöld*. However, as discussed earlier, the celebrated description of a pagan temple, for example, has been said to owe more to the influence of Christian church architecture than to knowledge of heathen temples.[158] Popular beliefs which are not attested elsewhere in medieval sources are also impossible to verify. In the same saga, for example, when the ghosts of drowned men return to the farmhouse at Fróðá to attend their own funeral feast, dripping with water, the living are pleased to see them, 'því at þetta þótti góðr fyrirburðr, því at þá höfðu menn þat fyrir satt, at þá væri mönnum vel fagnat at Ránar, ef sædauðir menn vitjuðu erfis síns; en þá var enn lítt af numin forneskjan, þó at menn væri skírðir ok kristnir at kalla' (because this was thought to be a good omen, because then people believed that drowned men had been well received by Rán [a sea goddess] if they came to their own funeral; there was then still some remaining heathen belief, even though people were baptized, and identified as Christians).[159] This particular belief is not otherwise attested in Old Icelandic literature, but may well have been a pre-Christian tradition associated with drownings. Elsewhere in the saga, when Steinþórr of Eyrr shoots a spear over the heads of his approaching enemies, we are told that this was 'at fornum sið til heilla sér' (according to the old custom, to get good luck).[160] In the eddic poem *Völuspá*, Óðinn shoots a spear above his enemies to inaugurate the very first battle that ever was; it is hard to know whether the saga author derived his detail from folk memory of traditional belief, or from a literary source.[161] In the same way, the narrator notes of the Swedish berserks in *Eyrbyggja saga* that they are completely exhausted once their *berserksgangr* (berserk fit) is over, 'sem háttr er þeira manna, sem eigi eru einhama' (as is customary with shape-shifters). Whatever about the actuality of berserks, here the casual present tense suggests a reference to an existing literary source.[162] On occasion, the narrator is keen to stress the gulf between past and present even when there is no specific knowledge to accompany it: for example, Þórólfr bægifótr's body is said to be made ready for burial 'eptir siðvenju' (according to custom) but no detail is given.[163] In all such instances, the narrator is stressing the pastness of the past – a very different place, if not a foreign country. Family sagas are not simply related in the conventional past tense of narrative; they are actually about the past.

Judgemental responses

Given that family saga authors are Christian, relating events set largely in the pre-Christian *söguöld*, it is not surprising that it is in connexion with reports of heathen beliefs and customs that we do, finally, hear an interventive narratorial voice breaking through the customary *impassibilité* of saga narration. Thus, for example, with regard to narratorial analepsis and interventive comment occurring together, the witchcraft of Þorgrímr nef (nose) in *Gísla saga* twice attracts the opprobrium of the narrator, who refers to it being practised 'með allri ergi ok skelmiskap' (with all possible perversity and devilry).[164] If the narrator or author were a cleric, this is just the sort of comment one might expect to break through the narratorial silence, but as I noted earlier, the response could just as well be scribal. There are also examples of narrators praising pre-Christian Icelanders for their virtue. In *Laxdœla saga,* for example, in the trial by ordeal I have already discussed, the defendant Þorkell trefill is so anxious about failing the trial (and thereby losing a large inheritance) that he rigs the fall of turf which would signify his guilt. The narrator notes, 'Ekki þóttusk heiðnir menn minna eiga í átbyrgð, þá er slíka hluti skyldi fremja, en nú þykkjask eiga kristnir men, þá er skírslur eru görvar' (heathens did not feel that they had less at stake when such practices were performed, than Christians do now when ordeals are set up).[165] Such endorsement of previous generations is evident also in the post-conversion setting of *Grettis saga*. Even though the farmers of Skagafjörðr have suffered marauding from Grettir, when they are fooled into making a truce with him they nevertheless keep to its terms, prompting the narrator to note – with a characteristically displaced judgement – that everyone felt that they had behaved honourably in this. But then a comment is added: 'ok má af slíku marka, hverir dyggðarmenn þá váru, slíkar sakar sem Grettir hafði gört við þá' (and this is a clear indication of what worthy men they were, given the trouble Grettir had caused them).[166]

There are also some rare occasions when we seem to hear a distinct narratorial voice reacting and responding directly to a narrative event or character. In *Laxdæla saga*, for example, we have the celebrated episode of the vengeful wife Auðr, whose husband divorces her on the grounds that she wears men's trousers. As she sets off on her mission to kill the husband, with what will prove to be a blatantly phallic sword thrust into him while he is asleep in his bed, the narrator describes how she leaps on to her horse, noting slyly: 'ok var hon þá at vísu í brókum' (and she was certainly wearing trousers then).[167] In *Gísla saga*, it is commented about Þórðr inn huglausi that 'þat var mjök jafnfœrt um vit ok hugrekki, því at hvárki var neitt til' (he had sense and courage in equal measure, because he had none of either).[168] And in the same saga, Gísli confesses publicly to the killing of his brother-in-law Þorgrímr by reciting a skaldic strophe 'er æva skyldi' (which should never have been [spoken]).[169]

In the two last cases, the comment seems to be an addition in a single manuscript – in other words, it may mark an individual scribal response. The distinction between grades of storyteller is a very speculative one. However, it logically holds true of all narratorial comment that, with an unknown and unknowable oral prehistory, sagas as they have come down to us may not be the product of one 'author', or one narrator, but the accumulated product of an unknown number of re-tellings, of equally unknowable extent. In the cases discussed above, we may very well be seeing a scribe responding to a pre-existing narrative, and being provoked into setting down a comment. Perhaps, then, the most remarkable thing is that such comments are so rare: in other words, that there seems to have existed a generally recognized – and near-consistently adhered to – set of stylistic conventions, featuring a self-effacing narrator, and the avoidance of such apparently off-the-cuff comments on the storyworld as the narrative unfolds.

Explanations

We have already seen examples of narrators guiding an audience through the complex interweaving and parallel stranding of the many individual narratives which make up a family saga, noting when a character may be making a final exit from the saga, for example, or when we should watch out for a reappearance. It is only a short step from this to narratorial comments which serve to explain what is happening in the narrative, comments which also mediate the substance of the narrative to an audience, helping readers and listeners through it. On the face of it, it might seem that any explanation of what was 'actually' going on might betray what I have called 'privileged epistemic access' on the part of the narrator – that is, a knowledge of character and event which an observer or reporter could not know (and which we as inhabitants of a real world cannot know about those around us). Such privileged knowledge marks a watershed, because it is symptomatic of fiction, and is essentially authorial privilege. I shall explore some remarkable instances at the end of this chapter. However, it may be helpful at this point to introduce the concept of the reasonable surmise: that is, an explanation which is helpful, but not revealing of something we or the narrator could not possibly know without the privileged knowledge which pertains to authorship.

There are examples of helpful – but not actually crucial – narratorial explanations in all of the sagas I have been considering in this book. In almost all cases, the comment makes clearer something which could fairly easily have been surmised by an attentive reader. When in *Grettis saga* we are told that Grettir makes a journey to seek out an outlaw called Grímr in order to take vengeance on him, only to find that he had left the district years ago, the narrator is careful to inform us that Grettir had not heard about Grímr's departure because he'd been in hiding for the past three years, and 'hafði enga menn fundit, þá er honum vildi nökkurar fréttir segja' (hadn't come across people who had wanted to tell him any news).[170] This looks very like a narrator – or a scribe, for that matter – anticipating an objection from an attentive listener, or querying Grettir's wasted journey, and stepping in to address the gap in the story: another strategy for managing the narrative, in fact.

In *Gísla saga*, Gísli's enemies send two spies to locate his hiding place, and we are told that they have been sent out to cut down timber, but that in fact, 'þó at þetta væri yfirbragð á þeira ferð, þá bjó hitt undir, at þeir skyldu leita at Gísli' (although that was the ostensible reason for their journey, the real reason was that they were to look for Gísli).[171] Given that this is the second attempt for one of spies, we do not really need the narrator's rather clumsy explanation of such a simple and obvious plan. In the third time of this narrative, as in real life, we can make reasonable assumptions about the motives of those around us.

But there is a very fine line between what we might infer from commonsensical surmise and what only the privileged knowledge of a narrator can reveal to us. To explore this boundary, I will look in further detail at the reasons given for Vermundr inn mjóvi's purchase of a pair of berserks in *Eyrbyggja saga*. Vermundr travels to Norway, and becomes a retainer of Hákon jarl (Earl Hákon Sigurðsson). Hákon has staying with him a pair of Swedish berserks, formidable warriors who 'fóru galnir sem hundar ok óttuðusk hvárki eld né járn' (raged like mad dogs and feared neither fire nor iron).[172] When Vermundr announces his intention of returning to Iceland, Hákon jarl offers to make him a gift of anything in his possession. Vermundr chooses the berserks. The narrator steps in here with an explanatory comment: Vermundr, we are told, is acting in the belief that he will get on better in Iceland if he has these fierce berserks as followers. It might be said that any reader or listener might reasonably infer this motivation without its being made explicit. But the narrator, crucially, goes further: Vermundr 'þótti Styrr bróðir sinn mjök sitja yfir sínum hlut ok hafa ójafnað við sik ... hugði hann, at Styr myndi þykkja ódælla við sik at eiga, ef hann hefði slíka fylgðarmenn sem þeir brœðr váru' (thought that his brother Styrr was lording it over him, and bullying him ... he reckoned that Styrr wouldn't find it so easy to take him on if he [Vermundr] had such supporters).[173]

We have not been told about such relations between these two brothers. This is a narratorial revelation – although significantly, it fits well with what we do know of the two Icelandic brothers. Styrr has been described in the saga as a man who has killed many men, and refused to pay compensation – a classic case of the *ójafnaðarmaðr*, the unjust man or bully. In addition, we need only attend to their names: Styrr is known in this saga and others as Víga-Styrr, literally Killer-Styrr, and the forename Styrr itself means 'disorder', or 'tumult'. A brother nicknamed *inn mjóvi* (the slender), the youngest in the family, would clearly benefit from the brawny support of two outsized berserks. One might argue that Vermundr's motivation in making what proves to be a very unwise choice of gift by requesting the berserks is so obvious that we do not need to be told about the relationship between the brothers. But what is significant is that the narrator has explicitly told us something which has required privileged access to a character's interiority. This access is of course most obviously gained by invention: relating what is going on in a character's mind requires authorial omniscience, which is one of the major elements of the rhetoric of fiction. One could argue that the narrator has here simply inferred in a commonsensical way an apparent interiority which amounts to little more than an insightful surmise. But in doing so, the saga narrator unequivocally ascribes a motivation to Vermundr – we are not left to draw our own conclusions, or to ponder possibilities, as we so often are in family saga narrative. By stating a motivation, the narrator has closed down speculation. I want to conclude this chapter with a close reading of more striking forays into this sort of fictionality, this time from *Hrafnkels saga*, looking especially at the way the narrator asserts authority rather than leaving matters to audience speculation.

When Hrafnkell's newly hired shepherd Einarr – the son of one of his neighbours – violates a taboo about riding Hrafnkell's sacred stallion Freyfaxi, Hrafnkell kills him. Hrafnkell has publicly vowed to kill anyone who rides the stallion, and he is making no exceptions, even though, as we have seen, immediately before delivering the fatal blow, he praises the boy's honesty in admitting the violation. It is at this moment that the narrator steps in to clarify exactly what is motivating Hrafnkell: 'En við þann átrúnað, at ekki verði at þeim mönnum, er heitstrengingar fella á sik, þá hljóp hann af baki til hans ok hjó hann banahögg' (and with the belief that no good comes of people who break solemn vows, he leapt down from his horse towards [the boy] and dealt him a fatal blow).[174] Since Hrafnkell has already told Einarr that he would have forgiven him one offence if he hadn't sworn the oath, then we might well surmise that the oath was uppermost in Hrafnkell's mind when he killed the boy. But having the narrator state this unequivocally makes a big difference to our reception of the narrative. In effect, the saga author has chosen *not* to allow an audience to speculate on a range of possibilities. And given that revelation of deep interiority is ineluctably fictional, the saga author could have invented, or the audience imagined, any number of alternative – or cumulative – motivations. Our attitude to Hrafnkell's character would be entirely different, for example, if we were told that Hrafnkell actively welcomed the opportunity to kill someone, or, by contrast, if we were told that Hrafnkell was reluctant, or regretful, about the killing. If Hrafnkell is shown as feeling he had no choice then effectively there is no need to show him making an ethical decision about the killing, and by the same token, this excuses us from judging him – at least in moral terms.

He did not have a motive as such – he simply had no choice, and the saga author, as I have said, closes down speculation with the explicit and extra-diegetic statement of this.

In his insightful study of ambiguity in *Hrafnkels saga*, William Ian Miller shows how the saga author cultivates ambiguity, rendering the narrative both complex and profoundly engaging for its audience.[175] It is all the more striking then, that it is in this saga that we have some instances of such marked disambiguation. Earlier in the saga, the narrator steps in to reveal (i.e. invent) Einarr's original motivation in riding the sacred stallion in spite of Hrafnkell's explicit warning not to. Having lost his sheep he at first tries to saddle one of Hrafnkell's mares. When, mysteriously, they all shy away from him, and only Freyfaxi stands still, he disobeys Hrafnkell's injunction not to ride the horse. His stated motivation is again highly significant for our reception of his character. Einarr 'hyggr, at Hrafnkell mundi eiga vita, þótt hann riði hestinum' (thinks that Hrafnkell wouldn't find out even if he did ride the horse).[176] Given that the saga author could have invented any motivation at this point in the narrative, we can imagine different motivations giving an audience very different views of Einarr's character. For instance, we might have been told, or supposed, that Einarr weighed up his options and decided (wrongly) that Hrafnkell would rather see Freyfaxi ridden than his sheep lost. Or we might have been told, or supposed, that Einarr, in contrast to Hrafnkell, did not set much store by solemn vows to pagan gods. Instead, we are shown in Einarr a character who knows that he is doing the wrong thing, but sneakily presumes that it doesn't matter because, in his remote pasture, he will not be found out. Interesting here is that the narrator's unambiguous statement of Einarr's motivation complicates rather than confirms our sympathies: Einarr is now not so much the victim of an autocratic and ruthless chieftain as a calculating and sly transgressor of an openly stated rule.

We see a similar guiding of the audience's sympathies in my third example of narratorial intervention. Hrafnkell is prosecuted for the killing by Einarr's ambitious lawyer cousin, Sámr. Hrafnkell is dismissive of Sámr's court case against him, and does not even bother to turn up to present a defence. But unexpectedly, and with help from a powerful chieftain and his brother, Sámr makes a persuasive case, and packs the area around the court with supporters. When Hrafnkell is told that things are going against him, he rushes to the court, and we are told what is in his mind: 'Hafði hann þat í hug sér at leiða smámönnum at sœkja mál á hendr honum. Ætlaði hann at hleypa upp dóminum fyrir Sámi ok hrekja hann af málinu' (His intention was to put off his inferiors from taking out court cases against him. He meant to break up the court in front of Sámr and drive him off the case).¹⁷⁷ But Hrafnkell cannot get near the judges to present his defence, and the decision goes with Sámr. Here, Hrafnkell is deprived of his legal rights, even though it was because he did not take Sámr's opposition seriously enough. This might shift audience sympathy in his favour. But countering this, Hrafnkell's bullying and disdainful attitude, as well as his contempt for legal process, one of the great achievements of *söguöld* society, are plainly stated. Here, the narratorial intervention expresses a fundamental feature of fictional narrative: the relationship between the inner life of the individual and the society around them. But in doing so, the narrator also asserts the ultimate control which is the preserve of the author of fiction.

5

Withheld knowledge

In this final chapter, I shall examine the imperfect knowledge which arises when the narrator purposefully omits or delays certain items of narrative information that are notably conspicuous by their absence, and this is evident either in the present moment of narration, or retrospectively. Sometimes the narrator even alludes, teasingly, to the act of omission. This is different from the imperfect knowledge of an audience moving through narrative time without the explicit guidance of a narrative voice. But it is also analogous to our experience of real lived time, of being situated in a present in which we do not know the full details of the past – that is, the circumstances which have created our present moment – or even the full circumstances of our present. And again, rather as in life, some things become clear with the passage of time, or are made known to us at some point, whilst others remain forever unknown: saga authors sometimes never do make known the missing elements. This is in contrast to most kinds of fictional narrative – especially novelistic ones – which typically reveal, by the time of the denouement of the story, all the information which has been withheld by some means. The revelation of missing information – whether gradually, in the course of a narrative, or dramatically, at its closure – is at the heart of what is generally experienced as plot. Plot involves the disarrangement and then 'tidying up' of the third time of narrative, so that our experience of a plotted narrative is clearly different from our sense of lived time, or, indeed, our experience of the majority of saga narrative.[1]

The withholding of information in conventional narratives can be accomplished in a number of ways: by simple, unremarked omission, or by some more obvious strategy, such as the delayed introduction of a character from the story so far who is in possession of some crucial fact, or the contrived absence of a witness to events because of illness, death or some other kind of silencing or removal from the present moment of the story. In the context of saga narratology, withholding knowledge can be facilitated by means of some of the familiar techniques of saga narrative I have outlined in previous chapters. It can be achieved, for instance, through the absence of narratorial comment on a puzzling or incomplete storyline, or the avoidance of interiority by an external narrator who typically reports only what can be observed or heard. But when the knowledge is at first delayed, and then revealed in due course in the narrative – though never at the very end of the saga, as a total, conclusive denouement – we may recognize self-contained elements of plots.[2]

I will begin with instances of the delaying of information with which, in hindsight, we can make sense of, or provide some closure to, what happened, because what has been absent in the story so far is suddenly revealed to us. Sometimes, the narrator may intervene directly in the narrative to allude to what is not being related, producing what might be called a 'conspicuous silence'.[3] As we shall see, the narrator sometimes rather oddly sets up what seems to herald a conspicuous silence by stating that certain characters had a private conversation which no one could hear, but then relates the dialogue. I will next move on to look at those very distinctive examples of withheld knowledge in which the narrative never supplies the missing element, and a pressing question remains unanswered. This equates to the experience of lived time in the real world when we never do find out what happened. I will then look at two examples of withheld knowledge involving the avoidance of interiority in the presentation of characters. Here, the narrative leaves open the question of motive – why did a character do (or not do) such and such? – rather like the absence of narratorial comment discussed in Chapter 4, and the omission serves to engage the audience in speculation. However, the fact that the question remains unanswered – even if only briefly – has here a clear and crucial bearing on the subsequent story: the silence which ensues is itself a narrative event which causes or allows what happens next. Finally, remaining with the absence of authorial omniscience and the avoidance of interiority, I will consider one stretch of narrative in which uncertainty, in this case concerning the attitude and motives of the main character, produces a classic example of narrative suspense. In due course, the uncertainty is clearly resolved, in the manner of all simple suspense plots.

To withhold knowledge, the saga author must manipulate the order of the narrative, choosing not only what to include (or not) but also, and most crucially, *when* to include it. This can only be done by a saga author with an apprehension of the whole saga – of the past, present and future of the story – from the *totum simul* perspective outside the saga. Of course, an audience who knows the story will, like its author, know what happens next, and how things will turn out. Their enjoyment of and engagement with the narrative will be different, but not, I shall argue, diminished. I shall address this issue of multiple readings or hearings as we go along, but especially in relation to the final, suspenseful episode.

Delayed disclosure

I begin with a narrative episode which illustrates very clearly the way in which silently withheld knowledge followed by a revelation later in the narrative seems to show the hallmarks of we might label as plot. In *Eyrbyggja saga*, Snorri Þorgrímsson, who will later become the formidable chieftain Snorri goði, travels abroad with his two foster-brothers; it is worth noting that here we have the familiar folk tale triad of three brothers.[4] Snorri is funded by his uncle, Börkr, who is also his stepfather, having married his brother's widow, Snorri's mother. Börkr very decently gives Snorri fifty ounces of silver to finance his travels. We hear little about their stay in Norway, but on their return to Iceland, the narrative voice describes the way one of Snorri's foster-brothers has decked himself out with showy purchases: he 'keypti þann hest, er hann fekk beztan; hann hafði ok steindan söðul allglæsiligan, hann hafði búit sverð ok gullrekit spjót, myrkblán skjöld ok mjök gyldan, vönduð öll klæði' (bought the best horse he could get; he had a decorated saddle too, all shiny, he had an ornamented sword and a spear inlaid with gold, a lavishly gilded dark blue shield [and] elaborate clothing).[5] This is in marked contrast to Snorri's appearance: he 'var í svartri kápu ok reið svörtu merhrossi góðu; hann hafði fornan trogsöðul ok vápn lítt til fegrðar búin' (wore a black cloak and rode a decent black mare; he had an old trough-shaped saddle and [his] weapons were not much decorated).[6] Goldilocks-style, the third brother's appearance is somewhere between the two.[7] The narrator makes no comment whatsoever on this difference, and there is no attempt to explain – at this point in the story – what its significance might be, although it is possible that a first-time reader or listener acutely sensitive to the norms of family saga narrative might be alerted by this inclusion of a passage of apparently gratuitous description.

We are told that when Snorri gets back to his stepfather's home at Helgafell, he is mocked for his poor appearance, and that Börkr believes that he must have spent all his travel money unwisely. The narrator makes no comment on whether Börkr is right in this assumption. The narrative then turns to a dramatic and apparently unrelated incident in which Börkr instructs Snorri and his mother Þórdís to welcome his cousin Eyjólfr, who was responsible for the killing of Gísli Súrsson, Þórdís's own brother. Þórdís tries to stab Eyjólfr, and Snorri is involved in the subsequent fracas when he defends his mother against a blow from Börkr.[8] The winter passes quietly, but at the spring assembly Snorri announces his decision to claim his inheritance and sever ties with Börkr. Börkr grants that they cannot share the farm at Helgafell, and suggests that he buy out Snorri, who agrees to the idea of a buy out, but reserves the right to decide who gets the whole farm whilst leaving the valuation of the property to Börkr. It is only now that Snorri's poorly equipped return from Norway assumes its significance, although the narrator does not make the connexion explicit. We are simply told that Börkr supposes that Snorri will not have enough money to buy the whole estate. He therefore makes a low valuation of the land, which he will of course benefit from if, as he expects, he buys Snorri's share. But Snorri has deceived him: he has more than enough ready money to pay for all the land, Börkr is bought out, and in spite of a last-ditch attempt by Börkr to go back to sharing the estate, he is forced to move out. Snorri takes charge, and Þórdís divorces her husband on grounds of his violence towards her.[9] If the denouement of this story thread is Snorri's appropriation of Helgafell, this is its closure. In retrospect, all the elements click into place.

The absence of comment on this clever and comprehensive outwitting of Börkr means that a first-time audience can only in retrospect realize the significance of Snorri's modest appearance on his return from Norway: he has been saving his money. For an audience who knows the story, there is a different pleasure in following the playing out of Snorri's plan: enjoying anticipating the discomfiture of Börkr, whose championing of Gísli's killers and threat of violence towards his wife Þórdís mark him out as an unsympathetic character.[10] Knowing the story in advance means that the audience knows what Börkr does not know – *yet* – which is that he has underestimated his stepson and nephew Snorri, and therefore made a tactical error in deliberately underestimating the value of Helgafell. Plot may function as a way of indicating which characters in a narrative should be accorded praise or blame.[11] As we know well, praise or blame is not routinely delivered in the narrative voice in family sagas.[12] Here, the silence of the narrative voice and the withholding of information create a miniature plot which has the effect of blaming Börkr, and either we can enjoy knowing more than he does, and anticipating his discomfiture, or just enjoy the revelation on a first hearing or reading.

But even advance knowledge of what happens is not enough to answer another question left unanswered by the silence of the narrative voice: did Snorri plan all this as early as the trip to Norway, or was it rather that his customary prudence, in contrast to the profligate ostentation of his foster-brother, happened to serve him well? Snorri's characteristic unreadability is already evident in this episode: his mother reacts angrily to the suggestion that her household welcome Gísli's killers, but Snorri 'lét sér fátt finnask um þessi tíðendi' (did not make much of this news).[13] However, it is only after he has settled at Helgafell that the narrative voice provides an explicit account of his calculating and inscrutable nature: 'fann lítt á honum, hvárt honum þótti vel eða illa' (it was hard to tell whether he thought well or ill of things).[14] This is the kind of character sketch which would more usually accompany the introduction of a figure into the narrative; here, this critical aspect of his character is shown to us in the narrative before we are told about it.

A second example of withheld knowledge which is retrospectively revealed also involves Snorri goði, but introduces the intriguing issue of the kind of conspicuous silence in which the narrator draws attention to what is not being reported in the narrative. I have already analysed the story line in *Eyrbyggja saga* concerning Vermundr inn mjóvi's unwise choice of a pair of berserks as a gift from the king of Sweden, and how back in Iceland he is forced to beg his brother Styrr to take them off his hands. As the saga proceeds, we learn that Styrr himself finds the berserks difficult to control, and when one of them announces that he wants to marry Styrr's daughter Ásdís, Styrr consults his friend and confidant Snorri goði about how best to proceed.[15] The narrator sets up the consultation in tantalizing detail: Styrr announces that he needs to talk, Snorri asks if it's a difficult problem, and Styrr ruefully concedes that it is. Snorri suggests that they climb the holy mountain Helgafell, because 'þau ráð hafa sízt at engu orðit, er þar hafa ráðin verit' (plans made there have less chance of coming to nothing).[16] But just when a first-time audience looks forward to hearing a cunning plan from Snorri, the saga author produces instead a conspicuous silence: 'sátu þar á tali allt til kvelds; vissi þat engi maðr, hvat þeir tölu ðu' (they sat there talking right until the evening, [and] no one knew what they were talking about).[17] This is a classic example of the conspicuous silence technique. And as Ruth Rosaler rightly notes, 'teasingly, conspicuously withheld information draws attention to the author's ultimate control of what is communicated and how it is communicated'.[18] Most obviously here, it also increases the tension, especially given the careful build-up to the silence. It also skilfully frees up the ensuing narrative so that how Snorri's advice is enacted – in this case, killing the berserks using some slapstick violence involving a sauna and an ox-hide – can be shown in all its comic drama without cluttering the narrative with explanation, or pre-empting it. And finally, it ostensibly preserves the stance of the external narrator, the narrator who stands outside the narrative and further, only relates what might be observed, heard or reported within the diegesis itself. Snorri's plan remains a secret within the storyworld, and also to the audience outside it, until we can retrospectively infer and thus reconstruct it.

However, saga authors do often breach this appearance of externality, and there are a number of instances of allusions to secret planning which are immediately followed by a full report of the content of the advice. In such cases, information, far from being withheld, is made known even when doing so involves overstepping the usual norms of saga narratology. Right at the beginning of the *Njáls saga,* for instance, when Unnr tells her father about her unsatisfactory sex life with Hrútr, it seems at first that the narrator is setting up a conspicuous silence: 'Þá gengu þau á tal, þar er engir menn heyrðu þeira viðrmæli' (then they went to speak where no one could hear what they said).[19] But their conversation – both Unnr's description of her husband's failed attempts at intercourse, and Mörðr's plan for a divorce – is then narrated in an extended detailed dialogue. To relate what Unnr and her father spoke about in private is to breach the externality of the narrative voice; the narrator seems to have claimed privileged access to their conversation, like a hidden camera or a fly on the wall. And in fact, almost all sagas contain plenty of instances of such privileged access, relating dialogue which could not have been observed or heard. In any case, common sense tells us that the long stretches of dialogue in saga narratives could not actually have been passed down intact in oral tradition, and must therefore be the saga author's invention, or at least, elaboration, even if they were openly spoken. Indeed, as I have noted, a high proportion of dialogue has been proposed as one of the indices of the fictionality of particular sagas.[20] But this is a long-standing convention of various kinds of non-fictional narratives. In biographical works, for example, dialogue (and even interiority) has always served to enliven the narrative for readers or listeners; as Paul Ricœur points out, 'the reader [has always been] prepared to accord the historian the exorbitant right to know other minds. In the name of this right, ancient historians did not hesitate to place in the mouths of their heroes invented discourses, which the documents did not guarantee, but only made plausible.'[21] If for 'documents' we read 'oral tradition', then we can say that saga authors are no different.

Why, then, the need for the gesture towards a conspicuous silence, inevitably drawing attention to the non-naturalistic reportage, and in any case undermined by the subsequent relation of what was said? Clearly, what is being discussed between Unnr and Mörðr is a delicate, private matter, and the saga author makes this evident by explicitly stressing the confidentiality of their talk. When invited by her father to make her case against Hrútr in front of her husband, his brother and other men, the year before, Unnr had been silent. The key point here is that the saga author is making a distinction between public utterance and private conversation *within the diegesis*. While we often take for granted the privacy of conversations in more modern narratives, in medieval societies with closely communal living conditions such confidentiality might well have needed to be specifically indicated. In narratological terms, indicating private conversation in the storyworld opens up a gap between what we, as audience, know, and what the other characters in the storyworld know – and in this case, it is vital for the subsequent storyline that neither the details of Unnr's failed sex life nor Mörðr's plans for her subsequent divorce from Hrútr are known by anyone else in the diegesis. To preserve the confidentiality of the plan within the storyworld, whilst at the same time apprising the audience of what will happen, the narrator has little option but to breach externality and open up that gap.

As it turns out, there is rarely a clear distinction between creating a conspicuous silence by withholding details of a private conversation and simply indicating in the narrative that a private conversation is taking place. Again in *Njáls saga*, Hallgerðr and Þráinn Sigfússon 'töluðu ... lengi hljótt, ok vissi engi, hvat þau höfðu í ráðagerðum' (spoke secretly for a long time, and no one knew what their plans were about).[22] We learn soon enough that, although Þráinn had earlier refused to kill one of Njáll's servants, in his secret conversation with Hallgerðr they must have agreed who else to ask, and Hallgerðr must have secured a promise from Þráinn to be at least present at the killing. But did they also hatch the plan for the killing itself during that conversation, a plan which Hallgerðr next outlines to the would-be killers? Here, then, our inference of 'what will have happened' is not precisely determined by what is later revealed; scope still remains for some speculation – and therefore, audience engagement – about the content of the secret conversation.

Njáls saga in particular is filled with instances of private or secret consultations which do not have a precise fulfilment in the subsequent narrative, but allow a reader or listener to speculate on what exactly might have been said. Thus, for example, when Hallgerðr insults Njáll's sons to their face by calling them 'little dungbeards' and their father 'old beardless', their mother Bergþóra begins to goad them about taking vengeance, but Njáll's son-in-law Kári advises restraint.[23] At this point, Njáll, his sons and Kári 'tala ... lengi hljótt' (speak secretly for a long time).[24] Presumably, Kári's advice to proceed cautiously was at least part of this secret conversation, but we as audience are inspired to speculate on what might have been said, and perhaps even wish we had been flies on their wall. Of course, if the conversation was a plan not to act, then by definition it could not be played out in the subsequent narrative, except implicitly, by omission.

The narrative of *Njáls saga* is dominated by secret plans and alliances, and a further intriguing example of secret conversations within the saga occurs in the context of rallying support and making alliances. After the burning, Flosi himself needs to recruit supporters. He approaches people from Ljósavatn, asking them for help, but they are not keen, and he berates them – presumably, publicly. However, we are told that he makes a second approach to them, this time privately, and bribes and flatters them.[25] We are not told in detail what he says, but it is effective, and again, we are left to speculate. The privacy of the conversation in itself casts suspicion on its integrity. Later in the saga, when support for the prosecution of Flosi for the burning of Njáll is being rallied at the Alþing, the distinction between what remains secret and what is known in the storyworld is again interestingly blurred. Ásgrímr Elliða-Grímsson is hoping to recruit the chieftain Guðmundr inn ríki to their cause, and at first, their negotiation is fully public: as Ásgrímr makes clear: 'Ekki þarf þetta á mutr at mæla: til þess eru vér komnir hér at biðja þik øruggrar liðveizlu' (There's no need to whisper this – what we've come here for is to ask for your firm support).[26] But when Guðmundr asks about their progress with other chieftains, they speak quietly – so that others cannot hear.[27] It is not clear whether Guðmundr's subsequent promise of support for them is also confidential, or whether he voices it publicly. But having thanked him, 'töluðu lengi síðan svá, at ekki heyrðu aðrir men til' (they talked for a long time in such a way that no one else could hear them).[28] Guðmundr advises them not to humiliate themselves doing any more begging for support, but again it is not clear whether the ensuing mixture of direct and indirect speech is a narratorial account of the secret conversation, or is spoken aloud.

By contrast, when Hjálti Skeggjason has a private talk with Njáll, he feels that the right thing to do is to make his position fully public: 'Þat mun ek sýna jafnan, at ek em ekki myrkr í skapi. Njáll hefir beðit mik liðveizlu; hefi ek ok í gingit ok heitit honum mínu liðsinni. Hefir hann áðr selt mér laun ... ' (I will always make it clear that I don't have hidden plans. Njáll has asked me for support; and I have agreed and promised him my help. He has already paid me ...).[29] This is in marked contrast to the secret plotting of characters like Hallgerðr or Flosi, which has the effect of creating an ominous tension and carries, as we have seen, distinct undertones of wrongdoing or deceit. In such cases as these, the secrecy of the conversation is not so much a narrative technique as an event in the diegesis. I have discussed in detail elsewhere the scene in *Njals saga* in which Hildigunnr tries to incite her uncle Flosi to take on the duty of blood vengeance for the killing of her husband Höskuldr.³⁰ She and Flosi, in a classic example of the conspicuous silence, are said to talk together privately for a long time. In spite of the best efforts of scholars, it is very far from clear what the substance of this secret talk might have been.³¹ Perhaps its function is simply to sustain an atmosphere of tension and uncertainty.

Finally, a confidential conversation may simply be a mark of the closeness of certain characters. In the first half of *Njáls saga*, the unshakeable alliance between Gunnarr and Njáll is highlighted by the number of times they are said to discuss matters one-to-one, and the narrative fact that they are speaking in relative privacy is the key point, not the effect of withholding of the content of what they said. This is clear because the content of their discussion is withheld for practically no time at all, but almost immediately reported, and in some detail.³² Perhaps the most celebrated instances of private conversations not as withheld information, but as a mark of something else entirely, are exemplified in *Njáls saga* by the intimate conversation of Gunnarr and Hallgerðr when they first meet at the Alþing. It does not matter what they talked about; the fact of their conversation is all we need to know.³³

A particularly noteworthy episode in family saga narrative featuring withheld information and one which comes closest to producing plot is the extended story of how Höskuldr Dala-Kollsson buys a mysterious slave woman. In chapter 12 of *Laxdœla saga*, we see Höskuldr at a big trading market associated with a royal assembly in Norway. Looking around with a group of companions, Höskuldr stops at the imposing tent of a Russian merchant called Gilli. Interestingly, this episode is focalized through Höskuldr: 'sá hann tjald' (he saw the tent) and entered it, and, when the curtain is drawn back, '[s]á Höskuldr at tólf konur sátu fyrir innan tjaldit' (Höskuldr saw that twelve women were sitting inside the tent). Throughout the scene, the narrator stresses that Höskuldr is doing all the looking: he is described as carefully scrutinizing one of the women Gilli has on sale, and passing judgement on her clothing.³⁴ As is often the (unremarked) case in family saga narrative, the saga author is not simply reporting in the narrative voice what anyone at the scene might have observed, but rather, what Höskuldr himself observed. Although such focalization might seem to afford us an artificially extended viewpoint because it tells us how the scene appears from the perspective of – and therefore, in the mind of – one of the characters, in some cases our view is actually restricted if the character is blinkered, or unreliable in judgement; the narrative is limited to his or her perception of what is happening. There is also an interesting physical limitation: we can only see what one individual might have in visual range. In this episode, we are drawn right into Gilli's tent via Höskuldr's individual visual perspective, but the degree to which we can trust the situation as focalized through him naturally depends on the degree to which we trust him as a character. And Höskuldr is not an exemplary protagonist.

At the opening of the scene, Höskuldr challenges Gilli to provide him with anything he might want to buy, and when invited to elaborate, specifies a slave woman. Gilli implies that Höskuldr doesn't really want a slave woman, but is only showing off in front of his companions, making himself look impressive by asking for something the trader doesn't have.[35] Their conversation is completely unmediated by the saga author, so it is left to us to judge whether Gilli's interpretation is unfair, or whether Höskuldr is indeed just showing off. Höskuldr is not a wholly impercipient character: he judges the woman he is scrutinizing to be good-looking in spite of her shabby dress – although by definition we only have the focalizer's judgement here! – and spots at once that the price Gilli is asking is extortionate. He is not completely the innocent abroad. Nevertheless, our confidence in Höskuldr's judgement is at least a little shaken by Gilli apparently calling his bluff, and their next exchange increases any doubts we might have. Gilli offers Höskuldr a cheaper slave woman, but Höskuldr – perhaps stung by Gilli's insinuation that he is not rich enough to buy the woman he has taken a fancy to – ignores the offer and waves his purse at the merchant. In response, Gilli warns Höskuldr that the woman cannot speak. Höskuldr again ignores Gilli's reservations about her, and simply presses him to weigh the silver in his purse.[36] We may read this as Höskuldr's fixation with proving that he is a man with enough money to buy even the most expensive slave woman. But the saga author leaves us with an important question unanswered: why has Gilli put such a high price on her if she cannot speak – a failure which Gilli himself calls a major flaw? Neither the saga author nor Höskuldr – through whom the narrative is focalized, and who is thus acting as the saga author's narrative stand-in – addresses this.

There is also a rather difficult-to-read moral dimension to this episode. It is hard to know what a contemporary audience might have thought about a married man like Höskuldr buying, and sleeping with, a slave woman.[37] Any disapproval we as post-medieval readers might feel may be simply anachronistic. The issue is not raised explicitly at this point in the narrative, and indeed we might even have forgotten about Höskuldr's wife Jórunn back in Iceland, were it not for Höskuldr's ostentatious action in dressing the slave woman in some fine women's clothes from a chest – surely clothes he planned to take back to Iceland for his wife. But the appearance of the slave woman in rich clothes serves another purpose. The saga author now presents the slave woman not from his own, or from Höskuldr's perspective, but in the judgement of public opinion: 'var þat ok allra manna mál, at henni semði góð klæði' (and everyone said that fine clothing suited her).[38] This is of course a significant, if oblique, clue to her identity – she does not look like a slave woman in fancy dress – but the saga author contrives to avoid intruding with his own opinion, whilst maintaining Höskuldr's ignorance. We – if we are a first-time audience – are kept in a tantalizing state of imperfect knowledge.

It's not until the later in the saga that the identity of Höskuldr's mysteriously over-priced slave woman is revealed, as I discussed in detail in my discussion of scene in Chapter 2. The information is withheld by means of Melkorka's refusal to talk. This contrivance is played off against the clues about her real identity which are carefully placed in the narrative. Once again, the pleasure is different, but perhaps not less, if we know the story in advance; as with the story of Börkr and Snorri, we can enjoy knowing more than some of the characters, and sharing the knowledge of a character – in this case, Melkorka – who is empowered by their control of silence. A first-time audience shares the ignorance of Börkr and Höskuldr. Those who know the story share what has not been expressed in the diegesis – the superior knowledge of Snorri and Melkorka – and Börkr and Höskuldr are implicitly deprecated.

We are never told why Gilli priced Melkorka so highly. Perhaps he knew her real identity (and would have disclosed it if Höskuldr had asked rather than being distracted by showing off how much silver he had). Perhaps he wanted to keep her for himself – or not give her to this Icelandic show-off. Perhaps the saga author expected his original audience to know the answer, and felt he didn't need to spell it out. Perhaps he simply forgot to say. I am well aware that speculation about what is not stated in the narrative contravenes the usual literary critical strictures laid down by most narrative analysts.[39] But precisely because of the saga author's withholding of knowledge, such speculative responses are not only justified, but even required. This implicit invitation to speculate is a consistent and characteristic feature of family saga narrative, and part of the way the audience is drawn in to engage with the narrative in the absence of the conventional rhetorical devices of fiction. But the sheer volume of unanswered questions throughout family saga narrative strongly suggests that keeping the audience in a state of imperfect knowledge by withholding crucial information is a purposeful literary technique in the Icelandic family saga, whether as a device for enlisting audience engagement, or as an aspect of emplotment.

Before leaving the story of Melkorka, it is worth noting that although the revelation to Höskuldr of her real identity and history, as a beautifully crafted narrative scene, constitutes a sort of closure, nonetheless it does not actually bring this particular storyline to a decisive conclusion. The narrative continues with Höskuldr in turn revealing Melkorka's identity to his wife Jórunn, the tension it creates in their household and, ultimately, the birth of the character on whom the saga narrative focuses thereafter as its dominant protagonist, Melkorka and Höskuldr's son Óláfr pái. The onward progress of the narrative – like life – continues, and is not tidied away. Elaine Showalter observes that Victorian novels traditionally end with a 'marriage, madness, or death'.[40] These are closures which, with the possible exclusion of death, are usually missing from saga ends, or are, by contrast, events which function as beginnings or continuations rather than as ends.

Unanswered questions

I turn now to two episodes in which disclosure is not merely delayed, clearing the way for a dramatic or satisfying revelation, but is in fact never made. As I have said, this is more like life than literature. Conventional fictions raise questions in order to answer them, creating and imposing artificial closure by means of plots, the 'means by which we re-configure our confused, unformed and at the limit mute temporal experience'.[41] Not answering a question which the narrative clearly raises has the effect of restricting the audience to the same imperfect knowledge as the characters in the storyworld, and mimicking our own imperfect knowledge of the real world. But the silence may at the same time create a series of different effects in the narrative, and I want now to consider three contrasting examples of the effects created when questions are raised but not answered.

In *Laxdæla saga,* before Kjartan leaves Norway for Iceland, the king's daughter Ingibjörg gives him a lavishly decorated gold headdress, instructing him to offer it to Guðrún as a wedding gift.[42] We have not – until now – been told that she knows about Kjartan's betrothal to Guðrún back in Iceland. Kjartan and his friend and trading partner Kálfr duly sail to Iceland, and Kjartan discovers on his return that, during his absence, Guðrún has married his foster-brother Bolli. On their arrival, Kálfr tells his sister Hrefna that she can have anything she likes from the goods he has brought back from Norway; Kjartan tells his sister Þuríðr the same. But the weather suddenly turns bad, and the two men are urgently called away to make their ship secure. At the very moment of their return to the farm, Hrefna is trying on the golden headdress. When Kjartan sees Hrefna in the headdress, he remarks that it suits her, and that perhaps he should own both the headdress and the woman.[43]

Whilst these two moments of chance coincidence – the men being called away, and returning just as Hrefna has donned the headdress – give the narrative a degree of drama and immediacy, they are not strictly necessary for the furtherance of the sequence of events in the saga. Nothing could be more natural – inevitable, even – than for Kjartan to marry the sister of his best friend, given that Guðrún has apparently rebuffed him by marrying his foster-brother Bolli. But the headdress will take on considerable significance as a symbol of Kjartan's betrayal of Guðrún, and her jealousy of Hrefna.

Kjartan duly marries Hrefna, and at a feast at his father's farm Guðrún, again by chance coincidence, hears Kjartan organizing the seating at the feast so that Hrefna will be placed in the seat of honour – a place which Guðrún felt to be rightfully hers. The attention here is sharply focused on Guðrún and Kjartan: 'Guðrún heyrði þetta ok leit til Kjartans ok brá lit, en svarar engu' (Guðrún heard this, and looked at Kjartan, and changed colour [i.e. most probably flushed], but makes no comment).[44] Again, this tense scene has no actual causal function; Guðrún might just as well have got to hear from someone else that Hrefna had been given the high seat, or even found out when the guests sat down to the feast. But by creating another moment of coincidence, the saga author has directed our attention to the private – and again, unspoken – relationship between Kjartan and Guðrún.

Similarly, the next day Guðrún asks Hrefna to put on the headdress. Again by chance Kjartan happens to be passing, and forbids his wife to wear it.[45] We can speculate as to why Guðrún wants her rival to wear the headdress, but we are not told. But the next day, Guðrún asks Hrefna to show her the headdress in private. This is a significant violation of Kjartan's prohibition: he has told Hrefna not to wear the headdress because he doesn't want it to be reduced to an 'augnagaman' (something for people to gape at).[46] Hrefna shows Guðrún the headdress, however, and Guðrún looks at it but says nothing. Shortly after, Hrefna is urged by Kjartan's mother to take the headdress to a return feast at Laugar, where Bolli and Guðrún live. The headdress is carefully stored away on their arrival, but the next morning, it has disappeared.[47]

Of course, although we are not told who stole the headdress, the identity of the thief is obvious. Guðrún has made plain her jealousy of Hrefna. She has not commented on the excellence of the treasure, nor expressed any wish that she had it, but we do not need any explicit acknowledgement of this to identify her as the culprit. She unhelpfully and unconvincingly suggests that maybe Hrefna left it at home, or lost it as she travelled to Laugar – even though the narrator specifically states that the headdress had gone from the place in which Hrefna had put it. Finally, in an indirect confession, Guðrún raises to the possibility that someone from her party may have taken the headdress, but that in doing so, they have only taken back what properly belonged to them, and further, that she herself is pleased that Hrefna has been deprived of it.[48] Significantly, however, no one accuses Guðrún of the theft and, although we are not told directly by the narrator what became of the headdress, '[þ]at höfðu margir men fyrir satt' (many people were sure) that Guðrún's brother Þorólfr burned it on his sister's instructions.[49] The narrator has again displaced what would otherwise be authorial judgement on to what is claimed to be popular opinion. There is also an interesting coda to this episode: Hrefna teases Kjartan about Guðrún wearing the headdress after the theft, and Kjartan angrily retorts that Guðrún doesn't need a golden headdress to look more beautiful than any other woman.[50]

A mystery has been created, a question which calls for an answer. But it is perfectly clear who has stolen the headdress. There is no other obvious suspect; this is no conventional 'whodunnit' mystery. Instead, through these carefully maintained silences, the saga author is putting the audience in the same position as the characters in the narrative. Like Höskuldr, we do not know who the overpriced slave woman is until the revelation later in the narrative. And like the guests and hosts at Laugar, we know very well who has stolen the headdress, but both intra- and extra-diegetically, the thief is not named. In fact, we may even understand – along with the people at Laugar – that if a direct accusation is made, the strained relationship between Bolli and Kjartan will be definitively severed, with who knows what consequences. In effect, we are living through the third time of narrative along with the characters, sharing their own imperfect knowledge, and experiencing the passage of events with them. We experience also the atmosphere of tension, hostility and suspicion, heightened by a culprit not being openly named. An open accusation – or, much less likely to happen, a confession from Guðrún – is the only way the culprit might be identified within the storyworld; otherwise, we would need the narrator to intervene explicitly with an answer from outside the diegesis, which would have the effect of defusing the tension, thus destroying a major element in the narrative. In addition, open identification of the thief from within the diegesis would call for some sort of response from other characters. And further, it does not matter how many times we hear or read the story of the headdress. Our engagement with the episode is not compromised, because our interest is not in finding out who stole it; that is to say, there is no conventional emplotment. The saga author is skilfully treading a fine line between withholding and disclosing information.

There is, as I have said, only one suspect in the case of the stolen headdress. But in *Gísla saga*, there are two suspects for the killing of Gísli's brother-in-law Vésteinn, and again, the saga author creates a careful and highly effective balance between withholding and disclosing the identity of the killer. We are never told whether it was Gísli's brother Þorkell or their brother-in-law Þorgrímr who killed Vésteinn, and in this case, there is no obvious inference to be made about which of the two was the culprit. In *Eyrbyggja saga*, we are casually and openly told that Þorgrímr killed Vésteinn; it is tempting to suppose that the author of *Gísla saga* has purposely created a non-committal stance in order to maintain the kind of imperfect knowledge I have been discussing so far, and provoke audience engagement.[51] I shall therefore look particularly closely at what effect the non-disclosure of the culprit has, especially within the storyworld, and at how the saga author creates and maintains the uncertainty.

The killing of Vésteinn is presented from the outset as being so inevitable as to be predestined. The two brothers Gísli and Þorkell, instead of sharing a fraternal bond, turn their backs on each other to form stronger alliances with their respective brothers-in-law: Gísli with his wife's brother Vésteinn, and Þorkell with his sister's husband Þorgrímr. A celebrated seer, Gestr Oddleifsson, predicts that the four men will be at odds before three years are up and, in a vain attempt to avert this prophecy, Gísli proposes that they all swear blood-brotherhood together. But this demonstration of and attempt to seal their alliance in fact exposes its weaknesses: Þorgrímr draws back from the ritual when he realizes that he has no direct affiliation with Vésteinn and, once Þorgrímr makes known his reluctance, Gísli's own commitment to an alliance with him evaporates.[52] The split in made very clear when all four go travelling and trading the next summer: Gísli and Vésteinn form one partnership, and Þorgrímr and Þorkell another.[53] When Vésteinn leaves Gísli to make a trip to England, Gísli himself predicts that their lives may in future be in danger, and gives Vésteinn one half of a coin which can be split into two, to be used so that one of them may warn the other if needs be.[54]

Hostility between the two parties is not long in coming. Þorkell overhears his and Gísli's wife discussing how his own wife once had hopes of marrying Vésteinn, while Gísli's wife once had a relationship with Þorgrímr. Þorkell's uncanny recitation of a doom-laden verse, which apparently betrays his presence to the women, prophesies that violent deaths will ensue.[55] But although we might assume that what he has overheard would inflame his jealousy of Vésteinn, Þorkell makes no threat. When Auðr tells her husband Gísli what has happened, again he resigns himself to the apparent inevitability of some unspecified fate: 'ok þat mun fram koma, sem auðit verðr' (and whatever is fated to happen will come to pass).[56] The brothers, Gísli and Þorkell, make a formal division of the property – ostensibly without rancour. The farms belonging to these two brothers on the one hand, and to Þorgrímr on the other, are actually adjoining, so that when Þorkell moves in with Þorgrímr, leaving the family farm for Gísli, the boundary between the two farms is a symbolic representation of the flawed fraternal bond, a party wall uniting as well as dividing the two brothers.

When Vésteinn returns to Iceland, he makes his way to Gísli, but hearing of Vésteinn's arrival, Gísli sends out their agreed warning token of the half coin. At this point, the saga author elaborately demonstrates the truth of what Gísli has maintained about fate: that it cannot be averted. Vésteinn at first narrowly misses the messengers with the token – but is delayed on his journey and they manage to catch up with him and present the half coin.[57] Vésteinn, however, is fatalistic in his turn: as we have seen, he says that if they had met him the first time, he would have heeded the warning, but 'nú falla vötn öll til Dýrafjarðar' (now all waters flow down towards Dýrafjörðr).[58] The pull of fate – like a strong current – is irresistible, and Vésteinn continues on to Gísli's. Three times along the way he is warned of the danger, even though there has been no indication that violence is being planned.[59] Curiously, a woman called Rannveig, one of the farmhands at Þorkell and Þorgrímr's farm, reports having seen Vésteinn, although another farmhand who used to work with Gísli, and who has already warned Vésteinn to be on his guard, tries to discredit the report. Þorgrímr sends Rannveig to Gísli's farm to see if Vésteinn has indeed arrived, but she fails to see him.[60] The upshot of this scene is not at all clear; perhaps the saga author is simply ratchetting up the tension.

Certainly the tension is increased when Vésteinn, settled in Gísli's farm, sends gifts to Þorkell which are roundly rejected. Gísli is again overcome by a sense of ineluctable fate, but it is notable that there have been no direct threats, insults or skirmishes, just a heavy and unshakeable sense of tragedy ahead.[61] Gísli's disquiet is conveyed by the fact that he sleeps badly for two nights in a row, and at this point the saga author produces a conspicuous silence: Gísli refuses to tell anyone what his nightmares were about.[62] On the third night, Vésteinn is murdered in his bed. The grammatical structure of the subjectless sentence allows the narrator to describe the killing without giving the least hint about the identity of the intruder and killer: 'Nú er gengit inn nökkut ... ok þangat at, sem Vésteinn hvílir' (now is entered somehow ... and [gone] to the place where Vésteinn is sleeping).[63]

The obvious suspects are either Þorgrímr or Þorkell. As we have seen, Þorkell's jealousy of Vésteinn would provide a motive, but without any intervening move or threat from him, the connexion to overhearing about his wife's early fondness for Vésteinn seems a tenuous one. I have already discussed the scene in which Gísli's wife Auðr urged a cowardly slave to pull the lethal spear out of Vésteinn's body, and questioned whether she might have had some legal reason to do this, since the narrator claims that at the time the person who withdrew a weapon was obliged to take on the revenge.[64] However, we should recall that Gísli claimed to have had bad dreams before Vésteinn's death, and later in the narrative, Gísli claims to have learnt the identity of the murderer in those dreams.[65] Thus any vengeance taken by Gísli could be understood to reveal that identity; one might speculate that Auðr realizes this, which is why she tries to persuade a slave to do it. Certainly Gísli shows that he knows it was one of the two, Þorkell or Þorgrímr, for he immediately sends his foster-daughter over to Sæból, the farm they share; she reports back that the men in the household are all fully armed and on the alert – just as, Gísli says, he expected.[66] But only Þorgrímr speaks: to ask for the news which, we must presume, he already knows. When he is told of Vésteinn's death, Þorkell wryly implies that this is not news – 'Tíðendi myndi oss þat hafa þótt eina stund' (that would have seemed news to us at one time) – but stops short of admitting that he already knows; he could conceivably be referring simply to the fateful inevitability of what has happened.[67]

Þorgrímr responds in a dignified and apparently wholly proper way, calling Vésteinn's death a great loss, and helping with the funerary rites.[68] Is this astonishing hypocrisy? Most remarkably, we are told in the narrative that he sits and talks with Gísli beside the gravemound: 'ok talask við ok láta allólíkliga, at nökkurr viti, hverr þenna glœp hefir gört' (and they discuss things, and reckon that it is totally improbable that anyone will [ever] know who committed the crime).[69] Is this a covert agreement to let the identity of the murderer lie? In the absence of openly naming of the perpetrator, we are left with Gísli's claim to know, and he makes it clear to his brother Þorkell that he knows. Þorkell repeatedly asks how Gísli's wife Auðr is taking the loss of her brother. Why does he want to know this? In the narrative itself, Gísli makes it clear what an inappropriate enquiry it is: 'Opt spyrr þú þessa, frændi ... ok er þér mikil forvitni á at vita þetta' (You keep asking this, kinsman ... and you are very curious to know this).[70] Is it perhaps because Þorkell needs to know whether Auðr, as a possible witness to Vésteinn's death (for they were the only people in the house when it happened) has revealed the identity of the intruder, and accused him of the murder? Or, perhaps, accused Þorgrímr?

All these unspoken – and, in fact, unsayable – resentments and suspicions are ostensibly set aside when Þorkell and Gísli agree shortly afterwards to behave as if nothing has happened.[71] Is this because it is in both their interests that Þorkell should not be revealed as the murderer? In any event, we could see the subsequent ball game as a symbolic rehearsal of the murder-and-due-vengeance sequence. Gísli brings Þorgrímr to the ground with a vicious tackle, and Þorgrímr fixes his gaze on Vésteinn's burial mound and recites two lines, including the phrase 'kannkat þat lasta' (I can't complain about that [or, I'm not sorry about that]). Gísli then knocks Þorgrímr to the ground and repeats the same phrase.[72] This looks like a perfect tit-for-tat exchange, but in fact, there is no actual admission or accusation of guilt: strictly speaking, Þorgrímr is simply saying that he is not sorry that Vésteinn has been murdered, and Gísli, that he is not sorry that he has knocked Þorgrímr to the ground. Þorkell rushes in to defuse the situation, but this could be because he does not want an escalation which might in the heat of the moment lead to the revelation of either himself or Þorgrímr as the murderer.[73] Gísli does in the end murder Þorgrímr. However, after their acrimonious dealings, including a maliciously provocative request from Þorgrímr to borrow from Gísli the tapestries which Vésteinn brought back from his travels, a gift which Þorkell controversially refused, this is not completely convincing as an unequivocal revelation of Þorgrímr as the killer.[74] Finally, much later on in the saga, the sons of Vésteinn carry out a bold revenge attack on Gísli's brother Þorkell.[75] Does this implicitly identify Þorkell as Vésteinn's murderer – an identification Gísli could never openly make, because after all, the fraternal bond, however much tested, is ultimately sacrosanct? And finally, we should return to another strange silence in the narrative. Why exactly was Vésteinn murdered? What was the trigger? In fact, the saga author cannot provide a motive, because of course providing a motive would serve to identify the culprit.

There have been many attempts by saga scholars to make a case for one or other of the two suspects as being the culprit.[76] My interest here is not to identify the culprit, but to consider how and why it is that his identity is withheld from the saga audience. What is very clear is that the saga author has gone to a great deal of effort to create and maintain ambivalence. What is the effect of withholding the identity of the murderer? Most obviously, the saga author is again engaging the audience in speculation about the narrative and the motives of the characters in it. Knowing the story in advance only deepens our connexion with it, since there is no revelation which would end the speculation. The saga author takes us deep into the third time of narrative, forcing us to slow or even halt our forward movement through its time, and to delve further into the complexity of the characters' interrelationships. And as with the scandal of Hrefna's headdress in *Laxdœla saga*, we can experience from the characters' perspective the social and psychological necessity of silence – of not making open accusations, but living with suspicion and doubt rather than bringing matters to a head, from which there may be no return. Here's a thought experiment – imagine a narrative which identified either Þorkell or Þorgrímr as the murderer. Significantly, it hardly matters which of them is named. The psychological depth of the narrative and our engagement with it is reduced either way. I would argue that the saga author's aim here is to convey the experience of living in a tightly knit – as I have described it elsewhere, over-bonded – community in which theft or murder is such a dangerous threat to the stability of society that its perpetrators cannot be named.[77] For the narrator to break the silence would be to cut off the saga audience from that experience, to present it from the outside. It would also, as with the episode of the stolen headdress, require a response from within the diegesis to a revelation or admission of guilt.

My final example of a missing piece of information which is never disclosed comes from *Grettis saga*. In chapter 16 of the saga, a young Grettir sets off to the Alþing with a large company of men. He has been given leave to travel rather against the better judgement of Grettir's father, who warns Þorkell that Grettir is 'þykkjumikill ok þungr' (obdurate and difficult to deal with), but is unwilling to do without his other son Atli who, unlike Grettir, is a hard worker.[78] We are thus prepared for trouble, and a certain amount of suspense is set up. On the way, Grettir loses a food bag which has been attached to his saddle, and goes looking for it. He meets a man called Skeggi who has also lost his bag. Grettir cordially suggests that they search together, and they do so. Skeggi suddenly rushes off and picks up a bag which he claims is his own. Grettir's response is an interesting one: he asks Skeggi who else can confirm that the bag is really his. This question might be asked of the whole episode: where are the witnesses who might have reported all this? Skeggi makes no attempt to justify his ownership of the bag but simply holds on to it. They tussle over it, insults are exchanged, and Skeggi brings up an incident which occurred earlier, when Grettir was bettered in a fight with an older boy, Auðunn. A fight breaks out, and Grettir kills Skeggi with an axe blow.[79]

This episode is not a random or free-standing event in the narrative; it occupies a crucial place in a chain of events. Grettir goes to the Alþing because his brother Atli is needed to look after the farm; and when Grettir kills Skeggi, it leads to his outlawry.[80] Furthermore, Skeggi taunts Grettir with mention of a fight he lost against Auðunn earlier in the saga, and a reminder of this lost fight has repercussions in succeeding chapters.[81] Further still, the fight itself echoes two other tussles in the saga, with its push-pull action: the famous tug of war with Glámr over the cloak, and Grettir's loss of the horse's reins in the struggle with Loptr.[82]

The altercation itself is tightly woven into the narrative line, but the ownership of the bag is oddly peripheral to it. The saga author never tells us who the disputed bag did in fact belong to, and has given us no hints. Does anything in the future of the narrative depend on knowing whose bag it was? Would it make any difference to our appreciation of Grettir's character? Of course, it may simply be that the saga author has forgotten to make clear who the bag belonged to. But in fact, the message of the extended episode seems to be precisely that, with only one witness, it is always hard to be sure of the facts. As Grettir comments to Skeggi in this episode, the testimony of one witness is a precarious thing, and 'mart er öðru líkt' (many things are not as they seem).[83] This is a recurring theme in the saga. For instance, as we have seen, later in the saga the wise lawspeaker Skapti Þóroddsson is reluctant to accede to demands for Grettir's outlawry, arguing that 'jafnan er hálfsögð saga, ef einn segir' (a story is always half told if only by one person).[84]

When Grettir rejoins the travelling group, they ask about Skeggi, and Grettir replies in an obliquely ambiguous verse that Skeggi has been felled by a 'hamartroll' (hammer-troll), which the listeners naively interpret as a sort of troll, while Grettir may rather be using a kenning for axe.[85] He then declares in the strophe 'vask hjá viðreign þeira' (I was present at their encounter), the implication being that he was an onlooker, not the perpetrator.[86] We are dependent on Grettir's account of the episode, since the only other witness is dead. Thus, the only way of finding out who the bag 'actually' belonged to (whilst bearing in mind that there is no necessary actuality behind the narrative, no *fabula* preceding the *sjuzhet*), in the absence of witnesses in the storyworld, is for Grettir himself to express this in the diegesis, but he has been notably enigmatic and unforthcoming about the whole affair. Of course as we have seen, saga authors do not invariably restrict the narration to what might have been seen or heard, but may silently adopt the stance of a fly on the wall, even in instances when the narrative voice makes clear that the reported discussion or event was witnessed by no one in the storyworld. And in *Grettis saga*, again as we have already seen, the narrator on occasion appeals to a surprising authority – Grettir himself, who is said to have later provided some information on which the narrative is based. In the episode of the lost bag, however, there is no such appeal. The only person who shows any interest in the ownership of the bag is Grettir himself, within the diegesis. If we try another thought experiment – this time, to imagine how the narrative would seem if the owner of the bag were explicitly identified – the result is interesting: a new moral dimension to the episode is opened up. Grettir would either be presented as being justified in claiming the bag, and killing a man who was trying to cheat him, or as finding himself embroiled in a pointless and unjustified killing, fulfilling the prophecies calling him an unlucky person. Without identifying ownership of the bag, the saga author presents an episode which shows that violence may flare at any moment, and uncertainty may be the spark; there is no moral high ground for either character to claim. Furthermore, as we have seen, random acts of violence may have repercussions in the succeeding narrative; their future may be of more significance than the circumstances of their present.

In this very minor episode in *Grettis saga*, the omission of an item of information – whose bag it actually was – both preserves the amorality of the ensuing violence and gives just enough narrative space – that is, time – for the situation to escalate into lethal violence. In the next section of this chapter, I want to explore two instances in which a brief and unexplained silence not only gives an uninformed audience the opportunity to engage in speculation, extra-diegetically, but also provides the narrative space/time for a crucial event to take place.

Undivulged motives

In *Laxdœla saga*, Kjartan, betrothed to Guðrún, goes to Norway for an agreed three years with his foster-brother Bolli. Bolli returns to Iceland at the appointed time, but Kjartan decides to stay on in Norway. He tells Bolli to pass on his regards to his kinsmen and friends, but makes no mention of any special message to Guðrún. When Bolli gets home, Guðrún makes a point of asking about Kjartan, but Bolli has no message for her. And bearing out the assertion repeated in *Grettis saga* that a story told by one person is only half told, Bolli relates a notably one-sided version of events in Norway: that Kjartan is doing well; that he may stay on in Norway; that marriage to the king's daughter Ingibjörg is very likely.[87] In the absence of a message from Kjartan to Guðrún – the silence at the heart of this storyline – Bolli is given an opportunity to pave the way for his own marriage proposal to Guðrún.

Why, then, does Kjartan not send a message? That his silence is significant is not in doubt. For instance, silence inevitably excites audience speculation, for which there is plenty of plausible scope here, as I shall shortly show. But it is also worth noting that the underlying story pattern – a wedding is agreed for a fixed time in the future but the bridegroom-to-be fails to return from a trip abroad at the appointed time – is common to most of the Old Icelandic *skáldsögur* (poet sagas), which strongly suggests fictionality.[88] Unless *Laxdœla saga* is the original archetype, which seems unlikely, we can assume that Kjartan's failure to return on time is a re-working of a familiar trope, and that Kjartan's silence is a twist on it – that is, that the saga author has purposefully created the silence with some end in mind.

We can base speculation about why Kjartan did not send a message on a close analysis of the whole episode. We may remember, for example, that in spite of the fact that they are a model match, and closely committed to each other, he and Guðrún part on bad terms. Specifically, Guðrún, nettled by Kjartan's out of hand rejection of her suggestion that he take her to Norway with him, refuses to agree to wait for him.[89] Might Kjartan's silence be retaliation for her show of temper? Or we may take note of the way Kjartan is presented during his stay in Norway: he is shown to be increasingly arrogant and cocksure, such that we could easily imagine that he would feel it beneath him to be bothered with events back in Iceland.[90] Indeed, it is even possible to conclude that his decision to stay on is part of an attempt to show that he is now an impressive and successful figure with little need to explain himself to those back home. Alternatively, and by contrast, one could suppose that Kjartan feels defensive to some extent about missing – or flouting – the deadline, and that his silence arises from that. And finally, we must take account of his relations with Bolli: throughout their time in Norway, Bolli is manifestly a subaltern figure, playing second fiddle to Kjartan.[91] We can imagine Kjartan feeling himself too grand to ask Bolli to take a hand in his personal affairs. These various possibilities are not, of course, mutually exclusive; we might even see them as cumulative, or mutually reinforcing.

The ostensible reason for Kjartan's extended stay in Norway is his relationship with the beautiful Ingibjörg, the king's daughter. This relationship is not entirely a malicious invention of Bolli's; Bolli accuses Kjartan to his face of forgetting about his obligations in Iceland because he is spending so much time 'sitting and talking with Ingibjörg', a common euphemism for flirtation or even sexual intimacy, and Kjartan does not exactly deny it, responding 'Haf ekki slíkt við'

(Don't be like that).[92] However, Bolli might be accused of exaggerating the relationship when he reports it to Guðrún as heralding a possible royal marriage. And Bolli certainly exploits Kjartan's silence to the full when he makes his first marriage proposal to Guðrún. Guðrún at once turns down his proposal, but Bolli smoothly counters her determination to marry no one but Kjartan by pointing out – rightly, as it happens – that Kjartan could very easily have sent her a message 'ef honum þœtti þat allmiklu máli skipta' (if he had thought it important).[93]

This begs another question: did it indeed matter to Kjartan? Again, the saga author is ambivalent. We learn that Princess Ingibjörg knows that Kjartan is betrothed to Guðrún, for when they part the following year, she gives him the golden headdress with instructions to give it to Guðrún. But is it perhaps part of her own bridal trousseau? If this were the case, then we might interpret the handover of the headdress as Ingibjörg relinquishing her hoped-for role as a potential bride for Kjartan when she discovers his intention to return to Iceland only at the very last moment, the moment of his departure. We would also see yet another reiteration of the trope of fine clothing or accessories being given to the 'other woman', as with Melkorka's new clothes, or the later history of the same headdress, given to Hrefna instead of Guðrún. As Kjartan and Ingibjörg part, the narrator falls back on a familiar non-committal device: 'höfðu menn þat fyrir satt, at þeim þœtti fyrir at skiljask' (people were sure that the parting was hard for them).[94] People might say so, but the narrator could not possibly comment.

I am not interested here in choosing or prioritizing one or other of these possible motives for Kjartan's silence, though some seem to me more persuasive or ingenious than others.[95] It is significant that the persuasiveness or otherwise of these speculations in the end comes down not to objective plausibility, but to subjective preference, to personal responses to Kjartan himself and his unexplained – but far from inexplicable – silence. I would argue that the saga author has created two quite separate literary effects by leaving Kjartan's feelings and motive unspoken here. Firstly, in purely structural narrative terms, Kjartan's silence allows Bolli the narrative time/space to take advantage of Guðrún's engineered lack of faith in Kjartan's faithfulness and, ultimately, to marry her in spite of her commitment to Kjartan and the apparent inevitability of their match hitherto. Secondly, the audience is inescapably drawn into the narrative, prompted not only to fill in the gaps but also to ponder in some depth the motivations and inner thought of the characters. This is a very rich receptive experience, and in the context of an original saga audience, we can also easily imagine the collective discussion and debate which might ensue.

My second example of unexplained motives creating silences in the narrative also gives scope for audience speculation, and the silence in question also causes an unexpected pause within the diegesis itself, in an otherwise smooth sequence of narrative events. This brief hiatus is rapidly and unwelcomely filled. In *Njáls saga*, it is agreed that compensation will be accepted for the killing of Höskuldr Hvítanessgoði, who was Njáll's beloved foster-son, murdered by Njáll's own sons. Impartial arbitrators are appointed to assess the amount to be paid, and they settle on the huge sum of six hundred ounces of silver. This far exceeds the resources of Njáll himself and all his sons, but the consequences of not reaching a deal are so perilous that other members of the community add to what Njáll and his family have contributed, bringing the total amount up to what has been specified. It is at this moment that Njáll adds to the heap of money – the collective wealth of the whole community – a pair of boots and a garment called in the saga *silkislæður*.[96] As I have discussed elsewhere, this garment, although a plural noun in Old Norse, appears in other saga contexts as a cloak or robe of some sort, distinguished by being of especially high quality.[97] At this point, Njáll's addition is remarked on by neither the narrator nor anyone in the storyworld, not even Hallr of Síðá, one of the leading arbitrators and moreover, the first choice of Flosi, Njáll's prosecutor and the recipient of the compensation. Hallr is specifically named as being present when the compensation is brought together. And Njáll himself seems to have no inkling that the addition may prove controversial, because as he and his sons gather to meet Flosi, he tells them 'Nú er máli váru komit í gott efni. Vér erum menn sáttir … skulu nú hvárirtveggju ganga til ok veita öðrum grið ok tryggðir. Vil ek nú biðja yðr, at þér spillið í engu um' (Now our case has turned out well. We are reconciled … [and] now both sides shall come together and offer each other peace and pledges of good faith. I now beg you not to do anything to spoil it).[98] If we are to take Njáll at his word, these are surely not the statements or the sentiments of someone who has himself knowingly wrecked the settlement.

But when Flosi inspects the compensation, while approving the monetary element, he stops short when he sees the *silkislæður*. He asks who gave them, and no one answers.[99] This is what creates our silence – most strikingly, a diegetical silence in the narrative itself, a literally unanswered question, and it raises questions unaddressed by the narrator. Why does Njáll not admit to donating the *silkislæður*? And if he thought they might be at all controversial, why did he add them to the pile? Did he only at this last moment realize their significance? Is this then a unique misjudgement by a man whose wisdom is a byword in the saga? Judith Jesch suggests, rightly in my view, that the *silkislæður* recall for Flosi the exceptionally fine cloak which he once presented to the murdered Höskuldr. Höskuldr's wife Hildigunnr used this cloak – which Höskuldr was wearing when he was murdered – as a prop in her elaborate and theatrical goading of Flosi to take blood vengeance for Höskuldr's death. Flosi repudiated this call for blood vengeance, leading to the legal settlement he is now on the point of accepting.[100] It has also been proposed that the garment was in some way not wholly manly.[101] Although this is not an issue in the other narratives in which it appears, the response its inclusion provokes – an exchange of sexual insults – might seem to bear this out. Alternatively, it might be argued that Flosi has understood the cloak as indeed referring to Hildigunnr's goading, and that his repudiation of violence and decision to take the legal route is in itself a slur on his masculinity which gives rise to the charges of effeminacy. But the issue remains unresolved: why did Njáll not foresee any of this?

Flosi twice asks who has given the cloak. This not only extends the tense silence, but also gives Njáll the opportunity to answer if he wants to, or can. But the silence endures. In an extraordinary moment, Flosi laughs. Inappropriate laughter, as we have seen, is a disturbing element elsewhere in Old Norse-Icelandic literature: we might recall Hallgerðr's laughter when she hears of the murder of her beloved second husband, and more distantly, the chilling laughter of Brynhildr in the *Poetic Edda*.[102] Here again, we as audience are called upon to interpret the meaning of Flosi's laughter, in the absence of narratorial comment. Is it an attempt to defuse the situation, to affect that this is no big deal, that an admission of having added the *silkislæður* will be taken in good part? Or is it an attempt to give this impression, to lull the culprit in to a false sense of security (as I suggested might have been the case with Hallgerðr's laughter)? Or is it, in an example of the saga author's psychological insight, a jittery response to a nerve-wracking situation? These are all plausible possibilities, and there may of course be others I haven't yet thought of. The act of interpretation is an end in itself, as with our response to the unanswered question of Kjartan's motive in not sending a message to Guðrún, although the issue of why Njáll added the *silkislæður* is of a different order: it remains a mystery, without any wholly satisfactory interpretation. Perhaps that very lack of an explanation is an expression of how in highly charged situations things can go badly wrong in spite of the good intentions and wise foresight of those present. Again, an eddic parallel comes to mind: the murder of their half-brother Erpr by Hamðir and Sörli in *Hamðismál*. There too an obscure insult gives rise to a disastrous escalation and the same rapid fire exchange of sexual insults we see in *Njáls saga*.[103] The actual narrative silence when no one answers Flosi's repeated question is structurally crucial, as it abruptly halts the apparently smooth running of the compensation and settlement narrative, and leaves narrative time/space for bottled up resentments to break out as offensive insults. These include Hallgerðr's old jibe about Njáll as 'karl inn skegglausi' (old beardless), and Skarpheðinn's double rejoinder: the wounding taunt that Flosi, unlike Njáll, has no sons – and indeed the saga narrative never mentions that Flosi had any children – and the fantastically offensive allegation that Flosi has regular sex with a male troll.[104]

The hard-won settlement of course collapses. Flosi renounces a peaceful settlement and vows to take blood vengeance for Höskuldr's death. Perhaps peace never had a chance in *Njáls saga* at this stage, although it came so tantalizingly close. Njáll foresees the horrors to come – ultimately, the burning of himself and his wife and grandson in the family home – but neither he nor the narrator makes any comment on what has happened, or any attempt to explain it. The money is set aside for when it will next be needed – a grim foretaste of continued wrangling. We never hear what happened to the *silkislœður*.

Uncertainty resolved

I conclude this chapter with an analysis of an episode in *Grettis saga* in which the persistent withholding of information – especially the motives and purposes of Grettir himself – creates an extended stretch of narrative suspense and uncertainty, an uncertainty resoundingly resolved in due course. Chapter 19 of *Grettis saga* opens with a detailed account of the movements and affairs of the rulers of England and Norway in the year leading up to the present moment of the saga's main narrative: Grettir's first winter in Norway.[105] This has the effect of anchoring the events of the saga to a familiar historical timeline, and as a technique it could be paralleled in most family sagas. As we have seen, narrative flashback – Genette's anachrony – is relatively uncommon in family sagas unless it arises from a character's recall within the diegesis. But the narrative of *Grettis saga* is something of a special case: Grettir's peregrinations often mean that, when he is shown as newly arrived somewhere, the saga author must bring us up-to-date, as it were, with the local state of affairs. And so it is at the beginning of chapter 19: we learn that before Eiríkr jarl Hákonarson had left Norway to visit his brother-in-law Canute in England, he had been busy outlawing berserks, and crucially, that he did so with the help of a landowner called Þorfinnr – with whom Grettir is now himself staying. The saga author notes, 'Gekk Þorfinnr mest manna fyrir sekð þeira; þóttusk þeir honum eiga fullan fjándskap at gjalda'

(Þorfinnr was the most prominent person pressing for their outlawry; they thought that he deserved to be paid back with their unqualified enmity).[106] This statement explicitly sets up a classic narrative mode familiar to many readers: suspense. The saga author's observation that the berserks are out for vengeance is a clear cataphor.[107] Narrative clues such as this create anticipation and thus suspense in the reader or listener, whether or not the attention aroused is satisfied or disappointed.

Noël Carroll usefully analyses an extended range of necessary preconditions for the creation of narrative suspense, and we can see at once how well these fit the episode of Grettir and the berserks.[108] Carroll notes that suspense is an emotional response to a narrative fiction and may arise as a reaction to 'discrete scenes or sequences within a larger narrative'.[109] He stresses that suspense is 'not a response to the outcome; it pertains to the moments leading up to the outcome'.[110] And one crucial feature is that the reader or listener (or viewer, in a cinematic context) must be induced to care about the uncertain outcome. As Carroll explains, 'one way in which the author can invest the audience with concern over a prospective outcome is to ensure that one of the logically opposed outcomes in the fiction is morally correct as well as uncertain'.[111] A dimension of some sort of physical danger will also intensify audience reaction, and a slowing up, or distension of the narrative may increase our suspense, although Carroll himself has certain reservations about this.[112] Finally, Carroll points out that, with regard to the ethical dimension of narrative suspense, an outcome which favours what he calls the morally 'correct' side is customarily presented as less likely than an anticipated outcome in which the morally incorrect, or evil, antagonists, triumph – in plainer terms, the more the odds are stacked against the hero, the greater the suspense.[113]

It is evident that the episode of Grettir and the berserks fulfils these conditions perfectly: as the narrative cataphor has led us to anticipate, the berserks do indeed arrive, and soon a second uncertain binary outcome is created and becomes the primary one: will they triumph, or will Grettir defeat them? The introduction to the chapter unequivocally identifies the berserks as a force for evil (as if our previous experience of Old Norse literature were not enough). The berserks are an intimidating force: their ship is painted and aggressively lined with shields, and, though there are only twelve of them, they easily move a ship which would normally require thirty men to launch. Their intentions are soon evident: they plainly plan to terrorize the women who have been left behind at the farm.

This opening scene is focalized through Grettir: 'Þá þóttisk Grettir sjá, at þeir myndi ætla at bjóða sér sjálfir beina' (Then Grettir supposed that they were intending to help themselves to what was on offer).[114] As we have seen, focalization through one of the characters in a narrative can have the effect of restricting the audience's view, especially if, as here, the narrator's own perspective is not made clear. And here, even though Grettir is a focalizer, and we see the berserks through his eyes, we are not privy to his inner thoughts – especially his intentions. What the saga author withholds from us – and also from the other characters, that is, the women left at home with Grettir as their only obvious male defender – is whether Grettir is minded to side with the berserks or defend the women. The story is familiar: Grettir pretends to befriend the berserks, gets them drunk and locks them in storehouse so that he can kill them one by one. But the women of the house – who are the berserks' intended victims – don't know what the plan is, and are very distressed.[115]

Carroll's extended analysis enables us confidently to distinguish between the suspense created by an uncertain and feared outcome, and the technique we examined earlier in this piece: the mystery created by withheld factual information (Who stole the headdress? Who is the overpriced slave woman? Was the food bag Grettir's or not?). And although they are theoretically distinct, I think we can see the two techniques operating in tandem, and interacting in a number of ways, in the account of Grettir's engagement with the berserks. For example, suspense is increased when our uncertain knowledge of Grettir's loyalties increases our sense of the unlikelihood of the women avoiding being raped by the berserks. Furthermore, his pretence at playing along with them effectively prolongs the narrative and thus the suspense. Finally, as Hans Wulff argues, '[t]here is a close correlation between the productivity connected with the formulation of given information and the intensity of the subjective experience' – again, more plainly, that having only imperfect information engages us more closely with the narrative, as I have argued throughout this and the previous chapter, and increases the suspense.[116] However, the question of what we know or not of Grettir's loyalties raises two very important issues. The attentive reader or listener will surely begin to suspect Grettir's plan if they play close attention to his ambiguous dialogue with the berserks. For example, Grettir makes a duplicitous offer to 'look after' to the men – 'gera skal ek yðr slíkan forbeina' (I will take care of you) – and also enacts a thinly veiled ploy to disarm them – 'Selið mér þat í hendr sem þér vilið af leggja, vápn ok vásklæði, því at eigi mun oss fólkit stýrilátt, meðan þat er óhrætt' (Give me whatever you wish to discard, weapons or rain-clothes, [but not everything] because the people will be not manageable for us, if they are not afraid).[117] There is a sense, then, that as with the question of Hrefna's headdress, the information in this case is not effectively withheld, but only cloaked, and this might be seen to decrease the suspense. But more significantly, our ability to predict Grettir's loyalties raises the whole issue of second and subsequent readings. We may have our suspicions about his good intentions confirmed, thus freeing us to enjoy his double meanings – the often very satisfying activity of reading with hindsight, which I shall discuss shortly. Here, as in the episodes with Börkr and Höskuldr discussed earlier in this chapter, the pleasure of knowing more than the deprecated figures – here, the berserks – is a significant gain. But if we also know what is going to happen – will the berserks triumph? – then what becomes of the suspense?

Of course, suspense theorists have confronted what Carroll calls 'the paradox of suspense': if suspense depends upon uncertain knowledge, how can it survive repeated reception of the text? William Brewer has made a useful list of the various theories which have been put forward to explain this apparent paradox.[118] I am engaging with that list here, because we have repeatedly come up against the same paradox in relation to imperfect knowledge in saga narratives. It might be argued, for example, that we willingly abandon our memories of a first reading, and re-experience the suspense as if it were happening for the first time – in effect, affecting not to know what happens. Or our memory of a narrative does not take in every detail, and suspense is engendered by details we missed first time round (though presumably, not quite as *much* suspense). Perhaps we re-read not 'for the story' but to enjoy the craft of the author, or to enjoy seeing how the author created the suspense.[119] Similarly, one might contend that when the suspense ceases to function, we shift our attention to the depiction of character. These suggestions all seem to me to be unsatisfactory in explaining the survival of suspense, even if they may describe well some responses to a narrative whose outcomes are known. But Carroll puts forward an intriguing solution to the 'paradox of suspense' which is strikingly relevant to our withheld knowledge problem, and brings us right back round to Ricœur's third time of narrative and its double temporality. Carroll argues that suspense is an emotion engendered in the reader, listener or viewer, and that 'an emotional response can rest on a thought'.[120] In other words, we do not need to *believe* that the women at the farm are in danger from berserks – after all, whether all this ever happened or not, it is now a narrative, distanced in time and not a 'real life' situation we are experiencing. We only need to *imagine* that it might be the case, and as a result we experience anxiety about the outcome, and feel consequent relief when the favoured outcome is secure. The mere formal structure of the narrative can engender this state of mind. Similarly, then, we can imagine what it is like not to know something, and in this way experience a situation along with one or more of the characters, as we move through the third time of narrative, whilst at the same time sharing the quasi-divine perspective Boethius called *totum simul*, from which we can see the past, present and future of the narrative as a single whole.

So, to return to Ricœur's double temporality, readers (or listeners – but it's clearer of course to readers) may envisage a narrative as a block of time, presented as *totum simul*, but they may also experience the passage of this third time along with the characters.[121] Ricœur calls this process 'a thought experiment by means of which we try to inhabit worlds foreign to us'.[122] Furthermore, this third time of narrative provides a decidedly collective experience – it's always available, and ideally it causes what William Dowling, following Ricœur, calls 'an alteration of consciousness' – a gradual or sudden insight into what the world looks like to others, and an insight which will stay with us.[123] For an original medieval Icelandic audience, living through the third time of saga narrative must have created a sense of extraordinarily close engagement with their forebears, and even today, the distinctive narrative strategies in the *Íslendingasögur* seem to bring us very near to figures from a now distant past.

Conclusion

This book has been concerned with the representation and production of time – what Paul Ricœur calls the third time of narrative – in a small selection of family sagas, and with how readers and listeners experience it. All narrators represent time, and in the very act of narrating, produce time. And all family saga narrators are always extra-diegetic, standing outside the third time of their narrative. They sometimes adopt what we might recognize as a fictional mode, offering privileged, quasi-authorial information about characters' inner lives, or evidently manipulating the order of events. More often, however, they are self-effacing, offering neither comment nor explanation, even seeming on occasion simply to be passing on a pre-existing story. The stance of the narrator, especially the degree to which narrators do intervene in their own narration, thus reminding an audience of their shared temporal externality, determines our experience of time in family sagas.

The narrative voice is at its most impersonal when ostensibly factual information is being related, and when external or 'historical' time is being represented. And yet as we have seen, even apparently factual genealogies and summary accounts of the settlement or events in Norway have been adapted to prefigure the themes and concerns of the sagas they preface. Narrators are also bound by actuality rather than exercising the freedom of fiction in their meticulously naturalistic depiction of the passing of years, seasons, days and nights, as if the passage of actual historical time were being documented. Time is skipped over when there are no relevant events to be narrated, but is invariably accounted for. Events are always shown against the appropriate historical or seasonal backdrop, and the appropriate alternation of night and day is always observed.

Like the authors of most extended prose narratives, saga authors vary the pace of narration. For example, with genealogical material the timespan covered is relatively extensive, while the time taken to record it is relatively short. Duration

– Genette's term for the relationship between the length of time narrated and the time taken to do the narrating – ranges from ellipsis and summary to scene and pause. It is with scene and pause, where the pace of the narrative slows, sometimes almost to isochrony, or actually halts, that we may become aware of a narrator not just as an abstract voice delivering the narrative, telling the story, but as an active force shaping that narrative, showing us what was happening, and how and why. The slow pace of scenic narrative gives scope for – or has expanded to accommodate – those effects which Wayne C. Booth has collectively termed 'the rhetoric of fiction': description, focalization, dialogue and the expression of a character's thoughts and feelings. The saga narrator does not simply summarize or mediate a known or pre-existing story or episode, but reimagines and recreates the past. Time is being produced in a manner typical of many works of fiction. Descriptive pauses too may rely on the intervention of a narrator, speaking directly to the audience. But as we have seen, saga authors often integrate such description into the diegesis itself, by having a character voice it. Displacement of the narrative voice into the diegesis in this way is most marked in the case of narratorial comment. Narrators do not need to intervene and pause the narrative themselves to offer an extra-diegetic comment, but may displace the judgement or information on to characters within the storyworld: 'this is what people said'. The narrator – who is, after all, articulating the whole narrative – is allowed to remain self-effaced and paradoxically, even silent.

Events in family sagas are almost always narrated in chronological order – that is, the order in which they would have happened had the subject of the narrative been an actual set of events. But by displacing evocations of past or future events – what Genette calls *anachrony* – on to characters in the storyworld as their prophecies or recall, narrators need not reveal themselves as speaking from a position outside of and above the narrative – the *totum simul* perspective, encompassing past, present and future. The consequent anachrony seems to come not from the narrator, but from within the diegesis itself. However, popular opinion, or prophecy, or recall, cannot carry the same authority as narratorial contributions. Uncertainty adds to the psychological depth of family sagas: a fallacious prophecy, or distorted recall, or misguided opinion may suggest a great deal about the motives and character of those in the storyworld. But even more importantly, the narrator's own 'silence' on these and so many other matters leaves scope for a considerable degree of ambiguity, and consequently, audience participation, in the interpretation of the narrative. Moreover, such ambiguity is clearly purposefully fostered by saga authors. If – as in real life – we do not have an authoritative voice explaining circumstances and guiding our responses, we are prompted to speculate about character and event in a way quite unlike the conventionally accepted response to fictional prose narratives.

Just as is the case with anachrony, family saga narrators necessarily, even if only implicitly, betray their awareness of the whole temporal scope – past, present and future – of the narrative in their use of conspicuous silences and the withholding or delaying of crucial elements in a set of events. Here, saga narrative comes close to exhibiting what is commonly recognized as *plot* – an overall configuration of events which make sense only in terms of that all-knowing authorial perspective. It is one of the staple elements of prose fiction.

Individual saga narratives constantly move between historicity and fictionality – whether we apply post-medieval understandings of the distinction, or speculate about medieval ones – and their narrators fade in and out of the narrative. No single family saga consistently adopts any one narrative mode. However, we can see distinctive temporalities expressed in individual sagas: *Njáls saga* with its heavy weight of a fated future, for example, or the events in *Gísla saga* so much a product of past silences. *Grettis saga* is dominated by emphasis on its own and its hero's place in a world outside the narrative: Icelandic literary tradition. *Laxdœla saga* is peopled by characters who are preoccupied by their status as compared with others before or after them, and *Eyrbyggja saga* focuses on the creation over time of a cohesive and stable community. The narrative of *Hrafnkels saga*, with its uniquely short time span, reveals an author acutely sensitive to the precise and economical relation of time, distance and action. I have confined the analysis in this book to a small handful of family saga texts. However, in exploring the double temporality of saga narrative – our apprehension of the narrative not only as a pre-conceived whole, but also as a stretch of time we move through, as we move through our lives – I hope I have set out a way of receiving and appreciating any saga narrative. Indeed, I hope that this sort of analysis might in future be applied to Old Norse-Icelandic prose in other genres.

Because, I think, novels are a contemporary form, it is tempting to assume that family saga forays into the rhetoric of fiction constitute an advance on the apparently artless reporting of 'what happened' by a self-effacing narrator who knows no more about the 'actual' events and characters in the narrative than a knowledgeable but disinterested observer or storyteller might. To adopt this assumption would be to regard family sagas as moving towards something akin to prehistoric novels. But in my view, this is very far from the case. The extraordinary feat of family saga authors is how their narrators manage to maintain – by and large – an impersonal stance, whilst at the same time drawing their audiences close in, allowing them to experience the present moment of the storyworld, apparently at first hand, without narratorial guidance, and to judge it for themselves, in all its uncertainty and ambiguity. This balance lies at the heart of the poetics of family saga prose and the remarkable achievement of its authors: the creation of the third time which is narrative, and thereby, the conditions for a revelatory thought experiment of what living in the *söguöld* might have been like, whilst nevertheless maintaining the fundamental status of sagas as representations of a passed past.

Notes

Chapter 1

1 M. C. van den Toorn, 'Zeit und Tempus in der Saga', *Arkiv för nordisk filologi* 76 (1961): 137.
2 Vésteinn Ólason, *Dialogues with the Viking Age: Narration and Representation in the Sagas of the Icelanders*, trans. Andrew Wawn (Reykjavík: Heimskringla, 1998), 85.
3 Kathryn Hume, 'Beginnings and Endings in the Icelandic Family Sagas', *Modern Language Review* 68, no. 3 (1973): 593.
4 Gísli Sigurðsson, *The Medieval Icelandic Saga and Oral Tradition: A Discourse on Method*, trans. Nicholas Jones (Cambridge, MA: Harvard University Press, 2004), 144, 191–201.
5 Hume, 'Beginnings and Endings', 593.
6 Vésteinn Ólason, *Dialogues with the Viking Age*, 87.
7 Hume, 'Beginnings and Endings', 593.
8 Vésteinn Ólason, *Dialogues with the Viking Age*, 85; Hume, 'Beginnings and Endings', 602.
9 Vésteinn Ólason, *Dialogues with the Viking Age*, 86–7.
10 Gísli Sigurðsson, *Medieval Icelandic Saga*, 144. Einar Haugen, ed., *First Grammatical Treatise: The Earliest Germanic Phonology: An Edition, Translation and Commentary* (London: Longman, 1972), 12–13.
11 Gísli Sigurðsson, *Medieval Icelandic Saga*, 194.
12 Margaret Clunies Ross, *The Cambridge Introduction to the Old Norse-Icelandic Saga* (Cambridge: Cambridge University Press, 2010), 136.
13 Gísli Sigurðsson, *Medieval Icelandic Saga*, 200.
14 Einar Ól. Sveinsson, ed., *Laxdæla saga*, Íslenzk fornrit, vol. 5 (Reykjavík: Hið íslenzka fornritfélag, 1934), 3. (Hereafter, *Laxdæla saga*.)
15 Einar Ól. Sveinsson, ed., *Brennu-Njáls saga*, Íslenzk fornrit, vol. 12 (Reykjavík: Hið íslenzka fornritfélag, 1954), 6. (Hereafter, *Njáls saga*.)
16 *Laxdæla saga*, 3.
17 Hermann Pálsson, *Keltar á Íslandi* (Reykjavík: Háskólaútgáfan, 1997), 94–5.
18 *Laxdæla saga*, 3.
19 Ibid., 8–13. On Unnr's commanding death pose, see Ármann Jakobsson, 'The Patriarch: Myth and Reality', in *Youth and Age in the Medieval North*, ed. Shannon Lewis-Simpson (Leiden: Brill, 2008), 270.

20 *Laxdœla saga*, 23. I shall discuss this scene further in Chapter 5.
21 *Laxdœla saga*, 57.
22 Ibid., 67–8.
23 Ibid., 199–201.
24 Ibid., 215–17.
25 Ibid., 4–7.
26 Einar Ól. Sveinsson and Matthías Þórðarson, ed., *Eyrbyggja saga*, Íslenzk fornrit, vol. 4 (Reykjavík: Hið íslenzka fornritfélag, 1935), 3–6. (Hereafter, *Eyrbyggja saga*.)
27 *Laxdœla saga*, 5.
28 *Eyrbyggja saga*, 6–7.
29 Ibid., 13.
30 Ibid., 12.
31 Guðni Jónsson, ed., *Grettis saga Ásmundarsonar*, Íslenzk fornrit, vol. 7 (Reykjavík: Hið íslenzka fornritfélag, 1936), 3. (Hereafter, *Grettis saga*.)
32 *Grettis saga*, 7.
33 Jakob Benediktsson, ed., '*Landnámabók*', in *Íslendingabók/Landnámabók*, Íslenzk fornrit, vol. 1 (Reykjavík: Hið íslenzka fornritfélag, 1986), 37, 146, 348, 380. (Hereafter, *Landnámabók*.)
34 *Grettis saga*, 4.
35 Ibid., 10–19.
36 Ibid., 6.
37 Ibid., 25–6.
38 Ibid., 261.
39 *Njáls saga*, 5.
40 Theodore M. Andersson, *The Growth of the Medieval Icelandic Sagas (1180–1280)* (Ithaca: Cornell University Press, 2006), 184.
41 See Ursula Dronke, *The Role of Sexual Themes in 'Njáls saga'* (London: Viking Society for Northern Research, 1981).
42 Jón Jóhannesson, ed., '*Hrafnkels saga Freysgoða*', in *Austfirðinga sǫgur*, Íslenzk fornrit, vol. 11 (Reykjavík: Hið íslenzka fornritfélag, 1950), 97. (Hereafter, *Hrafnkels saga*.)
43 *Njáls saga*, 75.
44 Ibid., 82.
45 Ibid., 197–8.
46 *Eyrbyggja saga*, 60.
47 *Laxdœla saga*, 16.
48 Ibid., 44.
49 Ibid., 78, 116–23.
50 Ibid., 215–17.
51 *Grettis saga*, 61. I will discuss this episode in more detail in Chapter 5.

52 *Njáls saga*, 438–9.
53 Ibid., 446–53.
54 *Eyrbyggja saga*, 80–1.
55 For a full account of how sagas variously represent this link, see Robert Avis, 'The Social Mythology of Medieval Icelandic Literature' (D.Phil. diss., University of Oxford, Oxford, 2011), 33–51.
56 *Njáls saga*, 255.
57 See Ólafia Einarsdóttir, *Studier i kronologisk metode: i tidlig islandsk historieskrivning* (Lund: CWK Gleerup, 1964).
58 Ibid., 165–83; Jakob Benediktsson, ed., '*Íslendingabók*', in *Íslendingabók/ Landnámabók*, Íslenzk fornrit, vol. 1 (Reykjavík: Hið íslenzka fornritfélag, 1986), 3. (Hereafter, *Íslendingabók*.)
59 *Eyrbyggja saga*, 183–4.
60 *Laxdæla saga*, 226. However, the date is not in fact specified in *Íslendingabók*.
61 *Laxdæla saga*, xlviii–lx, at l.
62 Ibid., 168.
63 Ibid., 176.
64 Magnus Magnusson and Hermann Pálsson, trans., *Laxdaela saga* (Harmondsworth: Penguin, 1969), 25.
65 Ibid.
66 *Grettis saga*, 35.
67 *Eyrbyggja saga*, 152–3.
68 *Laxdæla saga*, 196.
69 *Grettis saga*, 28–33.
70 *Íslendingabók*, xxxviii, 13.
71 *Grettis saga*, lxi.
72 *Njáls saga*, 236–48.
73 *Íslendingabók*, xxxviii, 19. See also Siân Grønlie, trans., *Íslendingabók, Kristni Saga: The Book of the Icelanders, The Story of the Conversion* (London: Viking Society for Northern Research, 2006), xlvii, 27 n. 80.
74 *Eyrbyggja saga*, 59–60.
75 *Íslendingabók*, 13–14.
76 Grønlie, trans., *Íslendingabók, Kristni Saga*, xxvi. Grønlie draws attention to the way Iceland is 'out here' in relation to Norway, but Greenland is 'out there', 'from here' in relation to Iceland.
77 *Hrafnkels saga*, 109.
78 Ibid., 125–30.
79 *Njáls saga*, 201.
80 Ibid., 460.
81 *Grettis saga*, 85.

82 *Laxdœla saga*, 77–80.
83 Ibid., 221–3.
84 *Hrafnkels saga*, 97.
85 *Laxdœla saga*, 197.
86 Ibid., 91, 196–7.
87 I will discuss the interplay of who knows what about this killing in a Chapter 5.
88 Björn K. Þórólfsson and Guðni Jónsson, ed., '*Gísla saga*', in *Vestfirðinga sögur*, Íslenzk fornrit, vol. 6 (Reykjavík: Hið íslenzka fornritfélag, 1943), 52–5. (Hereafter, *Gísla saga*.)
89 *Gísla saga*, 57.
90 *Njáls saga*, 233.
91 *Laxdœla saga*, 76.
92 Einar Ól. Sveinsson, ed., '*Kormáks saga*', in *Vatnsdœla saga*, Íslenzk fornrit, vol. 8 (Reykjavík: Hið íslenzka fornritfélag, 1939), 261. (Hereafter, *Kormáks saga*.)
93 *Njáls saga*, 185.
94 *Hrafnkels saga*, 126.
95 This is apparently a realistic depiction of unpredictable weather in Haukadalur; see *Gísla saga*, 43, n. 1.
96 *Gísla saga*, 43. I will discuss the way the identity of the killer is withheld in Chapter 5.
97 *Njáls saga*, 120–2.
98 Ibid., 122–5.
99 Ibid., 90.
100 *Hrafnkels saga*, 105–6.
101 For a detailed discussion of the ambiguities in the saga, see William Miller, *Hrafnkel or the Ambiguities: Hard Cases, Hard Choices* (Oxford: Oxford University Press, 2017).
102 *Laxdœla saga*, 11.
103 Ibid., 65.
104 Ibid., 73.
105 Ibid., 8–9. On the sources of *Lear*, see Meredith Skura, 'Dragon Fathers and Unnatural Children: Warring Generations in King Lear and Its Sources', *Comparative Drama* 42, no. 2 (2008): 141.
106 *Gísla saga*, 104.
107 Ibid., 109.
108 Ibid.
109 Ibid., 111.
110 Ibid., 115–16.
111 *Eyrbyggja saga*, 93.
112 Ibid., 93.

113 Ibid..
114 Ibid., 94.
115 *Grettis saga*, 110.
116 Ibid., 111.
117 Ibid., 111–12.
118 *Laxdœla saga*, 12.
119 Ibid., 13. See note n. 20 above.
120 *Njáls saga*, 323.
121 Ibid., 323–4.
122 Ibid., 330–1.
123 Ibid., 334.
124 *Gísla saga*, 97, n. 3.
125 Ibid., 97.
126 Ibid., 97–9.
127 *Eyrbyggja saga*, 116.
128 Ibid.
129 *Njáls saga*, 62.
130 *Hrafnkels saga*, 126.
131 Ibid., 131.
132 Ibid., 103–4
133 Ibid., 126.
134 Ibid., 120.
135 Ibid., 105.
136 Of course, a specific 'clock' time as marked by the sun would vary with the time of year. But perhaps what counted for shepherds as mid-afternoon in the middle of summer might be a different hour from mid-afternoon at the beginning or end of the summer season.
137 *Laxdœla saga*, 198–9.
138 *Eyrbyggja saga*, 99–100.
139 Ibid., 100.
140 Sigurður Nordal, ed., *Egils saga Skalla-Grímssonar*, Íslenzk fornrit, vol. 2 (Reykjavík: Hið íslenzka fornritfélag, 1933), 52 (hereafter *Egils saga*); Björn K. Þórólfsson and Guðni Jónsson, ed., '*Fóstbrœðra saga*', in *Vestfirðinga sögur*, Íslenzk fornrit, vol. 6 (Reykjavík: Hið íslenzka fornritfélag, 1943), 244.
141 *Gísla saga*, 75. I am very grateful to Gareth Lloyd Evans for these references.
142 See Christopher Abram, *Evergreen Ash: Ecology and Catastrophe in Old Norse Myth and Literature* (Charlottesville: University of Virginia Press, 2019), 37.
143 Grønlie, trans., *Íslendingabók, Kristni Saga*, 20, n. 36.
144 *Hrafnkels saga*, 108. See also, for instance, *Gísla saga*, 63.
145 Ibid., 118.

146 Ibid., 109.
147 Andrew Dennis, Peter Foote, and Richard Perkins, ed., *Laws of Early Iceland: Grágás*, 2 vols (Winnipeg: University of Manitoba Press, 1980–2000), 1.92–5, 1.250. (Hereafter, *Grágás*.)
148 *Gísla saga*, 4.
149 *Eyrbyggja saga*, 146.
150 *Grettis saga*, 226.
151 Ibid., 289.
152 Ibid., 244–5.
153 Ibid., 164.
154 *Grágás*, 1.125–6, 1.250.
155 *Gísla saga*, 34–5.
156 Ibid., 36.
157 Ibid.
158 *Grettis saga*, 111.
159 Gabriel Turville-Petre, *Myth and Religion of the North: The Religion of Ancient Scandinavia* (London: Weidenfeld and Nicolson, 1964), 243.
160 *Laxdœla saga*, xlvi.
161 I have discussed elsewhere the bold collocation of the heroic and the Christian, or biblical, in family sagas; Heather O'Donoghue, 'Figura in *Njáls saga*: The Dorothea Coke Memorial Lecture 2018', *Saga-Book* 42 (2018): 156–8.
162 *Laxdœla saga*, 118.
163 Ibid., 121.
164 Ibid., 122.
165 Ibid.
166 Ibid., 147.
167 Ibid.
168 Ibid., 154.

Chapter 2

1 Gérard Genette, *Narrative Discourse: An Essay in Method*, trans. Jane E. Lewin (Ithaca: Cornell University Press, 1980), 27.
2 Paul Ricœur, *Time and Narrative*, trans. Kathleen McLaughlin and David Pellauer, 3 vols (Chicago: University of Chicago Press, 1984–8), 2.77.
3 Jonathan Culler, *The Pursuit of Signs: Semiotics, Literature, Deconstruction* (Ithaca: Cornell University Press, 1981), 171. The application of post-medieval literary theory to medieval texts is of course controversial. I would argue that at the level of basic narratological features such as these, the theory is applicable to all kinds of narrative, if used with care.

4   Genette, *Narrative Discourse*, 86–112.
5   It is worth noting that theoretically all narratives are to some degree elliptical, since no narrative could possibly relate everything that happened in every single moment of an event. See Seymour Chatman, *Story and Discourse: Narrative Structure in Fiction and Film* (Ithaca: Cornell University Press, 1978), 30.
6   Genette, *Narrative Discourse*, 106.
7   See ibid., 87. For most readers, even relatively slow ones, passages can usually be read much more quickly than recited. Speed of recitation perhaps varies a little less than reading time and so provides a reasonable measure of story time as against narrative time.
8   Genette, *Narrative Discourse*, 93.
9   Ibid.
10 See however, Slavica Ranković, 'Golden Ages and Fishing Grounds: The Emergent Past in the *Íslendingasögur*', *Saga-Book of the Viking Society* XXX (2006): 39–64. In a wide-ranging article, Ranković also considers the stance of saga narrators, and their avoidance of responsibility for the narrative, drawing together some of the other issues I discuss in this book.
11 Jamie Cochrane, 'Passing Time and the Past in Grettis Saga Ásmundarsonar', in *The Preprint Papers of the 14th International Saga Conference*, ed. Agneta Ney, Henrik Williams and Fredrik Charpentier Ljungqvist, 2 vols (Gävle: Gävle University Press, 2009), 1.194–5.
12 See, for instance, '[V]ar kyrrt allan þann vetr' (It was quiet all that winter); *Laxdœla saga*, 22.
13 *Njáls saga*, 63, 51, 33, 129. See Cochrane's illustrative list of similar examples from *Grettis saga*; Cochrane, 'Passing Time', 194–5.
14 *Grettis saga*, 210.
15 *Eyrbyggja saga*, 11.
16 Ibid., 11.
17 *Laxdœla saga*, 38.
18 Ibid., 77.
19 *Eyrbyggja saga*, 172. This feature – being roughly twice as advanced than the norm for his chronological age – is one Glæsir shares with prodigious human heroes: see, for example, *Egils saga*, 80; *Laxdœla saga*, 27.
20 *Eyrbyggja saga*, 173–6.
21 I noted in the previous chapter how accelerating one narrative strand – the maturing of Bolli Bollason so as to credit him with taking vengeance on his father's killer – can cause a lack of synchronicity with the chronology of other strands.
22 In fact, saga authors do not often use this technique, but I shall discuss some instances of it Chapter 3.
23 *Njáls saga*, 85, 48, 7.
24 *Laxdœla saga*, 170.

25 Ibid., 108.
26 *Eyrbyggja saga*, 96.
27 Ibid., 97.
28 Ibid., 97–103.
29 *Grettis saga*, 147.
30 Ibid., 124. See also ibid., 201.
31 Ibid., 104.
32 Ibid., 174. For a fuller discussion of 'tíðendi' denoting a pre-existing narrative, see Chapter 4.
33 On the 'rhetoric of fiction', see further Wayne C. Booth, *The Rhetoric of Fiction* (Chicago: University of Chicago Press, 1961). In commonsensical terms, it is unlikely that substantial stretches of dialogue in medieval narrative could represent what was actually said on some occasion, whatever an audience might have felt about its authenticity.
34 See Percy Lubbock, *The Craft of Fiction* (London: Jonathan Cape, 1921), 62.
35 Carol Clover, 'Scene in Saga Composition', *Arkiv för nordisk filologi* 89 (1974): 58.
36 *Laxdœla saga*, 5.
37 *Njáls saga*, 7.
38 Ibid., 7.
39 Ibid., 7–124.
40 Dronke, *Role of Sexual Themes*.
41 See O'Donoghue, 'Figura in *Njáls saga*', 153.
42 Hans Wulff, 'Suspense and the Influence of Cataphora on Viewers' Expectations', in *Suspense: Conceptualizations, Theoretical Analyses and Empirical Explorations*, ed. Peter Vorderer, Hans Wulff and Mike Friedrichsen (Manwah, NJ: Erlbaum, 1996), 2.
43 Even if the audience – whether medieval or modern – is familiar with the story of Gunnarr and Hallgerðr, the cataphor still makes us impatient to go on with the narrative. For a persuasive demonstration that narrative suspense still functions if an audience is aware of the outcome – and many saga receivers were and are – see Noël Carroll, 'The Paradox of Suspense', in *Suspense: Conceptualizations, Theoretical Analyses and Empirical Explorations*, ed. Peter Vorderer, Hans Wulff and Mike Friedrichsen (Manwah, NJ: Erlbaum, 1996), 71–91.
44 See Anne Saxon Slater, 'From Rhetoric and Structure to Psychology in *Hrafnkels Saga Freysgoða*', *Scandinavian Studies* 40, no. 1 (1968): 36–7, and Sigurður Nordal, *Hrafnkels saga Freysgoða: A Study*, trans. George Thomas (Cardiff: University of Wales Press, 1958), 40, 55.
45 *Hrafnkels saga*, 103–4.
46 Ibid., 105.
47 Ibid.

48 Ibid.
49 See this chapter, footnotes 41 and 42.
50 *Grettis saga*, 112.
51 Ibid., 119.
52 Ibid.
53 Ibid., 120.
54 Ibid.
55 Ibid., 121-2.
56 Ibid., 122. It is worth mention that in the scenes previously discussed, the narrative has allowed for witnesses who might plausibly have recorded and transmitted events: Ketill's followers; the other feasters in Höskuldr's hall; the women who were milking when Hrafnkell killed Einarr. These scenes are, strictly speaking, public events within the world of the narrative.
57 *Grettis saga*, 5-6.
58 This trope is not confined to Old Norse literature; the Old English poem 'The Battle of Maldon' offers a very celebrated example; E. V. K. Dobbie, ed., 'The Battle of Maldon', in *The Anglo-Saxon Minor Poems* (London: Routledge, 1942), 15-16 (ll. 312-19).
59 *Grettis saga*, 6.
60 Ibid., 251. See also the discussion of apparently themed details in genealogies in Chapter 1.
61 See, for example, Sigurður Nordal and Guðni Jónsson, ed., '*Heiðarvíga saga*', in *Borgfirðinga sögur*, Íslenzk fornrit, vol. 3 (Reykjavík: Hið íslenzka fornritfélag, 1938), 301-9, and Einar Ól. Sveinsson, ed., *Vatnsdæla saga*, Íslenzk fornrit, vol. 8 (Reykjavík: Hið íslenzka fornritfélag, 1939), 79-80.
62 *Grágás*, 1.139-42; 2.24-5.
63 *Laxdæla saga*, 27.
64 As Genette rightly warns, not all passages of description constitute a narrative pause – see Gérard Genette, *Narrative Discourse Revisited*, trans. Jane E. Lewin (Ithaca: Cornell University Press, 1988), 36.
65 *Hrafnkels saga*, 99, 128.
66 Ibid., 129.
67 Ibid., 99.
68 *Grettis saga*, 186.
69 Ibid., 199. This description does not fit present-day Þórisdalr; see Ibid., n. 1.
70 *Grettis saga*, 225-6.
71 Ibid., 225.
72 *Laxdæla saga*, 55.
73 Ibid., 63-6.
74 Ibid., 76-7.

75 Ibid., 77.
76 T. M. Andersson also draws attention to the practice of such eulogistic characterization, but associates it with the impending death of the saga hero, and does not relate it to narrative time. See T. M. Andersson, *The Icelandic Family Saga: An Analytic Reading* (Cambridge, MA: Harvard University Press, 1967), 60–2.
77 *Laxdœla saga*, 77. See also Chapter 4.
78 Ibid., 134–5.
79 *Eyrbyggja saga*, 8–9. See also the discussion of the temple in Chapter 1.
80 Ibid., 26–7, 139.
81 Ibid., 120–1.
82 *Laxdœla saga*, 186–91. Andersson and Miller note the frequency with which saga characters are identified by their clothing but are not concerned with description and narrative time. See T. M. Andersson and William I. Miller, *Law and Literature in Medieval Iceland: Ljósvetninga Saga and Valla-Ljóts Saga* (Stanford, CA: Stanford University Press, 1989), 141–42, n. 38.
83 *Hrafnkels saga*, 128.
84 This catalogue of the appearances of several attackers is clearly an echo of an established literary trope. Consider, for example, its appearance in the Irish *Togail Bruidne Da Derga*; see Ralph O'Connor, *The Destruction of Da Derga's Hostel: Kingship and Narrative Artistry in a Mediaeval Irish Saga* (Oxford: Oxford University Press, 2013).
85 Sigurður Nordal and Guðni Jónsson, ed., 'Bjarnar saga Hítdœlakappa', in *Borgfirðinga sögur*, Íslenzk fornrit, vol. 3 (Reykjavík: Hið íslenzka fornritfélag, 1938), 197–200. (Hereafter, *Bjarnar saga*.)
86 But see Tom Morcom, 'Insult and Insight: Skarpheðinn's Performance at the Alþingi', *Viking and Medieval Scandinavia*, vol. 16 (2020), for another interpretation of the function of the descriptions.
87 *Njáls saga*, 298.
88 Ibid.
89 I will discuss Skarpheðinn's insult in Chapter 3, as an example of analepsis as recall: alluding to something in the narrative past which was not mentioned at the time.
90 *Njáls saga*, 299.
91 Ibid., 301.
92 Ibid., 301–2.
93 Ibid., 303.
94 Ibid., 304.
95 Ibid., 304–5.
96 Ibid., 306.
97 For verses as pauses in the narrative, see Hallvard Magerøy, 'Skaldestrofer som retardasjonmiddel i islendingesogene', in *Sjötíu ritgerðir helgaðar Jakobi*

Benediktssyni 20. Júlí 1977, ed. Einar G. Pétursson and Jónas Kristjánsson, 2 vols (Reykjavík: Stofnun Árna Magnússonar, 1977), 586–99.

98 Heather O'Donoghue, *Skaldic Verse and the Poetics of Saga Narrative* (Oxford: Oxford University Press, 2005).

99 O'Donoghue, *Skaldic Verse*, 3–4. It should be noted that this is not, as some scholars have implied, a distinction inherent in the verses themselves, but a distinction in the way they are presented in the narrative.

100 Whether or not a verse is quoted in a saga text – either in full, or with a first-line reference – varies in the manuscript tradition, so it's impossible to be certain whether the effect of the placement is authorial or scribal, and which audience the effect is available to.

Chapter 3

1 Genette, *Narrative Discourse*, 40.
2 Ibid., 49–50.
3 Vésteinn Ólason, *Dialogues with the Viking Age*, 96.
4 Peter Brooks, *Reading for the Plot: Design and Intention in Narrative* (Cambridge, MA: Harvard University Press, 1984), 13.
5 For this reason, proleptic irony, a direct and knowing communication between a temporally omniscient narrator and readers or listeners, is rare in family sagas.
6 Booth, *The Rhetoric of Fiction*, 191.
7 Genette, *Narrative Discourse*, 40.
8 Ibid., 205.
9 *Eyrbyggja saga*, 28–53. For reservations about the literary quality of this episode, see O'Donoghue, *Skaldic Verse*, 128–9.
10 *Eyrbyggja saga*, 54.
11 Ibid.
12 *Grettis saga*, 121.
13 *Njáls saga*, 136, 173.
14 Ibid., 57. See also Jónas Kristjánsson and Vésteinn Ólason, ed., '*Völuspá*', in *Eddukvæði I: Goðakvæði*, Íslenzk fornrit (Eddukvæði), vol. 1 (Reykjavík: Hið íslenzka fornritfélag, 2014), 291–321. (Hereafter, *Völuspá*.)
15 *Njáls saga*, 57, n. 3.
16 Ibid., 84.
17 Ibid., 87.
18 Ibid., 104–5.
19 Ibid., 139.
20 Ibid., 274.

21 Ibid., 139.
22 Ibid., 206.
23 Ibid..
24 Ibid., 267.
25 *Eyrbyggja saga*, 34.
26 *Njáls saga*, 59–63.
27 Ibid., 24–5.
28 Ibid., 26, 59.
29 *Laxdœla saga*, 174, 178–9.
30 *Eyrbyggja saga*, 87–8.
31 Ibid., 81.
32 Ibid., 133.
33 Ibid., 119.
34 *Njáls saga*, 42.
35 Ibid., 364.
36 Ibid., 369.
37 Ibid., 177.
38 *Gísla saga*, 28–9.
39 *Laxdœla saga*, 112.
40 Ibid., 25.
41 *Njáls saga*, 82.
42 *Laxdœla saga*, 37, 111.
43 *Eyrbyggja saga*, 27, 26. For a fuller discussion of this sort of management of the narrative line, see Chapter 4.
44 *Grettis saga*, 26, 88, 94.
45 See Bettina Sommer, 'The Norse Concept of Luck', *Scandinavian Studies* 79, no. 3 (2007): 275–94.
46 *Grettis saga*, 134.
47 Ibid., 38–9, 82, 117, 172.
48 *Njáls saga*, 210.
49 Ibid., 209.
50 Ibid., 7.
51 Ibid., 32–3.
52 Ibid., 87.
53 Ibid., 160.
54 Ibid., 154.
55 Ibid., 160, 187.
56 *Eyrbyggja saga*, 141–2.
57 Ibid., 142.
58 *Njáls saga*, 186.
59 Ibid., 183.

60 Ibid., 101.
61 Ibid., 235.
62 Ibid., 237.
63 It's hard to see the relevance of the compound 'marlíðendr' (literally, sea-travellers). Rather, is tempting to interpret the first element as relating not to the sea, but to the *mara*, or female night-spirit. See Ármann Jakobsson, 'The Fearless Vampire Killers: A Note about the Icelandic *Draugr* and Demonic Contamination in *Grettis Saga*', in *Nine Saga Studies: The Critical Interpretation of the Icelandic Sagas*, ed. Ármann Jakobsson (Reykjavík: University of Iceland Press, 2013), 125–137, 128. For an authoritative analysis of the *mara*, see Caroline R. Batten 'Dark Riders: Disease, Sexual Violence, and Gender Performance in the Old English Maere and Old Norse Mara', *JEGP*, vol. 120 (2021).
64 Jónas Kristjánsson, ed., '*Víga-Glúms saga*', in *Eyfirðinga sögur*, Íslenzk fornrit, vol. 9 (Reykjavík: Hið íslenzka fornritfélag, 1956), 30–1.
65 *Njáls saga*, 106.
66 Ibid., 170.
67 Ibid., 324.
68 Ibid.
69 *Laxdœla saga*, 84.
70 Ibid., 84.
71 Ibid., 85.
72 See Georgia Dunham Kelchner, *Dreams in Old Norse Literature and Their Affinities in Folklore* (Cambridge: Cambridge University Press, 1935), 77–144 and Gabriel Turville-Petre, 'Dreams in Icelandic Tradition', *Folklore* 69, no. 2 (1958): 93–111.
73 See O'Donoghue, *Skaldic Verse*, 136–79.
74 *Gísla saga*, 70.
75 Ibid., 70.
76 Ibid., 77.
77 Ibid., 94.
78 Ibid., 94.
79 O'Donoghue, *Skaldic Verse*, 165.
80 *Gísla saga*, 105.
81 See I. A. Richards, *The Philosophy of Rhetoric* (London: Oxford University Press, 1936).
82 *Njáls saga*, 155–6.
83 Ibid., 159.
84 Ibid., 351–2.
85 Ibid., 352.
86 Ibid., 93–4.
87 *Laxdœla saga*, 88–9.

88 Ibid., 87. For an excellent critique of the strangeness and possible significance of a teenaged Guðrún conversing on apparently equal terms with Gestr, see Ármann Jakobsson, 'Laxdœla Dreaming: A Saga Heroine Invents Her Own Life', in *Nine Saga Studies: The Critical Interpretation of the Icelandic Sagas*, ed. Ármann Jakobsson (Reykjavík: University of Iceland Press, 2013), 173–89. In this article, Ármann also makes the surprising claim that Guðrún invents the substance of these dreams.
89 *Laxdœla saga*, 91.
90 Ibid., 215.
91 Ibid.
92 Ibid., 222.
93 See Einar Ól. Sveinsson, '*Njáls saga*': *A Literary Masterpiece* (Lincoln: University of Nebraska Press, 1971), 205–6.
94 *Njáls saga*, 346.
95 Ibid., 346.
96 There is only one minor discrepancy between the dream and later events: Glúmr himself is included in the wrong group. See ibid., 347, n. 7.
97 *Njáls saga*, 362–413.
98 *Eyrbyggja saga*, 140–52 at 145–6.
99 Ibid., 145.
100 Ibid., 146.
101 Ibid., 147–8.
102 Ibid., 116.
103 Ibid., 115.
104 Ibid., 171.
105 Ibid., 172.
106 O'Donoghue, *Skaldic Verse*, 129.
107 *Eyrbyggja saga*, 173–6.
108 O'Donoghue, 'Figura in *Njáls saga*', 160.
109 *Eyrbyggja saga*, 140.
110 *Njáls saga*, 175.
111 Discrepancies in the MS tradition contribute to our sense that this was not a familiar idea to at least one scribe; see ibid., n. 4, and the reference to the kenning *benrögn* (wound-rain) in a verse later in the saga; ibid., 193.
112 *Njáls saga*, 454–9. See also Russell Poole, *Viking Poems of War and Peace: A Study in Skaldic Narrative* (Toronto: University of Toronto Press, 1991), 120–42.
113 *Njáls saga*, 291. See also O'Donoghue, 'Figura in *Njáls saga*', 161–3.
114 *Njáls saga*, 459.
115 Ibid.
116 Ibid., 459–60.

117 See also O'Donoghue, 'Figura in *Njáls saga*', 160–5.
118 *Eyrbyggja saga*, 141.
119 *Njáls saga*, 172.
120 Ibid., 329.
121 Ibid., 274.
122 Ibid., 168.
123 *Gísla saga*, 34.
124 Ibid., 40.
125 *Grettis saga*, 57.
126 *Laxdœla saga*, 27–8.
127 Characters might also be depicted as the recipients of social memory, knowing about occurrences before their own lives if not actually remembering them personally. For an example, the legal case about the whale, discussed later in this chapter, as well as *Grettis saga*, 31–2 and. On social or cultural memory in the sagas, see also Vésteinn Ólason, 'Dialogues with the Past', in *Handbook of Pre-Modern Nordic Memory Studies: Interdisciplinary Approaches*, ed. Jürg Glauser, Pernille Hermann and Stephen A. Mitchell, vol. 1 (Berlin: De Gruyter, 2018), 489–94.
128 *Njáls saga*, 189.
129 Ibid., 189–91.
130 *Grettis saga*, 46.
131 *Njáls saga*, 297–303. For a celebrated instance of similar 'blasts from the past' see also *Ölkofra þáttr*; Jón Jóhannesson, ed., '*Ölkofra þáttr*', in *Austfirðinga sögur*, Íslenzk fornrit, vol. 11 (Reykjavík: Hið íslenzka fornritfélag, 1950), 90–3.
132 *Gísla saga*, 30–1.
133 *Njáls saga*, 194.
134 Ibid., 330.
135 *Laxdœla saga*, 150.
136 Ibid.
137 Genette, *Narrative Discourse*, 37.
138 O'Donoghue, *Skaldic Verse*, 145, n. 21.
139 *Gísla saga*, 5.
140 Ibid., 58. The significance of this confession was not lost on the scribe/author of one version of the saga, who adds that the verse 'æva skyldi' (should never have been [recited]); see ibid., n. 1.
141 *Gísla saga*, 61.
142 *Grettis saga*, 31–2.
143 Ibid., 88–9, 93.
144 *Njáls saga*, 374–5.
145 *Hrafnkels saga*, 116–17.

146 Ibid., 107.
147 Genette, *Narrative Discourse*, 205.
148 *Laxdœla saga*, 151.
149 *Eyrbyggja saga*, 61–75. See also my discussion of this sibling dynamic in Chapter 4.
150 *Hrafnkels saga*, 103.
151 Ibid., 102.
152 Ibid., 108, 113.
153 *Grettis saga*, 130.
154 Ibid., 124.
155 Ibid., 126.
156 Ibid., 127.
157 Ibid., 272.
158 Ibid.
159 Ibid., 251–61.
160 Ibid., 273.
161 *Njáls saga*, 443.
162 Ibid., 333.
163 Ibid., 443.
164 Ibid.
165 Ibid., 277.
166 Ibid.
167 Ibid., 278.
168 Ibid.
169 Ibid.
170 Ibid., 22–8.
171 Ibid., 29.
172 Ibid.
173 *Laxdœla saga*, 51.
174 See Stith Thompson, ed., *Motif-Index of Folk-literature: A Classification of Narrative Elements in Folktales, Ballads, Myths, Fables, Mediaeval Romances, Exempla, Fabliaux, Jest-Books and Local Legends* (Bloomington: Indiana University Press, 1955), H80–H149, esp. H82.6 and H94.
175 *Njáls saga*, 64.
176 *Gísla saga*, 56–7, 69.
177 Ibid., 84.
178 *Laxdœla saga*, 42.
179 Ibid.
180 Ibid., 42–3.
181 *Gísla saga*, 56–7.
182 *Laxdœla saga*, 42–3.

Chapter 4

1. Ricœur, *Time and Narrative*, 2.99.
2. On possible composition by dictation in other medieval contexts, see, for example, Malcolm Godden, 'Did King Alfred Write Anything?', *Medium Ævum* 76, no. 1 (2007): 1.
3. *Stjörnu-Odda draumr* is a fascinating exception. It contains a complex layering of narrative voices, some of whom are individuated characters. It is set in Iceland, but shortly after the traditionally accepted end of the *söguöld*, and so is perhaps not strictly a family saga at all; see Ralph O'Connor, 'Astronomy and Dream Visions in Late Medieval Iceland: *Stjörnu-Odda draumr* and the Emergence of Norse Legendary Fiction', *JEGP* 111, no. 4 (2012): 474–512.
4. The best recent account of the saga narrator's neutrality and objectivity is Vésteinn Ólason, *Dialogues with the Viking Age*, 101. See also Carol Clover, 'Icelandic Family Sagas (Íslendingasögur)', in *Old Norse-Icelandic Literature: A Critical Guide*, ed. Carol Clover and John Lindow (Ithaca: Cornell University Press, 1985), 265 for a summary of the conventional view of the narrator, as nuanced by Lars Lönnroth.
5. Although the concept of a self-effacing narrator objectively relating events is widely accepted in saga studies, there are in fact obvious examples of narrators passing judgement on characters, most notably in the brief character sketches accompanying the introduction of new characters. See Jónas Kristjánsson, *Eddas and Sagas: Iceland's Medieval Literature*, trans. Peter Foote (Reykjavík: Hið íslenzka bókmenntafélag, 1988), 207. I will consider these introductory character sketches in the course of this chapter.
6. Booth, *Rhetoric of Fiction*, 71–6, 151. The phrase 'the organizing principle of the text' comes from Paul Cobley, *Narrative* (London: Routledge, 2014), 125. Mieke Bal discusses the limitations of Booth's definition, and H. Porter Abbott notes that 'inferred author' might be a better term, since the concept is constructed by the reader or listener; see Mieke Bal, *Narratology: Introduction to the Theory of Narrative*, 4th edn (Toronto: University of Toronto Press, 2017), 61, and H. Porter Abbott, *The Cambridge Introduction to Narrative* (Cambridge: Cambridge University Press, 2002), 77–8. With regard to family sagas, Margaret Clunies Ross claims that 'the stance of the Icelandic saga writer ... is self-effacing' – a clear conflation of the two roles; see Margaret Clunies Ross, *The Cambridge Introduction to the Old Norse-Icelandic Saga* (Cambridge: Cambridge University Press, 2010), 51.
7. For the concept of the immanent saga, see Carol Clover, 'The Long Prose Form', *Arkiv för nordisk filologi* 101 (1986): 36. See also Ranković, 'Golden Ages'.
8. See *Eyrbyggja saga*, 98–103.
9. Vésteinn Ólason, *Dialogues with the Viking Age*, 101.
10. Ibid., 102.

11 Ibid., 103.
12 *Njáls saga*, 29–35.
13 Ibid., 45–50.
14 Ibid., 50.
15 Sif Ríkharðsdóttir, *Emotion in Old Norse Literature: Translations, Voices, Contexts* (Cambridge: D. S. Brewer, 2017), 117 ff.
16 Ibid., 120.
17 Ibid.
18 *Njáls saga*, 48.
19 Ibid., 50–1.
20 Ibid., 183.
21 Ibid., 95.
22 Ibid., 96.
23 Ibid., 98, 102.
24 *Laxdœla saga*, 104–6.
25 Ibid., 110–11.
26 Ibid., 111.
27 Ibid., 16.
28 What Wayne Booth calls, after Flaubert, *impassibilité*; Booth, *Rhetoric of Fiction*, 81–3.
29 *Grettis saga*, 155.
30 Matthew Roby, 'Troll Sex: Youth, Old Age, and the Erotic in Old Norse-Icelandic Narratives of the Supernatural' (D.Phil. diss., University of Oxford, Oxford, 2019), 32–7.
31 *Hrafnkels saga*, 120.
32 Ibid., 121.
33 *Njáls saga*, 241–2.
34 *Laxdœla saga*, 68.
35 Ibid., 74.
36 Ibid., 66.
37 *Njáls saga*, 310.
38 Ibid., 311–12.
39 *Laxdœla saga*, 7.
40 See Chapter 1.
41 *Njáls saga*, 52.
42 *Eyrbyggja saga*, 19.
43 *Laxdœla saga*, 16.
44 *Grettis saga*, 146.
45 Ibid., 146.
46 Ibid., 147.

47 Ibid., 127.
48 *Eyrbyggja saga*, 54.
49 *Laxdœla saga*, 100.
50 Ibid., 138.
51 *Gísla saga*, 70.
52 *Eyrbyggja saga*, 139. For further analysis of this particular instance of displacement, including its implication that Þórgunna's age is a source of surreptitious gossip, see also Matthew Roby, 'Menopausal Marvels: Elderly Female Sexuality in the *Fróðárundur* of *Eyrbyggja saga*', *Saga-Book*, Saga-Book vol. XLIV (2020).
53 *Eyrbyggja saga*, 138–9.
54 *Laxdœla saga*, 93.
55 *Njáls saga*, 211.
56 Ibid., 211.
57 *Gísla saga*, 7.
58 Ibid., 7.
59 *Njáls saga*, 30.
60 Ibid., 32.
61 Ibid.
62 Ibid.
63 Ibid., 33.
64 Ibid.
65 *Eyrbyggja saga*, 78.
66 Ibid., 77. On dissimilarities between the content or implication of verse and prose in sagas, see O'Donoghue, *Skaldic Verse*.
67 *Eyrbyggja saga*, 80.
68 Ibid., 108.
69 Ibid., 108–9.
70 Ibid., 84.
71 *Gísla saga*, 57.
72 *Njáls saga*, 46.
73 Ibid.
74 *Eyrbyggja saga*, 170.
75 Ibid.
76 *Laxdœla saga*, 198.
77 Ibid., 198.
78 See Roby, 'Troll Sex', 52–66.
79 *Eyrbyggja saga*, 29.
80 Ibid.
81 Ibid., 30.
82 Ibid., 54.

83 *Grettis saga*, 118.
84 Ibid., 249.
85 Ibid., 249–51.
86 *Gísla saga*, 89–92.
87 Ibid., 117.
88 Ibid., 92.
89 Ibid., n. 4.
90 *Eyrbyggja saga*, 97.
91 Ibid., 98.
92 Ibid., 103.
93 *Gísla saga*, 88.
94 *Grettis saga*, 289–90.
95 *Gísla saga*, 116; *Njáls saga*, 189.
96 *Laxdæla saga*, 76, 86.
97 *Hrafnkels saga*, 99. For an analysis of the stock character of the *ójafnaðarmaðr*, see Joanne Shortt-Butler, 'Narrative Structure and the Individual in the *Íslendingasögur*: Motivation, Provocation and Characterisation' (Ph.D. diss., University of Cambridge, Cambridge, 2016).
98 I will address the issue of multiple readings in my Chapter 5; see also Rita Felski, *Uses of Literature* (Oxford: Blackwell, 2008), 113.
99 Carol Clover, *The Medieval Saga* (Ithaca: Cornell University Press, 1982), 89.
100 *Grettis saga*, 43.
101 Ibid., 95.
102 Ibid., 219.
103 See *Laxdæla saga*, 5, as well as, for instance, 49, 62, 86, 101, 125. See *Eyrbyggja saga*, 70.
104 See, for instance, *Njáls saga*, 80.
105 Ibid., 196. See also *Njáls saga*, 235, 278.
106 *Laxdæla saga*, 37.
107 Ibid., 83. See also George Manning for an analysis of the exchange of gender roles symbolically enacted here; George Manning, 'Scripts and Props: Saga-Women Staging Rage against Saga-Men' (unpublished conference paper, Bergen International Postgraduate Symposium in Old Norse Studies, Bergen, 2019).
108 *Laxdæla saga*, 49.
109 *Njáls saga*, 26.
110 Ibid., 57.
111 *Grettis saga*, 138.
112 Ibid., 237.
113 *Gísla saga*, 60.
114 Ibid., 65.

115 Ibid., 70.
116 Ibid., 80.
117 *Grettis saga*, 106–7, 162.
118 Ibid., 104.
119 *Laxdœla saga*, 48.
120 *Njáls saga*, 419.
121 See O'Donoghue, *Skaldic Verse*.
122 *Grettis saga*, 107.
123 Ibid., 200.
124 Ibid., 213.
125 Ibid., 169–70.
126 Ibid., 35.
127 Ibid., 42.
128 Ibid., 243.
129 *Laxdœla saga*, 229.
130 *Eyrbyggja saga*, 180.
131 *Grettis saga*, 205.
132 *Laxdœla saga*, 199.
133 *Grettis saga*, 33.
134 Ibid., 219.
135 *Njáls saga*, 239.
136 *Grettis saga*, 168; *Laxdœla saga*, 80.
137 This distinction mirrors a distinction I made earlier with regard to description: a passage of description may simply function as scene-setting, or it may help the audience to understand the circumstances of some event. See Chapter 2.
138 *Eyrbyggja saga*, 117.
139 *Laxdœla saga*, 219.
140 *Grettis saga*, 38.
141 *Laxdœla saga*, 145. See Jón Johannesson, *Sturlunga saga*, 2 vols (Reykjavík: Sturluútgáfan, 1946), 1.235. Interestingly, both these editors, and a recent translator of the saga, *do* note that the facilities were separate from the farmhouse.
142 See *Grettis saga* 55, n. 1.
143 *Gísla saga*, 44.
144 The standard distinction is between *víg*, a killing which is announced, and *morð*, which is kept secret; see, for instance, *Egils saga*, 181, n. 1.
145 *Hrafnkels saga*, 118.
146 *Grágás*, 2.212, n. 110.
147 *Eyrbyggja saga*, 104.
148 Similar laws appear in *Grágás*, 1.151, 1.156–7. See also *Eyrbyggja saga*, 104, n. 4.
149 *Hrafnkels saga*, 119. This name has apparently not survived.

150 *Laxdœla saga*, 9.
151 See references to, for instance, a hut Grettir allegedly once stayed in on Arnavatnsheiðr; a wall built by two berserks in *Eyrbyggja saga*; another wall in the same saga, built by Arnkell; and a temple built by Hrútr in *Laxdœla saga*. *Grettis saga* 178; *Eyrbyggja saga*, 72, 95; *Laxdœla saga*, 48.
152 *Hrafnkels saga*, 99, 127.
153 *Grettis saga*, 48, 102, 192.
154 Ibid., 157.
155 Ibid.
156 Emily Lethbridge points out that certain aspects of Icelandic geography and topography have changed a great deal since the Middle Ages, and therefore cautions readers (and scholars) against presuming exact correspondences between modern and medieval Icelandic landscapes; see Emily Lethbridge, 'Icelandic Saga Map: The Seduction of Landscape and the Digital' (unpublished conference paper, Medieval English Research Seminar, Oxford, 2016). The 'Icelandic Saga Map', an invaluable tool resulting from the research of Lethbridge and others, can be found at http://sagamap.hi.is/is/.
157 *Íslendingabók*, 17; Sigurgeir Steingrímsson, Ólafur Halldórsson, and Peter Foote, ed., 'Kristni saga', in *Biskupa sögur I*, Íslenzk Fornrit, vol. 15, 2 vols (Reykjavík: Hið íslenzka fornritafélag, 2003), 2.36.
158 Turville-Petre, *Myth and Religion*, 243.
159 *Eyrbyggja saga*, 148.
160 Ibid., 122.
161 Ibid., 122, n. 2. See also *Völuspá*, 297.
162 *Eyrbyggja saga*, 74. See too, for example, the mention of King Haraldr's berserks, who are said to be resistant to weaponry; *Grettis saga*, 5.
163 *Eyrbyggja saga*, 92.
164 *Gísla saga*, 56–7, 69.
165 *Laxdœla saga*, 42–3. On trials by ordeal following the conversion, see *Laxdœla saga*, 43, n. 1.
166 *Grettis saga*, 236.
167 *Laxdœla saga*, 97.
168 *Gísla saga*, 65.
169 Ibid., 58.
170 *Grettis saga*, 219.
171 *Gísla saga*, 97.
172 *Eyrbyggja saga*, 61.
173 Ibid., 61–2. See my discussion of imperfect anachrony, in this case a false prediction, in Chapter 3.
174 *Hrafnkels saga*, 105.

175 Miller, *Hrafnkel or the Ambiguities*.
176 *Hrafnkels saga*, 103.
177 Ibid., 117.

Chapter 5

1 The 'slice of life' short story form may also feature a plotless narrative which typically eschews narrative closure, and often involves withheld or merely implied information. In plotted narratives, failure to 'tie up loose ends' is generally regarded as a flaw.
2 It is of course important to recognize that what I am terming, for convenience, 'withheld information', does not actually exist if a narrative is fictional; its status is purely implicational. It is rather part of an author's un-narrated imagining of the story. See the discussion of *fabula* and *sjuzhet* at the beginning of Chapter 3.
3 See Ruth Rosaler, *Conspicuous Silences: Implicature and Fictionality in the Victorian Novel* (Oxford: Oxford University Press, 2016). I confine my discussion of conspicuous silence at this point to instances in which the narrator explicitly draws attention to the omission. In Rosaler's work, any silence evident to the reader is designated as conspicuous.
4 See, for instance, Thompson, *Motif-Index*, H507.3.1, J2037.2, T69.1.1.
5 *Eyrbyggja saga*, 22–3.
6 Ibid., 23.
7 Ibid.
8 Ibid., 23–4.
9 Ibid., 24–6.
10 Börkr also appears in *Gísla saga*, again as an unsympathetic character who is often in ignorance of what is going on.
11 For a detailed analysis of how plot works, see Brooks, *Reading for the Plot*.
12 I have discussed historically sanctioned praise, as in either introductory character sketches or summative commendations; see Chapter 4.
13 *Eyrbyggja saga*, 24.
14 Ibid., 26.
15 Ibid., 70–1.
16 Ibid., 72.
17 Ibid.
18 Rosaler, *Conspicuous Silences*, 132.
19 *Njáls saga*, 24.
20 See the discussion of 'scene' in Chapter 2.
21 Ricœur, *Time and Narrative*, 3.186.

22 *Njáls saga*, 107.
23 Ibid., 229.
24 Ibid.
25 Ibid., 365.
26 Ibid., 373. The phrase 'mæla á mutr' (to speak quietly or with reserve) may also function as a pun on 'múta' (bribe) here.
27 *Njáls saga*, 373.
28 Ibid., 374.
29 Ibid., 296.
30 See O'Donoghue, 'Figura in *Njáls saga*'. See also *Njáls saga*, 290–2.
31 See, for instance, Miller, *Why Is Your Axe Bloody? A reading of* Njáls saga', ed. William Ian Miller (Oxford University Press, 2016), 205.
32 *Njáls saga*, 58, 94, 99, 160. There is no specific allusion to secrecy, but Gunnarr and Njáll are said on each occasion to go off together for a conversation.
33 *Njáls saga*, 85–6.
34 *Laxdœla saga*, 22–3.
35 Ibid., 23.
36 Ibid., 24.
37 As Jochens notes, male extra-marital affairs and even formal concubinage seem to have been commonplace, and perhaps therefore permissible, at least as late as the thirteenth century. However, as both she and Auður Magnúsdóttir have argued, the absence of such affairs from many saga genres might indicate discomfort with such activities; see Jenny Jochens, *Women in Old Norse Society* (Ithaca: Cornell University Press, 1995), 31–6, and Auður Magnúsdóttir, 'Kingship, Women, and Politics in Morkinskinna', in *Disputing Strategies in Medieval Scandinavia*, ed. Kim Esmark, Lars Hermanson, Hans Jacob Orning and Helle Vogt (Leiden: Brill, 2013), 86–7.
38 *Laxdœla saga*, 24–5.
39 Such speculation is most famously mocked in L. C. Knights, *How Many Children Had Lady Macbeth? An Essay in the Theory and Practice of Shakespeare Criticism* (Cambridge: Minority Press, 1933). Incidentally, there is to my mind a distinction between 'facts' belonging to an unnarrated backstory, and speculation about unstated motives or unexplained actions in the narrative.
40 Elaine Showalter, *Hystories: Hysterical Epidemics and Modern Culture* (New York: Picador, 1997), 95.
41 Ricœur, *Time and Narrative*, 1.xi.
42 *Laxdœla saga*, 131.
43 Ibid., 133. There are of course echoes of Höskuldr's slave woman and her fine clothes here – clothes given not to their intended recipient, but to her rival, whom they are said to suit.

44 *Laxdœla saga*, 139.
45 Ibid., 139-40.
46 Ibid., 140.
47 Ibid., 142-3.
48 Ibid., 143-4.
49 Ibid., 144.
50 Ibid., 145.
51 *Eyrbyggja saga*, 20.
52 *Gísla saga*, 20-4.
53 Ibid., 26.
54 Ibid., 28-9.
55 Ibid., 30-1. See also O'Donoghue, *Skaldic Verse*, 150.
56 *Gísla saga*, 34.
57 Ibid., 38-40.
58 Ibid., 40. See also Chapter 3.
59 Ibid., 40-1.
60 Ibid., 41-2.
61 Ibid., 42.
62 Ibid., 43.
63 Ibid.
64 See my discussion of legal information in Chapter 4.
65 *Gísla saga*, 46.
66 Ibid., 44-5.
67 Ibid., 45.
68 Ibid.
69 Ibid., 46.
70 Ibid., 47.
71 Ibid., 48-9.
72 Ibid., 50.
73 Ibid.
74 Ibid., 51-4.
75 Ibid., 90-1.
76 See, for instance, Riti Kroesen, 'The Enmity between Þorgrímr and Vésteinn in the *Gísla Saga Súrssonar*', *Neophilologus* 66 (1982), 386-90; Eiríkur Björnsson, 'Enn um vígið Vésteins', *Andvari* 18 (1976), 114-17; Hermann Pálsson, 'Hver myrti Véstein í *Gísla sögu*?', *Andvari* 17 (1975), 133-7; Claiborne W. Thompson, '*Gísla saga*: The Identity of Véstein's Slayer', *Arkiv för nordisk filologi* 88 (1973), 85-95; and Theodore Andersson, 'Some Ambiguities in *Gísla saga*: A Balance Sheet', *Bibliography of Old Norse-Icelandic Studies* 6 (1968): 7-42.
77 O'Donoghue, *Skaldic Verse*, 142.

78 *Grettis saga*, 45.
79 Ibid., 45–6.
80 Ibid., 48.
81 Ibid., 43–4, 95.
82 Ibid., 120, 176. See also O'Donoghue, 'Figura in *Njáls saga*'.
83 *Grettis saga*, 46.
84 Ibid., 146.
85 Ibid., 47.
86 Ibid., 47.
87 *Laxdœla saga*, 114–28.
88 See, for example, *Bjarnar saga*, 113–23 and Sigurður Nordal and Guðni Jónsson, ed., 'Gunnlaugs saga ormstungu', in *Borgfirðinga sögur*, Íslenzk fornrit, vol. 3 (Reykjavík: Hið íslenzka fornritfélag, 1938), 67–82.
89 *Laxdœla saga*, 115.
90 Ibid., 117–23.
91 Ibid., 117–23.
92 Ibid., 126.
93 Ibid., 128.
94 Ibid., 131.
95 See for instance Ursula Dronke, 'Narrative Insight in *Laxdœla saga*', in *J.R.R. Tolkien, Scholar and Storyteller: Essays in Memoriam*, ed. Mary Salu and Robert Farrell (Ithaca: Cornell University Press, 1979), 120–37.
96 *Njáls saga*, 312.
97 O'Donoghue, 'Figura in *Njáls saga*', 158–9.
98 *Njáls saga*, 313.
99 Ibid.
100 See Judith Jesch, 'Good Men and Peace in *Njáls saga*', in *Introductory Essays on 'Egils saga' and 'Njáls saga'*, ed. John Hines and Desmond Slay (London: Viking Society for Northern Research, 1992), 72–3, and O'Donoghue, 'Figura in *Njáls saga*', 158–60. See *Njáls saga*, 290–2.
101 See Ármann Jakobsson, 'Masculinity and Politics in *Njáls saga*', *Viator* 38, no. 1 (2007): 198–200, and Jesch, 'Good Men and Peace', 72.
102 *Njáls saga*, 50; see also Jónas Kristjánsson and Vésteinn Ólason, ed., '*Sigurðarkviða in skamma*', in *Eddukvæði II: Hetjukvæði*, Íslenzk fornrit (Reykjavík: Hið íslenzka fornritafélag, 2014), 340.
103 Jónas Kristjánsson and Vésteinn Ólason, ed., '*Hamðismál*', in *Eddukvæði II: Hetjukvæði*, Íslenzk fornrit (Reykjavík: Hið íslenzka fornritafélag, 2014), 409–10.
104 *Njáls saga*, 314. On the legal status of exaggerated insults, see Robert Cook, ed., *Njals saga* (London: Penguin, 1997), 333, n. 4.
105 *Grettis saga*, 61–2.

106 Ibid., 62.
107 Wulff, 'Suspense and the Influence of Cataphora', 2.
108 Carroll, 'The Paradox of Suspense', 71–91.
109 Ibid., 74.
110 Ibid.
111 Ibid., 77.
112 Ibid., 83.
113 Ibid., 78.
114 *Grettis saga*, 63. This focalization incidentally gives the impression that Grettir is the ultimate author of the account, which the saga author is merely relaying.
115 See Seymour Chatman's sympathetic analysis of the way we yearn to tell characters what is going to happen to them; Seymour Chatman, *Story and Discourse: Narrative Structure in Fiction and Film* (Ithaca: Cornell University Press, 1978), 59.
116 Wulff, 'Suspense and the Influence of Cataphora', 15.
117 *Grettis saga*, 64–5.
118 William F. Brewer, 'The Nature of Narrative Suspense and the Problem of Rereading', in *Suspense: Conceptualizations, Theoretical Analyses and Empirical Explorations*, ed. Peter Vorderer, Hans Wulff and Mike Friedrichsen (Manwah, NJ: Erlbaum, 1996), 119–23.
119 This theory is often held to account for the 'one read only' limitation of the cheap thriller. It has even been proposed that sheer suspense, rather than a more thoughtful engagement with the text, is primarily enjoyed only by undiscriminating or fundamentally unserious readers. Brewer attributes this view to C.S. Lewis; see Brewer, 'Nature of Narrative Suspense', 121.
120 Carroll, 'The Paradox of Suspense', 87.
121 This is not the same as identifying psychologically with characters. Rita Felski further distinguishes two varieties of intellectual identification, the first of which relates the more closely to our engagement with saga characters: 'Identification can denote a formal *alignment* with a character, as encouraged by techniques of focalization, point of view or narrative structure, while also referencing an experiential *allegiance* with a character, as manifested in a felt sense of affinity or attachment'; Felski, *Uses of Literature*, 34.
122 Ricœur, *Time and Narrative*, 3.249.
123 William C. Dowling, *Ricoeur on Time and Narrative: An Introduction to 'Temps et récit'* (Notre Dame, IN: University of Notre Dame Press, 2011), 51.

Further reading

Saga translations

Njal's Saga (*Njáls saga*), translated by Robert Cook (Penguin Classics)
The Saga of the People of Laxardal (*Laxdœla Saga*) *and Bolli Bollason's Tale,* translated by Keneva Kunz (Penguin Classics)
Eyrbyggja Saga, translated by Hermann Palsson and Paul Edwards (Penguin Classics)
The Saga of Gisli (*Gísla saga*) and *The Saga of Grettir* (*Grettis saga*) in *Three Icelandic Outlaw Sagas*, translated by Anthony Faulkes and George Johnston (Viking Society for Northern Research)
Hrafnkel's Saga (*Hrafnkels saga*) *and Other Stories*, translated by Hermann Palsson (Penguin Classics)
Or: the above sagas, and any others in:
The Complete Sagas of Icelanders, edited by Víðar Hreinsson (5 vols, various translators) (Leifur Eiríksson Publishing)
Or in: *The Sagas of Icelanders* (a selection of family sagas including *Hrafnkels saga*, *Gísla saga* and *Laxdœla Saga* – various translators with a preface by Jane Smiley) (Penguin Classics)

Secondary literature

Carl Phelpstead, *An Introduction to the Sagas of Icelanders* (University Press of Florida, 2020)
Heather O'Donoghue, *Old Norse-Icelandic Literature: A Short Introduction* (Blackwell, 2004)
Margaret Clunies Ross, *The Cambridge Introduction to the Old Norse-Icelandic saga* (Cambridge University Press, 2010)
The Routledge Research Companion to the Medieval Icelandic Sagas, ed. Ármann Jakobsson and Sverrir Jakobsson (Routledge, 2019)

Background

Magnus Magnusson, *Iceland Saga* (The History Press, 2005)
Peter Foote and David Wilson, *The Viking Achievement* (Sidgwick and Jackson, 1970)

Judith Jesch, *Women in the Viking Age* (Boydell and Brewer, 1991)
Jesse Byock, *Viking Age Iceland* (Penguin, 2001)

Narratology

Gérard Genette, *Narrative Discourse*, translated by Jane E. Lewin, foreword by Jonathan Culler (Blackwell, 1980)

Gérard Genette, *Narrative Discourse Revisited*, translated by Jane E. Lewin (Cornell University Press, 1988)

Paul Ricœur, *Time and Narrative*, 3 vols, translated by Kathleen McLaughlin and David Pellauer (University of Chicago Press, 1984–8)

Index

Locators followed by 'n.' indicate endnotes

Abbott, H. Porter 203 n.6
Á la Recherche du Temps Perdu (Proust) 49, 77
alteration of consciousness 10, 182
ambiguity 8, 28, 150, 184, 186, 190 n.101
anachrony 71, 75, 178, 184–5
   analeptic (*see* analepsis)
   diegetic 76–7
   imperfect 104–9
   proleptic (*see* prolepsis)
   unsuccessful 109–12
analepsis 75, 77, 92, 109–10, 145
   allusions 101–2, 196 n.89
   imperfect 106
   legal proceedings 102–3, 111
   in *Njáls saga* 100, 110
   prolepsis and 98–9, 109
Andersson, T. M. 13, 21, 196 n.76, 196 n.82
Ari Þorgilsson 18, 24–5, 27–8, 42, 102
Aristotle 4
Arnórr (*Grettis saga*) 119–20
Arnþrúðarstaðir 30
Ásdís (*Eyrbyggja saga*) 157
Ásgautr (*Laxdœla saga*) 84, 134
Ásgrímr Elliða-Grímsson 69–71, 160
Ásmundr skegglauss 20, 138
Atli (*Grettis saga*) 87, 118–19, 171–2
Atli (*Njáls saga*) 171–2
audience 9, 58, 60, 63, 72, 76, 101, 113, 121, 130, 177, 179–80, 194 n.33, 194 n.43, 197 n.100
   engagement 117–18, 139, 150, 154, 159, 163, 167, 170
   first-time 5, 7, 92, 129, 155–7, 163
   guidance 120, 125, 133, 147, 150
   mediating 114, 133, 147
   original 8, 11, 36, 97, 140–1, 144, 163, 175

   post-medieval 8, 115
   sympathies 123, 150–1
Auðr (*Gísla saga*) 36, 89–90, 100, 141–2, 168–9
Auðr (*Laxdœla saga*) 146
Auðunn jarl geit (nanny-goat earl) 20, 100, 134, 171–2
Auður Magnúsdóttir 210 n.37
Augustine 4–5, 7, 133

Bakhtin, Mikhail 6
Bal, Mieke 8, 203 n.6
Bárðr (*Gísla saga*) 125
Batten, Caroline 199 n.63
Bergþóra (*Njáls saga*) 39, 79, 87–8, 92, 101, 118, 159
Bersi Véleifsson 33
Bjarnar saga Hítdœlakappa 69, 196 n.85, 212 n.88
Bjarni (*Njáls saga*) 82–3
Björn Breiðvíkingakappi 24, 82, 84, 126–7
Björn Hítdœlakappi 64, 69
Björn inn austrœni 17–18, 36, 51, 56
block of time 4–5, 9, 182
Boethius 4, 6, 182
Bolli Bollason 25–6, 45–6, 66, 101–2, 104–5, 164–6, 173–5, 193 n.21
Bolli Þorleiksson 26, 51–2, 68, 81
Booth, Wayne C. 2, 55, 76, 114, 116, 184, 194 n.33, 203 n.6, 204 n.28
Börkr inn digri (the fat) 84, 102, 136, 155–6, 163, 181, 209 n.10
Brandr 96
Brennu-Njáll (Burnt Njáll). *See* Njáll
Brewer, William 181, 213 n.118, 213 n.119
Brooks, Peter 76
Brynjólfr (*Njáls saga*) 87

Canute, King 178
Carroll, Noël 179–81, 194 n.43
Caves 64
Cearbhall, Irish King 15
chance coincidence 165
Christianity 1, 11, 50, 139, 145
　Christmas 36–8, 44, 51
　cultural time 28, 45–6
　external time 12
　Iceland's conversion to 24–6, 48, 139, 144
　pre-Christian to Christian 144
Christian martyrdom 45–6
'clock' time 41, 191 n.136
Clover, Carol 55, 133, 203 n.4
Clunies Ross, Margaret 14, 203 n.6
Cochrane, Jamie 49, 51, 193 n.11
colouring 8
conspicuous silence 130, 154, 157, 185, 209 n.3
　Eyrbyggja saga 157
　Gísla saga 168
　Njáls saga 158–9, 161
Culler, Jonathan 47, 76, 192 n.3
cultural times 28, 42–6

Darraðarljóð (the song of Dörruðr) 96
definite ellipses 50–1
descriptive pause 48–9, 64, 66–7, 69, 72–3, 76, 84, 100, 184
Dialogues (Gregory) 93
discourse time 49, 55
displaced comments 114, 121–30, 146
distentio anima (the time of the soul) 4
Dögurðarnes 143
Dörruðr 96–7
double temporality of narrative 5, 9, 78, 181–2, 185
Dronke, Ursula 57
duration 6–7, 47, 73, 183–4. See also
　ellipses/ellipsis; pause; scene; summary
　relationships 47–8

Egill (*Eyrbyggja saga*) 40, 140
Egill Skalla-Grímsson 66
Egils saga 42, 191 n.140
Einar Ólafur Sveinsson 14, 25
Einarr (*Hrafnkels saga*) 41, 58–9, 105, 149–50, 195 n.56

Eiríkr blóðøx (blood-axe) 23
Eiríkr inn rauði (the red) 28
Eiríkr jarl Hákonarson 23, 178
Eiríkr ölfúss (ale-eager) 20
ellipses/ellipsis 47–9, 184
　characterizing 50, 52, 55
　definite 50–1
　explicit 48, 50–1
　Eyrbyggja saga 51, 53
　Hrafnkels saga 52
　impression of historicity 54
　longer 51
　'meanwhile' strategy 52
　Njáls saga 50
　virtual 47, 55
environmental time. See natural time
Erpr (*Hamðismál*) 177
erzählte Zeit 47, 58, 69, 73
Erzählzeit 47, 73
events 49, 53, 58, 75–6, 80, 91, 97–9, 102, 183–4, 203 n.5
　diegetic 85, 93
　in Iceland 24–8, 30, 174
　newsworthy 53, 138
　outside Iceland 21–4
　recalling 98, 103–4
　supernatural 94–5, 124, 127–8
　surprising/shocking 114–15, 119
external time 5, 11–12, 47, 50, 183
　rhythms and patterns 7
Eyjólfr (*Eyrbyggja saga*) 155
Eyjólfr (*Gísla saga*) 32, 90
Eyjólfr Bölverksson 82–3
Eyrbyggja saga 4, 22, 115, 167, 185, 193 n.19, 205 n.52, 208 n.151, 208 n.162
　conditions and beliefs 144–5
　conspicuous silence 157
　conventional judgements 131
　cultural time 43, 45
　day and night (natural time) 40–1
　delayed disclosure 155
　descriptive pause 67
　discourse, managing 134, 138
　displacement 122–4, 126–30
　ellipsis 51, 53
　events 24–6
　genealogy 15, 17–19
　imperfect anachrony 105
　information 142
　and *Laxdæla saga* 17, 27

narratorial explanations 148
prophecy 78, 80-2, 84, 86-7
'scene-setting' description 140
season (natural time) 37-8
settlement of Greenland 28
supernatural events 94-5
Eyvindr (*Hrafnkels saga*) 29, 33, 41, 63, 69

fabula and *sjuzhet* 2, 5, 7, 75-6, 139, 209 n.2
family sagas (*Íslendingasögur*) 1, 4, 11-12, 55, 182. *See also specific saga*
   the future in 7
   genealogy (*see* genealogies (*Íslendingasögur*))
   narrative mode 1-2, 8, 131
   silent speech 113
fardagar (moving days) 44
Felski, Rita 213 n.121
Fifth Court 27-8
fjörbaugsgarður (lesser outlawry) 43
Flosi 23, 27, 38-9, 82-3, 91-4, 96, 101, 103, 121, 160-1, 176-8
fornaldarsögur (sagas of olden times) 6, 20
Fóstbrœðra saga 42
Freyr (the god) 31-2, 127
Freysteinn (*Eyrbyggja saga*) 94
Friðrekr, Bishop 26, 138
Fyrsta málfrœðiritgerðin (*First Grammatical Treatise*) 14

games with time 6
Gautr (*Grettis saga*) 84
Geirmundr (*Laxdœla saga*) 134
Geirmundr heljarskinn (Hel-skin) 20
Geirríðr (*Eyrbyggja saga*) 87, 129
Gellir (*Laxdœla saga*) 25, 138
genealogies (*Íslendingasögur*) 12
   the conflict story 14
   Eyrbyggja saga 15, 17-19
   function of 13
   Grettis saga 19-20
   historicity 14
   Hrafnkels saga 21-2
   Laxdœla saga 15-18, 21, 55-6
   Njáls saga 15, 21
   post-ending 13
   pre-beginning 13, 15
   primary effect 13

Genette, Gérard 3, 6, 47-50, 52, 55, 73, 75, 77, 91, 97, 99, 101, 104, 195 n.64
   anachrony 75, 178, 184
   characterizing ellipsis 50, 52
   duration 47, 73, 184
   explicit ellipsis 48
   order 73, 75
   pause 48
   prolepsis 77
   scene 48
   story and discourse 47, 49
Gestr Oddleifsson 30-1, 39, 80, 92-3, 130, 167, 200 n.88
Gilli (*Laxdœla saga*) 161-3
Gilli (*Njáls saga*) 97
Gísla saga 4, 83, 98, 185, 209 n.10
   analepsis and interventive comment 100-1, 111, 145-6
   cultural time 43
   day and night (natural time) 42
   discourse, managing 136
   displacement 124-5, 129-30
   immutability 98
   moving days 44
   narratorial explanations 148
   'scene-setting' description 141-2
   seasons (natural time) 31, 33
   superstition 127
   withholding and disclosing information 167, 171
Gísli Sigurðsson 14, 83, 131, 136, 141-2, 146, 148, 167-70, 187 n.4
   analepsis 100, 102, 111-12
   cultural time 14, 44
   day and night (natural time) 39-40, 42
   displacement 124-5, 127, 129-30
   experience of dreaming 89-90
   prolepsis 83, 89-90, 98
   seasons (natural time) 31-3, 36-7
Gísli Súrsson 36, 155-6
Gizurr Teitsson 100
Glámr 37-8, 60-1, 79, 106, 129, 172
Glæsir 51, 193 n.19
Glúmr (*Njáls saga*) 93, 200 n.96
Glúmr Óleifsson 82
Grettir 6, 19-20, 129, 133-7, 139, 141, 143-4, 146, 171-3, 208 n.151, 213 n.114

outlawry 20, 23, 54, 64–5, 79, 123, 131, 134, 172
Grettisfærsla 139
Grettis saga 4, 6, 129, 185, 201 n.127, 208 n.151, 213 n.114
  analepsis 98, 100, 103
  conventional judgements 131
  cultural time 43
  descriptive passages 64–5
  discourse, managing 133, 135–9
  displacement 123
  ellipsis 51, 54
  events in Iceland 26–7
  genealogy 19–20
  impassive narrator 119–20
  imperfect anachrony 106–7
  information, omission 171, 173
  narratorial explanations 147
  post-conversion setting 146
  prolepsis 84–5
  prophecy 78, 84–5
  scene 61–2, 79
  'scene-setting' description 141
  seasons (natural time) 29–30
  summary mode 61
  topographical features 143–4
  uncertainty 178–81
  undivulged motives 173
  winter hauntings in 37, 51
  withholding of information 178
Grímr (*Grettis saga*) 134, 138, 147
Grímr (*Njáls saga*) 88
Grønlie, Siân 28, 42, 189 n.73, 189 n.76
Guðbrandr í Dölum 85
Guðmundr inn ríki (the powerful) 70–1, 85, 111, 160
Guðríðr (*Gísla saga*) 36
Guðrún Ósvífrsdóttir 7, 15–17, 23, 52, 83, 92, 101, 105, 123–5, 128, 131, 164–6, 173–5, 177, 200 n.88
  cultural time 43, 45
  dreams 92–4
  events 25–7
  seasons 30–1
Gunnarr (*Njáls saga*) 22, 57, 79–81, 83, 85–8, 117–18, 131, 161, 194 n.43, 210 n.32
  analepsis 99–101
  day and night (natural time) 40

  dreams 91, 96–7
  implausible analepsis 110
  prophecy 79–81, 83, 85–8
  seasons (natural time) 29, 33–4
  vision of *fylgja* 110
Gunnarr Lambason 107
Gunnlaugr 87, 129

Hákon Aðalsteinsfóstri, King 23
Hákon jarl Sigurðsson 22–4, 30, 83, 105, 148
Halldórr (*Laxdœla saga*) 141
Hallfreðargata 64
Hallgerðr 34–5, 56–7, 79, 82–3, 85–7, 92, 99–100, 116–18, 125–6, 159–61, 177–8, 194 n.43
Hallmundr (*Grettis saga*) 134
Hallr of Síðá 121, 176
Hamðir (*Hamðismál*) 177
Hamðismál 177
hamingja, concept of 87–8
Haraldr Gormsson, King 17–19, 21–2, 24, 42, 56, 61–2, 66, 83, 208 n.162
Haraldr gráfeldr 22–3
Haraldr inn hárfagri 23, 26, 55
Hartley, L. P. 143
Hávarðr (*Gísla saga*) 39–40
Heiðarvíga saga 138
Heidegger, Martin 4
Helgi bjólan 35–6
Helgi Harðbeinsson 25–6, 68–9, 128
Helgi inn magri 15, 17
Helgi Njálsson 23, 79–80, 88, 103
Herjólfr (*Laxdœla saga*) 123
Hermann Pálsson 26
Hildigunnr (*Njáls saga*) 27–8, 96, 161, 177
Historia Britonum 36
history and fiction 2, 72, 185
Hjálti Skeggjason 160
Hjörtr (*Njáls saga*) 91
'höfðingi' (chieftain) 45
Högni (*Njáls saga*) 100
Höskuldr Dala-Kollsson 15–16, 21, 23, 35, 56–7, 62–3, 82, 83, 86, 109–10, 119, 121, 134, 161–4, 166, 195 n.56, 210 n.43
Höskuldr Hvítanessgoði 176–8
Höskuldr Þráinsson 27–8, 87, 107–8
Hrafn inn rauði (the red) 29

Hrafnkell 21–2, 58–9, 63–4, 69, 105, 120, 132, 142–3, 149–51, 195 n.56
Hrafnkels saga 4, 29, 185, 206 n.97
  analepsis 103–4
  cultural time 42
  day and night (natural time) 40–1
  descriptive passages 63–4
  descriptive pause 69
  ellipsis 52
  food supplies 34
  genealogy 21–2
  impassive narrator 120
  imperfect anachrony 105
  information 142
  landscape 63–4
  motivations 149–50
  narratorial intervention 150–1
  natural topography 143
  scenes 58–9
  seasons (natural time) 29–30, 33, 35
Hrappr (*Njáls saga*) 85, 125
Hrefna (*Laxdæla saga*) 124, 164–6, 171, 175, 180
Hrossageilar 143
Hrútr Herjólfsson 15, 23, 40, 53, 56–7, 81–2, 85, 108–10, 117–19, 123, 134, 136, 158–9, 208 n.151
human time 4–5, 7
Hume, Kathryn 13–15
Húsdrápa 139
Husserl, Edmund 4

Illugi (*Grettis saga*) 65
immanent saga 114, 136
imperfect anachrony 102, 104–9
imperfect knowledge 7–9, 115, 133, 153, 163–4, 166–7, 181
implied author 114
indefinite ellipses 50, 52
Ingibjörg (*Gísla saga*) 102
Ingibjörg (*Laxdæla saga*) 164, 173–5
Ingjaldr (*Gísla saga*) 111
Ingólfr Arnason 18, 27, 103
interiority 8, 60, 76, 89–90, 101, 104–5, 137, 149, 158
Íslendingabók (Ari Þorgilsson) 24, 28, 42, 189 n.73, 208 n.157
Íslendinga saga 43, 141
Íslendingasögur. See family sagas (*Íslendingasögur*)

Jesch, Judith 176
Jochens, Jenny 210 n.37
Jökull Bárðarson 85
Jól (Yule) 44–5
Jórunn (*Laxdæla saga*) 162, 164
Jórunn manvitsbrekka (wisdom-slope) 15

Kálfr (*Laxdæla saga*) 164
Kambsnes 143
Kári (*Laxdæla saga*) 119
Kári (*Njáls saga*) 83, 107, 136, 159
Kárr inn gamli (the old) 98
Katalak, Michael 23
Katla (*Eyrbyggja saga*) 78, 87, 123, 129
Ker, W. P. 13–14
Ketill flatnefr 15–21, 51, 55–6, 195 n.56
Killer-Styrr. *See* Víga-Styrr
Kjalleklingar (Kjallakr) 18
Kjartan Óláfsson 15, 23, 43, 45–6, 51, 66–7, 83, 89, 93, 101, 104, 124, 127, 131, 141, 164–6, 173–5, 177
Kjötvi inn auðgi (the rich) 20
Kolbeinn (*Njáls saga*) 85
Kolr (*Njáls saga*) 92
Kolskeggr (*Njáls saga*) 22, 86, 96
Kormáks saga 33

Landnámabók 20
Laxdæla saga 4, 6–7, 23, 38, 41, 51, 161, 185, 196 n.82, 207 n.141, 208 n.151
  analepsis 98–9, 111
  conventional judgements 131
  cultural time 43, 45
  discourse, managing 134, 136, 138
  displacement 121–5
  double displacement 128
  dramatic portraits 67
  dreams 92
  ellipsis 51–2
  events 24–7
  Eyrbyggja saga and 17, 27
  genealogy 15–18, 21
  headdress 164–5, 171
  imperfect anachrony 104–5
  inconsistencies 26
  internal chronology 25
  narrative voice 119, 146
  pause 66–8
  pre-Christian Icelanders 145–6
  prophecy 81, 83–4, 88–9

'scene-setting' description 141, 207 n.137
scenic mode 55–7, 62–3
seasons (natural time) 30–1, 33, 35
settlement in Iceland 143
undivulged motives 173–4
unsuccesful anachrony 110
Lear, King 35, 190 n.105
Lethbridge, Emily 208 n.156
Ljósavatn 160
Lönnroth, Lars 203 n.4
Lýtingr (*Njáls saga*) 97

Magnus Magnusson 26
Manning, George 206 n.107
'marlíðendr' (sea-travellers) 87, 199 n.63
'meanwhile' strategy 52
Melkorka (*Laxdœla saga*) 15–16, 62–3, 98–9, 110, 163–4, 175
Miller, William I. 117, 150, 196 n.82
moment of attention 5, 7, 133
Morcom, Tom 196 n.86
Mörðr gígja (fiddle) 21, 56, 81, 122, 158–9
Mörðr Valgarðson 103, 107–9
Müller, Günther 47
Myrkjartan, King 16, 66, 99, 110

narrative/narrator voice 3, 55, 72–3, 129–30, 183
　controlling 2
　discourse, managing 132–40
　displacement 121, 129, 184
　explanations 147–51
　information 140–5
　judgemental responses 145–7
　prediction 96
　recounting 6
　self-effacing 2–3, 8, 114, 133, 147, 203 n.5
　silence of 156, 172
　silent speech 113 (*see also* silent narrator)
　stylistic mode 114
　totum simul perspective 104
narratorial prolepsis 77, 83–5, 106, 133
natural time 28
　night and day 11–12, 38–42
　seasons 11–12, 29–38
newsworthy event 53, 94, 138

Njáll 23, 34, 69, 80, 101, 107, 110, 118, 120–1, 135–6, 159–61, 176–8, 210 n.32
Njáls saga 4, 15, 23–4, 56–7, 96, 185, 201 n.131, 210 n.32, 212 n.102, 212 n.104
　analepsis 100, 103–4
　conspicuous silence 158–61
　conventional judgements 131
　day and night (natural time) 38–40
　diegetic prolepsis 84
　discourse, managing 134–6, 138
　displacement 121, 125–7
　dream and vision 91, 93
　ellipses 50, 52
　events 27–8
　food supplies 34
　future, allusions to 79–84
　genealogy 15, 21
　haymaking 33
　impassive narrator 120
　imperfect anachrony 107–9
　implausible analepsis 110
　narrative climax of 38
　narratorial comment, absence 116–18
　private/secret conversations 159–60
　prolepsis 79–83, 85–8, 91, 97, 108
　prophecy 85–6
　realistic intervals of time 29
　scenes 57–8
　supernatural events 95–6
　superstition 127
　undivulged motives 176–8
　vision of *fylgjur* 88
Njósnar-Helgi (spy-Helgi) 39–40
Noregskonungstal (List of Norwegian Kings) 24

Oddr Kötluson 78, 129
Óðinn 145
Ófeigr burlufót 19, 61
Ófeigr Grettir Einarsson 19
ójafnaðarmaðr 148
St. Óláfr 19, 24–5
Óláfr feilan (wolf) 16, 18
Óláfr inn helgi. *See* St. Óláfr
Óláfr inn hvíti (the white) 15
Óláfr pái (peacock) 16–18, 23, 30, 35, 51, 53, 65–6, 68, 83, 88–9, 110, 121, 134, 141, 164

222 Index

Óláfr Tryggvason, King 23–4, 45, 67, 85
Ölvir barnakarl (child-man) 19
Öndóttr kráka (crow) 20
Önundr (*Grettis saga*) 19–20, 27, 61–2
order 2, 7, 73, 75, 177, 184
Ósk (*Laxdœla saga*) 111
Ósvífr (*Laxdœla saga*) 30–1
Otkell (*Njáls saga*) 34, 79
Oxmýr 63

pace/rhythm 48–9, 60, 183–4
the paradox of suspense 181, 194 n.43
paradox of time 4–5
pause 48
    descriptive 48–9, 64, 66–7, 69, 72–3, 76, 84, 100, 184
    fleeting 63, 65
    narrative 61, 71–2, 195 n.64
Þiðrandi (*Njáls saga*) 138
Þjóstólfr (*Njáls saga*) 125–6
Poetic Edda 6, 45, 177
Þórarinn (*Eyrbyggja saga*) 22
Þórarinn (*Laxdœla saga*) 111
Þórarinn (*Njáls saga*) 82
Þorbjörn ferðalangr (far traveller) 106
Þorbjörn (*Grettis saga*) 123, 144
Þorbjörn (*Hrafnkels saga*) 35, 103–5
Þorbjörn laxakarl (salmon-man) 19
Þorbjörn öngull (hook) 107
Þorbjörn øxnamegin (oxen-might) 119
Þórdís (*Eyrbyggja saga*) 84, 155–6
Þórdís (*Gísla saga*) 32, 100, 102, 125, 136
Þórðr (*Laxdœla saga*) 125
Þórðr inn huglausi 141–2, 146
Þórðr leysingjason 88
Þorfinnr (*Grettis saga*) 178–9
Þorgeirr Hávarsson 84
Þorgerðr (*Gísla saga*) 39, 66
Þorgils Hölluson 41, 128, 138
Þorgrímr (*Gísla saga*) 31–3, 36, 44, 100, 102, 136, 146, 167–71, 211 n.76
Þorgrímr (*Njáls saga*) 86
Þorgrímr nef (nose) 145
Þórgunna (*Eyrbyggja saga*) 67, 86, 94–5, 97, 99, 124, 205 n.52
Þorhallr (*Grettis saga*) 37, 60–1
Þórir haklangr (long chin) 20, 61
Þórir of Garðr 123

Þórir viðleggr (wooden leg) 94
Þórisdalr 64
Þorkell Eyjólfsson 16–17, 23, 25–6, 30–2, 44, 93, 100, 167–71
Þorkell hákr (the bully) 71
Þorkell krafla (scrabbler) 26
Þorkell máni (moon) 27
Þorkell trefill (fringe) 111–12, 146
Þorleikr Höskuldsson 84, 118–19
Þóroddr (*Eyrbyggja saga*) 94–5
Þórólfr (*Eyrbyggja saga*) 18
Þórólfr (*Laxdœla saga*) 166
Þórólfr bægifótr (twisted foot) 37, 81–2, 95, 128, 145
Þórólfr Mostrarskeggi 67
Þorsteinn (*Laxdœla saga*) 111
Þorsteinn inn rauði (the red) 16, 18
Þorsteinn þorskabítr 123
Þorvaldr (*Njáls saga*) 91, 126
Þorvaldr Koðránsson 26, 138
post-medieval literary theory 192 n.3
Þráinn Sigfússon 22, 32, 71, 87, 159
presentiments of death 78, 86, 105
privacy of conversations 159–60
privileged epistemic access 115, 147
privileged knowledge 81–2, 104, 124, 140, 147–8
prolepsis 75, 77–98, 109
    diegetic 84
    Eyrbyggja saga 78, 80, 82, 86–7, 95
    Gísla saga 83, 98
    Grettis saga 79, 84–5
    Laxdœla saga 81, 83–4, 92
    narratorial 84–5
    Njáls saga 79–83, 85–6, 88, 96–7
    'passed past' 78
    pessimism 78, 91
    plan 81
    prophecy 78–9
    prophetic dream and vision 88–91, 93, 97
Proust, Marcel 49, 77
Þuríðr (*Eyrbyggja saga*) 126–7
Þuríðr (*Laxdœla saga*) 134, 164

Rafarta (*Laxdœla saga*) 15
Ragnarr loðbrók 19
Rannveig (*Gísla saga*) 168
Rannveig (*Njals saga*) 83, 100

the rhetoric of fiction 2, 4, 55, 61, 63, 73, 75, 116, 149, 184–5, 194 n.33
Rhetoric of Fiction (Booth) 203 n.6
Ricœur, Paul 2–4, 7, 9, 47, 113, 115, 158
   alteration of consciousness 10, 182
   double temporality 5, 9, 78, 182
   imperfect knowledge 7–8, 115, 133
   third time 4, 9–10, 181, 183
Rimmugýgi 71
Roby, Matthew 120
Rosaler, Ruth 157, 209 n.3

saga author 3, 5, 9, 12, 15, 20, 24–6, 51–2, 59, 64–6, 72, 78, 90, 99, 114, 117, 145, 158, 167, 171, 175, 177–9, 184–5, 213 n.114
Sámr (*Hrafnkels saga*) 29, 40–3, 69, 103, 120, 142–3, 150–1
Sámr (*Njáls saga*) 79, 86
Sæmundr 24
scene 48, 69, 127, 179, 184, 195 n.56
   as compositional unit 55
   emotional intensity 92
   Grettis saga 61–2, 79
   Hrafnkels saga 58–9
   Laxdæla saga 55–7, 62–3, 141
   Njáls saga 57–8, 161
   summary and 50, 55
'scene-setting' description 63, 140, 207 n.137
'semi-legal' dates 44
Showalter, Elaine 164
Sif Ríkharðsdóttir 116–17
Sigtryggr, Earl 107
Sigurðr Hlöðvísson 23, 80, 107
Sigurðr jarl 97
Sigvatr inn rauði (the red) 56
silent narrator 113, 184
   conventional judgements 114, 130–2
   displacement 121–30
   impassive narrator 119–21
   neutrality 115
   no comment 115–19
silkislæður 176–8
sjuzhet, fabula and 2, 5, 7, 75–6, 139, 209 n.2
Skaldic Verse and the Poetics of Saga Narrative (O'Donoghue) 72
Skamkell (*Njáls saga*) 79

Skapti Þóroddsson 28, 37, 44, 70, 123, 138, 172
Skarpheðinn 27, 32, 87, 100, 107–8, 118, 178, 196 n.89
Skeggi (*Grettis saga*) 171–2
Snorri goði (the chieftain) 24–6, 28, 30, 40, 52–3, 67–8, 70, 81–3, 115–16, 121, 130, 138, 155–8, 163
Snorri Þorgrímsson. *See* Snorri goði (the chieftain)
Snorri Sturluson 24
söguöld (saga age) 6, 11, 25, 135, 140, 142–5, 151, 186, 203 n.3
Sörli (*Hamðismál*) 177
Spá-Gils (prophecy-Gils) 80–1
Spjótsmýrr (Spear-Swamp) 144
Stefan Einarsson 13
stefnudagar (summonsing days) 43
Steinþórr Þorláksson of Eyrr 67–8, 82, 145
Steinvör (*Njáls saga*) 86
Stjörnu-Odda draumr 203 n.3
story 47, 76, 154
   and discourse 47, 49, 55, 75
   and narrative 47, 75
   time 48–50, 55
Sturla Þorðarson 43, 131, 144
Styrr. *See* Víga-Styrr
summary 48–9, 54–63, 131
   and scene 55
   settlement of Iceland 55–6
supernatural events 94–5, 124, 127–8
Svanr (*Laxdæla saga*) 126–8
Svartr (*Njáls saga*) 92
Sveinn jarl Hákonarson 30, 85
Sveinn tjúguskegg (forkbeard), King 22

temporal ellipsis 51–3
third time of narrative 4, 9–10, 99, 109, 115, 132–3, 139, 148, 153, 166, 171, 181–3, 186
thought experiment 10, 171, 173, 182, 186
Time and Narrative (*Temps et Récit*) (Ricœur) 2–3
the time of the world 4–5
totum simul (everything at once) 4–6, 9, 76, 78, 104, 115, 133, 139, 154, 182, 184
travelling times 29
Turville-Petre, Gabriel 45

Úlfarr (*Eyrbyggja saga*) 81–2
Úlfr Uggason 139
undivulged motives 173–8
Unnr in djúpúðga 51, 56–7, 81, 108, 110, 122, 134, 143, 158–9, 161
   day and night (natural time) 38, 40
   genealogy 15–19, 21
   season (natural time) 35–6
unsuccessful anachrony 109–12

van den Toorn, M. C. 12
vápnatak 142
Vatnsdœla saga 26
Vermundr (*Grettis saga*) 85
Vermundr inn mjóvi (the slender) 22, 105, 148–9, 157
Vésteinn (*Gísla saga*) 31, 33–4, 83, 98, 100, 129–30, 141–2, 167–70
Vésteinn Ólason 13–14, 75, 77, 91, 115–16, 122, 203 n.4
Vestmarr (*Grettis saga*) 20

Víga-Glúms saga 87
Víga-Styrr 105, 148, 157
Vígbjóðr (*Grettis saga*) 20
Vigdís (*Laxdœla saga*) 134
Völsunga saga 45
Völuspá 79, 145

Winter Nights 31, 33, 44
withheld knowledge/information 99, 153–4, 209 n.2
   authorial omniscience, absence of 154
   avoidance of interiority 154
   conspicuous silence 157–9
   unanswered questions 154, 162–3, 164–73
   uncertainty, resolved 154, 178–82
Wulff, Hans 180

Yngvildr (*Laxdœla saga*) 15
Yngvildr (*Njáls saga*) 91–2

www.ingramcontent.com/pod-product-compliance
Lightning Source LLC
Chambersburg PA
CBHW072231290426

44111CB00012B/2054